Letters to God from the Wilderness

Letters to God from the Wilderness

Ronald Beasley

Shoving Leopard

Published by
Shoving Leopard
8 Edina Street (2f3)
Edinburgh,
EH2 5PN,
Scotland

http://www.shovingleopard.com

Cover design by NialSmithDesign, Copyright © 2006

Every effort has been made to trace possible copyright holders and to obtain their permission for the use of any copyright material.
The publishers will gladly receive information enabling them to rectify any error or omission for subsequent editions.

ISBN 978-1-905565-09-2 Paperback

Acknowledgements and thanks

To Pam my wife, companion and lover, who has accompanied me all the way on my journey of discovery.

To Elizabeth Templeton a sojourner, for her convictions and her questions which have fertilised my own understanding of theology, and has quickened my imagination.

To Eric Savage for his readiness and patience, who with his technical skills transformed my tentative text into a script that invites responses.

Contents

Introduction

I have spent a considerable proportion of my life thinking about God – the Enigma of God. As a child I attended Sunday School. My mother was a thinker and was mildly interested in religion. My father, as far as I know, had no religious belief. I attended the local Church, and became a Sunday School teacher, joined the Youth Fellowship, became a church member, and eventually took over the leadership of the Youth Club.

As an only child the Church environment suited me. As well as other things it enlarged my horizon. Leaving school in 1939 meant initially having odd jobs before I eventually trained as a costing accountant in a large industrial company. Some years later the Youth department of the then Presbyterian Church of England encouraged me to enrol for the two year Course in Youth & Community Work and Christian Education at the Selly Oak Colleges in Birmingham. I was resident in Westhill College and enjoyed the experience enormously.

This fostered and developed my insight into the scriptures, and I had my first 'brush with theology'! My view on pacifism and non-violence crystallized. I was ordained an Elder in the Presbyterian Church of England in my mid 20s. I worked at the Presbyterian Settlement in Poplar, East London. Thereafter I joined the staff of the Y.M.C.A., first in Halifax and then in North Shields on Tyneside, as a Youth & Community Worker. This eventually led me to join the staff of the Youth Department of the Church of Scotland as Senior Youth Organiser, based in Edinburgh. I also became a member of the Iona Community.

My life has not been short of pain; and frequently my marriage has been a bulwark for me. But again and again my searching and contemplation could not find any credible explanation for the way the world was – and still is! Truth appeared to have endless elasticity – love seemed too vulnerable and uncertain – violence was deeply embedded in the fabric of society, and injustice, as I discovered was rampant. Somehow or other, God – what I thought was God – did not seem to fit in at all. Any notion of God seemed incoherent. I was confused. I did my best to pose relevant questions, but they went largely unanswered by myself and others around me. This is not to say that I have not been greatly blessed. But I was also aware of my growing sense of doubt when it came to facing up to the meaning of religion, and particularly the Christian religion. I wondered why it was all so complex, and why was it difficult, even just to talk comfortably about God?

So over the years in a busy life, from time to time, I have been, as it were, rehearsing LETTERS TO GOD, in my imagination. I recall my first attempt when quietly attending a Retreat in Iona Abbey. My searching has continued over the years. It was some twelve or so years ago that Patrick Rodger, a past Bishop of Manchester, and then of Oxford, who when he retired came back to Edinburgh to live nearby. Our evolving relationship provided some of the most fertile and 'mind blowing' occasions for me. My questions from 'the depths' could be posed without embarrassment. Patrick was a sensitive listener, so we were able to probe, and to meditate in a creative mode, seeking answers and possibilities. And if on occasion there were none, then we placed these issues 'on the shelf', to await further consideration at a later date. Nothing was evaded. Nothing was 'verboten'. Our mutual exchange enabled me to feel that my questions did have their validity.

As I grew into living theology as one of the Laity, I was stimulated further when I joined a group for questioners, called Threshold. This was an open meeting place for those who had questions that would not go away. It was a relaxed and informal setting where no holds were barred intellectually. We explored evolving perceptions and insights about truth and human experience. On occasion we would face the inevitable 'stone wall'. There was ambiguity and complexity. Elizabeth Templeton with Patrick Rodger facilitated the searching so that we felt liberated enough to be able to think more vigorously, gradually discarding inhibition and guilt. We faced the contradictions within the theological struggle. It became clear that it was not the doctrine and belief that was of primary importance. Rather, it was the listening, the sharing, the openness and commitment, each of us at our own pace, discovering that the evolving relationship of shared doubt strengthened each of us.

As I grow older many of the questions remain. What follows in this slender volume of Letters is my attempt to explore the enigma of God, probing the possibility of discovering a personal relationship with God. I have come to realise that this could not be done in a hurry. My hope is that these Letters will enable fellow travellers to discover a more incisive and exciting discernment of life, as it is 'fired' and eventually 'fashioned' into a vessel of beauty and integrity. I make no apology for the passion of these Letters. George Steiner once commented that 'the trouble with this people is the poverty of their desire'. Exploration into God through these Letters has been written out of a compelling passion. With their intellectual rigour I hope that they will be infectious!

Letter 1: Looking for God

Dear God,

As I woke in the early dawn, my ears were tuned to a solitary blackbird. His exquisite song, vibrating on the fresh morning air captivated me. As the light strengthened, and my senses fully awoke, I lay there very still. My ears alert to a new experience of great simplicity. I lay with my breath quietly ebbing and flowing with its own assuring rhythm. The lifting throb of the song took over my space, and the quietness of the morning. As minute followed minute effortlessly the bird's glorious anthem of melody and tender rhythm were fused together into an ecstatic symbol so sublime, so delicate, yet strong enough it seemed, to last the whole promised day. As I lay there I wanted to do nothing else but to listen, and listen, and go on listening.

I pictured the bird high up there in the branches, hidden by leaves, black feathers, orange yellow beak, clear forward piercing eyes, stretched neck, it moved from branch to branch. This song needed no adornment. Nothing interrupted this priceless melody – no traffic, no radio, no shouting or babble. No – just the bird's own song. It felt like an endless tune. A gift, a delight, a metaphor perhaps about the day that was dawning. The night had enfolded me with what seemed impenetrable darkness. I had been uneasy in the stillness – the darkness – restless and with my spirit taut, yet uncertain. But the bird's song heralded a pristine beginning, filling me with joy.

Little bird, your song has taken over my mind, moving my brain into action. You have offered to me an exciting expectation. Hearing you this once can now never be enough. I need more of your solitary sonata. I'm insatiable, needing it at this very moment. And I'll need it tomorrow as well. The prospect of living without your song would leave me diminished. To me your beauty is an endless joy. You offer the world your own sense of harmony. You arouse me to a new hope, and a new thankfulness. Fragile songster, what a miracle you are!

Dear God, are you listening too? Listening to the bird and to me? I hope you are tuned into this delicious wonder. Does this bird excite your own sense of wonder? In your own secret and mysterious being do you respond with a deep surge of excitement? Its sounds are so perfect, and so special. For me it is unique for ever.

This bird is its own magnificat - without words - a song so complete that I'm left wondering if it might not even out-sing the song of angels, which sadly I have never heard. I'm just musing – what an occasion it would be if all the song birds across our Earth all sang together! What a flood of scintillating music would embrace and surround this precious globe. Yet humanity's teeming millions play out their lives sadly in ignorance of these melody makers of the trees and hedgerows. I know this is a fantasy, but its seductiveness pleases my soul, and is a needed relief from the harshness of my every day. There is too much sordidness, violence, ugly vulgarity, of society hammering in my ears with ceaseless chronic noise, and meaningless babble. This goes on with breakneck speed – with little space and no time to reflect, and sadly the present all too soon has become the quickly forgotten past.

This morning in the quietness, I surprised myself as I became acutely aware of the single and yet profound gift given to me. In a sense I knew this already in my head. But this morning it took over my whole being. Stopping and waiting and attuning myself to the quiet noises and murmurings of the world, as they revealed their secret of contentment. It is strange, but since this morning, I now know my own profound need to listen, and to listen deeply. Those gentle vibrating sounds – the ticking clock, the upstairs washing machine, the faint echo of quick steps of a neighbour, the 'click' of the central heating switch, and then the slight rumble as the breeze caught the top of the poplar in the garden, with its gracious sway. All of this was so strangely quiet, so different, from my usual bustling around, struggling to keep a tight schedule, clearly unplanned. Now I'm wondering if all my busy-ness without the listening ear misses the point – that creative point which the blackbird symbolises? Since this morning a deeper insight is dawning, simply because I listened. In a way I don't understand, I was made to listen. The blackbird's song, pointed beyond itself and provided me with what I can only call a song-laced silence, which has nourished me. The poet Averil Stedeford captures this creative mood –

When you attend to me,

When you really listen,

My words are drawn into your waiting silence I'd almost say enticed.

When you listen like that I find myself saying things I never said before,

Hearing things I never thought I'd hear,

Coming from the other side of me I scarcely know.

When I sit here in my consulting room, with a pained woman, or a disillusioned man, I think I know how to be sensitive to the therapy from the silence between us. But those ears are not tuned to the blackbird. They are harassed and overcome with fears and hesitations. They look back with regret and for them the silence is unfamiliar and uncomfortable. They are tuned into a sense of inevitable chaos, argument, gridlocked frustration. Then comes the dawning horror of isolation. Can there be anything worse than absolute aloneness, which seems to go on for ever. Chronic rejection blanks out the mind. So, how can I, as it were, clear an audio path so that they can hear the new sound – the song of the blackbird? These clients are a part of me. I sense their desperate and unconscious yearning. Tenderly, in the silence I try to match their feeling with the words that reflect their sorrow and their fears. The image of the blackbird fertilises my imagination hopefully for them.

Suddenly, my mood is broken by the digital radio from the flat above. It's tuned up so that everyone will hear it! Across the world of sound there are no frontiers. Then the postman on his early round whistles his tune as he climbs the stairs to deliver the letters. My letters fall on the mat and arrive as a diversion from my reflections. But then, almost like a miracle, the ubiquitous radio transmits another song – a clever violin impersonates the bird's song – this time the skylark – 'The Lark Ascending' by Vaughan Williams. It lingers. My tortured soul and mind and my worn out body glide into a peace beyond description. How much I wish it could be quietly transmitted to the occupants of my consulting room. Deep listening for them has yet to be discovered.

Looking back on the morning I feel a sense of liberation and surprise. I hope this will stay with me for the entire day. Meanwhile life has to be lived, relationships made, work to be done – learning, growing, flowering, with a ministry of caring which in itself tests my sense of purpose and hope. And then – the countdown to death. What listening can I find to illuminate this deepest of mysteries?

Dear God I'm wondering! Seeping into my heart at this moment is a worrying realisation that I do not feel any nearer to you. This morning's oratorio has brought so much to me. I feel flooded with sensitivity. Secretly I suppose I had hoped that I would feel nearer to you. But I don't! It is all so tantalising, for in a sense this morning has been something of a vision, that clearly has enriched me, and given me a revived motivation to a deeper ministry of listening – a deeper listening. I'm conscious of a mindfulness that values each moment. And this could fertilise the pastoral caring vocation, coping more effectively with the most desperate need of others as well as of myself.

I hoped the uninvited songster would help me to traverse the void of everyday life and reduce 'the distance' between you and me. If I could hear your heartbeat, or even dimly discern in the shadows your divine profile, then today would be for ever in my memory, and my step on the road quicker and surer. I suppose fleetingly I hoped that the horizon of the bird's song would have shown me real communication with you. I wondered if I might have discovered a deeper grasp on the reality that is sure and stretches even beyond this temporary world. The hope that my sense of isolation would diminish, even a little, is disappointed. So I am asking myself, am I expecting too much? Is it, in fact, even possible to expect too much of you? My desire is for a greater sense of intimacy with you. But I'm left wondering if your silence will be forever? This is a puzzle, of you and me, and there are missing pieces, but I don't know how many. But hoping perhaps this morning I might have found just a few of the missing pieces. I feel I have, but it remains uncomfortable to know that there remain gaps, whose void fills me with anxiety. I know I am listening - I am searching – and I am expectant. But for how long, well, it is hard to say. The deeper sense of listening has some sense of illumination, particularly with regard to my neighbours, my clients, and even those who in closeness love me. But you? You remain beyond my grasp. I'm hoping that deeper listening will provide a new bridge for us – a new bridge of knowing. Can you – will you meet me on this bridge?

Letter 2: Who are You, God?

Dear God,

I will begin this letter by admitting that I am confused and I hardly know where to begin. I feel I have a lot 'to get off my chest'. You see - well, I'm saying 'you' - but this is part of the strangeness of my feelings - because I've not seen you, heard you, or, as far as I know, I've not touched you. So how do I know that you are you, if you see what I mean? Yet, I can hardly call you 'It'. This would seem hardly right. I want to be personal to you, even though part of my perception is that you do not feel personal to me. I've had a strange sense of ambivalence about writing to you, and not knowing really if I'll find the right words. For me, the religious words used to describe you feel so inadequate. Inside myself, in my inner being the words traditionally used to describe you feel like a barrier, rather than like a path, or a door, to give access. I'm thinking that being divine changes everything, doesn't it? Clearly I'm not divine. Likewise you are not human. Or is it rather that you are more than human? How much more? And the question that pops into my head is whether or not you have 'tasted' being human? I want to know how the non-divine, the human, is able to be in touch with the divine? Some would say that this is the ultimate '64,000 dollar question'. I'm clear that it is the most important question for me. Can I know you? If so, how? I'm hoping these letters, such as they are, will help, in a way to penetrate my deepest understanding. I'm left wondering if you understand how millions of people share my question, feeling near desolate, living on our planet Earth, with no belief in anything or anyone. Life for me is a struggle, without much hope. I feel utterly alone in a shallow endless fear about tomorrow. Sometimes I have little motivation to survive. This is something of my sense of wilderness. Yet, inspite of my gloom and my informed despair, I feel driven to search for a coherent belief about my life. Yet I'm unsatisfied. I have this hunch that if I found you - or you found me, then, perhaps, life and the future would have the chance of being optimistic. I'm hoping this letter will feed my optimism.

Although sometimes it does not seem like it, deep down I want to love life. Yes, I want to love my own one unrepeatable life. I want to love living, and I want to love the world. I want to love people -

well, I suppose, most of them. In moments of quiet sombre reflection I find myself astonished at the colour, variety, beauty, profundity, that surrounds so much of my daily experience. This recognition makes me feel alive. But my mind rushes on to the endless vastness of space - of time - and how the entire universe is still evolving - after millions of years. Frankly I can hardly comprehend it. Time seems so elastic! And then you have been around all this time too? I'm intrigued to know how it feels to have been around for such a long time? How, I wonder can this all become real to me? However on this cold winter day, for a moment I'm stopped in my meditation when in the front garden I can see in its simplicity a fresh snowflake- so fragile, and a few inches away a snowdrop thrusting its fragile leaves up through the frozen earth. The snowflake quickly melts in my hand, to a dribble of water. In a sense I feel like that snowflake – precarious! From the snowflake to the single speck of sand on the seashore. It has no identity, but it is real. And I'm sensing my own insignificance, which is tinged with despair, knowing that I do not know! However my mood fluctuates, and I tell myself that I am a tiny part of something - something that feels big, which again leads me into a smallness that is rather frightening. Feeling a little bolder, I'm even now daring to wonder if the recognition of my own solo understanding could be, dare I even say it, be of you? Whatever it is, it is a mystery. Tantalising, evocative, disturbing! It's hard finding the right words, as I try to express my mixed up thoughts. I shudder when I recall how frequently I have felt utterly alone in my life. Alone on the outside, and alone on the inside. My World seems to be estranged from any sense of personal comfort, or personal knowledge. God, in what sense can I say 'my God?' Do you understand this? Have you experienced what I am experiencing? There are others, braver than me, who have faced what it has felt like to drink the dregs of utter aloneness, in the face of demoralised helplessness. Reason, I find is fragile and inadequate, and I'm left with a sinking feeling. You God appear to be so chillingly silent - so absent. This is my wilderness!

When I take time to look inside myself, I'm struck by my own complexity- in my body - in my mind - and in my inner personal self, the most private part of me. I find it hard to grapple with my own inner self. On occasion, I know I choose to hide from my own complexity, because it almost frightens me. But again, there are occasions when I have soaring desires. Alas too soon I find myself plummeting into despair more quickly than the speed of light, because I'm disillusioned by my own fragility. It's like a kaleidoscope of immediate wonder, quickly followed by a searing sense of isolation. My exasperation being a sense of lostness, with no understanding of what is really happening to me. I feel I have no control. I'm defeated. It is so baffling, and I can only tell myself, it's a mystery, too profound for my understanding. Yet as I write the words, I doubt them!

So I'm wondering where are you in all this, mysterious God? Can you enter into the bafflement I feel? I open up myself with my best intellectual honesty, but at the end of it all I'm left in an ocean of doubt. What is the ultimate meaning of life?

Since the beginning of time and space, whenever that was, life here on earth has not stopped. Creation appears continuous. Humanity as far as I can see, feels overwhelmed with a sense of endless searching for understanding. I have no sense of there being a map or a guide to the complex task of exploration. My own curiosity remains undimmed. However I search for signposts but they have disappeared. It was Pascal who suggested that "You would not be seeking me unless you had already found me". And I'm wondering if the signposts were ever visible anyway? You see, I'm trying to assure myself that I could be at the beginning of a new - wonderfully new - phase of knowing. Can I understand the signs from my search? Can I find the key to the code of life on Earth? If I could find you, then I'd hope you would enlighten me from my present inhibiting ignorance, and to say the least, I might feel a little more comfortable in my present skin. In Psalm 139 with its sensitive language, the psalmist writes 'Such knowledge is too wonderful for me, it is high, I cannot attain unto it!' This puts my feeling into a verbal shape that fits my mood. But I'm dissatisfied, because I do want to attain to some deeper understanding of the meaning of my life, and my relationship to you, if there can be one. I cannot call myself an atheist. I may not have the knowledge, but I would like to believe that I have some vision. I want to move on in this journey of discovery, but I can only do so with the assurance of intellectual integrity. I say this because I hope you God are the source of intellectual integrity. This integrity also has to possess my feelings, which are touched with a genuine warmth generated by the prospect that eventually truth will be discovered. If truth cannot be discovered, then truth will have no point, and thereby will be meaningless, and this is hard to believe.

I'm clearing my mind so as to face the hope that I will find you. Can you be found? I have to explore the intellectual space where you might be discovered. But I suppose this space between you and me is the actual barrier that prevents me from coming closer to knowing you. I have done my best to read the scriptures, even though for me they seem to be in a time warp. But even just to read them is an achievement for me. I'm aware too of the Jesus event, in actual history, but which has its own sense of mystery as well. Yet, with all the wisdom of the saints and my own honest objective, your divine being still evades me. In my desperation I can just simply ask - God can you, will you be 'in touch' with me?

I recall that Moses was not allowed to see you when he stood on Mount Horeb. But at least he heard you. How wonderful that must have been. Is the story actually true and not just a metaphor? There is a sense in which I'm jealous of Moses. Why, I wonder, has he had what seems to be preferential treatment? There's a popular gimmick used today in advertising and business parlance. It's called 'direct line'. Among its many uses there's one which allows two persons to be in direct contact with each other, without actually seeing each other but clearly hearing each other! Some friends facetiously speak about someone who has 'a direct line to God'. It sounds a wonderful idea, except that it is frequently spiritual pride. On the other hand it could be a wonderful position provided it is not reserved for special guests like the Pope! I know of some 'chatty Christians' who speak as if they have 'God in their pocket'. Again, this can be either flippant or even superior, but for me, I find it unimpressive. I'm desiring something far more authentic - a real relationship, reciprocal, informed, and one in which I'd be quite ready to be the lesser partner. I simply wish to be close to you, God. Finite me, actually in touch with infinite you?

As I approach my later years I'm more aware of what appears to have been a sequence of mistakes. I feel it is a part of being human, and I know that it is in making mistakes that on many occasions I have learnt so much. But it is a hard way to learn. I have tried to take seriously and value this process of learning. I know some mistakes are accidental and not meant, while others are premeditated and meant. Some are even downright evil, and make me cringe. These can be absolved only by forgiveness. I count myself fortunate that in my life I have known the intimacy of personal forgiveness. This has enabled me to be a much more understanding and sensitive person. However now, as I reflect, this is not enough for me, and I'm aware of a re-surfacing question. It is hard to pose, but it remains. When I contemplate you, your very Being, I'm wondering and perhaps speculating when you, God, have made mistakes? Do you know anything of this frailty, first hand? In fact do you make choices at all? Can you I wonder know anything of this experience, within yourself? I know that some will think these questions are out of order. But I want to stay with it. It's a hard question to ask. I'm not sure if anthropomorphic images will help. I'm aware that you are not human, and you cannot be defined by human attributes. But the gap of recognition between you and humanity itself seems to be immensely wide - wide as the ocean in my limited imaging.

A visualisation of you in my head, in a sense, can only add to my already known sense of confusion. I hesitate to impose upon you human characteristics, which in themselves are bound to be limiting, though I would hasten to add they are not meant to be in any sense disrespectful.

Nonetheless these images come from my deepest yearning to know you. But I'm already feeling defeated, because it seems to me that my yearning in itself has become a block to my divine learning about you. Pictures of you, and sundry adjectives of you that attempt to give you a human guise, for me, only compound my problem. And yet, without them, I appear to have nothing to put in their place. What a dilemma!

In this search of mine I know the Scriptures are precious. But they are also complex. The Bible is no ordinary book. It requires what I can only describe as 'a deep reading'. These writings more than deserve a lifetime of study. I can readily feel that within the Old and New Testaments that much is written of you, God. The myth, metaphor, parable, poetry, and graphic fiction as well as non-fiction all contribute to a potentially greater understanding of you and the world. But its writings require of the reader a readiness to grapple with not only the actual text, but with the complex circumstances in which the entire text has been written. Though not a biblical scholar, I have spent time reflecting and exploring and sharing insights and bafflement with others. So I might, even at this stage, consider myself a beginner, as I feel my grappling will still be a long journey. And because of the size of the task will not be completed by me, in this earthly life. The wells of knowledge and understanding remain yet to be discovered. I have something of the same sense when I study the creeds of the Church. Down the annals of history creeds were formulated to give guidance for belief and behaviour. However I find them limited in both their language and substance. Humanity only has its own language, in its diversity. But in a sense I'm left thinking that the task is so immense because it feels as though the objective is to describe the indescribable, or to speak of the unspeakable. However, large numbers of people regularly recite the creed(s) in the belief that this is for them the only way of trying to declare something of their own perception about what hopefully is for the present the nearest approximation of the truth for them of you, God. For me the creeds can only be provisional. I know that for some of my friends reciting the creeds only reminds them of what they do not believe! And this must have its own meaning! My own uncertainties, I think are partially fed by the mystery of your Being. Sacred texts do give comfort and guidance to the faithful. But for those who are searching with enquiring yet perhaps doubtful minds they will continue to struggle with the dilemmas of daily behaviour, ethics, and belief, in the hope of accruing some fresh illumination, fired with a growing sense of recognition, that every discovery, no matter how small, will point to a future in which we can all have some confidence. For myself I'm looking for the satisfaction that hopefully comes from exploration. So if it is true that you have a gift of almightiness, why is it that you seem to withhold using it? I'm tantalised by what seems like an unlikely guess, that you might find yourself willingly impotent? It's a hard question I know, but it has a human touch about it. But again, I am open to the prospect that you are particularly motivated in all things here on earth by love. This has with it a generosity of spirit which on occasion puts the effort of humanity almost to shame. Human love is so frail. It is our everyday experience to see women, children, and those who cannot help themselves being cut down by catastrophes both from nature and human evil. From the beginning humanity has had no option but to face widespread undeserved suffering. Can this be reconciled with that belief which affirms your love for everyone? I have a distasteful fear that humanity is not, and will not be able to explain the inexplicable - whether the mistakes are human or divine. From experience we know suffering is inevitable in this world.

This letter is trying to establish some kind of dialogue with you, but of course I'm also wondering if my expectation is beyond realisation? In the thrust of attempted dialogue I'm aware of the danger and trap of jargon, religious or otherwise. This can be a retreat from reason. But I'm assuming that reason is necessary when I pursue the path which I hope will lead to a greater understanding of you. I want to value the wisdom of the saints, living and departed. Some of them encourage me to keep trying to find a breakthrough to your own unutterable wisdom, glory and meaning. But in my own frailty I'm pursued by the doubt that this can only be mission impossible!

I'm remembering a frightening experience which made me so aware that I have very little control in the face of the immensity of living. I stood on an exposed headland at the height of a terrifying storm. I had not been aware that it was imminent. Winds were at gale force, and across the rocks the sea had waves thirty feet high. Every fragile thing bent before the power of the raging wind and the sweeping rain. I had, thankfully, a concrete post designed to support a feeble fence. The fence collapsed, but the post was secure. But I realised how fragile was my own security. Yes, I was frightened. Along with the rocks, the shrubs and the trees, and the unkempt outhouses I could have been swept away and smashed to smithereens.

I sensed that death was near at hand. I was feeling pitiably insignificant. I had no control whatsoever, and I was frightened. There appears to be violence at the very heart of our creation. Why is this? What message has this uncontrolled natural violence for humanity? It brings undeserved suffering and despair, with a frightening sense of the inevitable. No wonder civilisation feels apprehensive Clearly it is part of your plan, but you have yet to disclose why natural violence is necessary? And if you were to describe, how would your disclosure be conveyed to humanity

– to ordinary women and men? Even were I to know what to look for, - or to listen for – or how else to be sensitive to the deepest awareness of my heart – I will only know when it happens, and the revelation, whatever the form, floods my soul.

Now I'm feeling that I'm locked into a sense of inadequate articulation. Nonetheless my search for the truth will not be abandoned, so hopefully this will lead to a more mutual relationship of increasing exchange and, for me, greater confidence. Issues of control, the desire for power, with the frailty of our loving with the shallowness of our present understanding, can these still become a means for my own growth and insight and awareness of the recognition of your spirit in me? This would imply some growing awareness as far as I am concerned. This letter, along with others can only take me so far on a complex journey of hopeful discovery. As far as I know, no one has yet penetrated the veil of your presence, and the mystery of your Being.

I'm not going to retreat either into silence, or into isolation. My search will be in and through the 'everyday-ness' of my life. It will demonstrate, I hope, my desire to serve, to grow, and to love. So I hope God you will attend to this longing of mine - and the others who share this exploration with me. I wish nothing more than that you companion me into my unknown future, within a close distance. If I am to look forward to loving you more deeply, and more fully, then I have a fear that this will be 'mission impossible' unless you disclose yourself to the inner being of my own person? Because for me, to love presumes to know.

I'm remembering a joke told by Woody Allan, a drole American film star and director. In a moment of reflection he said that if you want to make God laugh, then tell him about the plans you have for tomorrow! You'll see the implication? Yes? Of course I do have plans- lots of them but I hope they can be in tune with yours, if you will come close enough to share them with me.

I will not be surprised if yours outstretches mine. My plea for communication and a revelation is laid out. Perhaps you will light it up and even garnish it with some sign or indication which hopefully will bring a smile to your face. I'm waiting. – It's a difficult discipline to master, but I'm not giving up - and this is a promise.

Letter 3: Is my suffering God's suffering, too?

Dear God,

Back in 1996 I recall I was sitting in the corner of this quiet Cathedral. My brain was sodden with the wettest tears. My thinking was water-logged. Pain vibrated in my head and down my spine. I was unable to think clearly, or to express my deep sense of bewilderment and chaos. I wonder if you recall the shooting of those Primary School children and their teacher at Dunblane? I think it was my sense of utter dereliction that made me doubt even the possibility that you would have, maybe, your own concerns for the victims and their murderer.

The question on the minds of many was why those kids in Dunblane had to die in that way? So unexpectedly and savagely? Even though I know it happened all those years ago, today it feels as if it was only yesterday. The memories are not blurred – they remain quite sharp. There were the injured children too, choked with pain and confusion, and feeling frighteningly alone. Was it all a fantasy, they wondered, or a bad dream, or was it for real? There was the agony of wondering how long it would last? These thoughts and fears vibrated through the hospital wards on that fateful morning. Parents waited. The police were harassed. The traumatised gave up. Life, as it were, came to a full stop. So even now this feels like a dire tragedy, a wicked calamity, an experience that did not have a vestige of logic or purpose about it. Strangely it still feels frighteningly present.

Over the intervening years there have been more tragedies, and the sharp pain from them infiltrates my very being, and in a strange way drives me on in my search for you, God. In my search there is a sense of mystery within myself which feels so close, and yet I am unsure whether or not it is about you at all. Clarity is hard to find in this search. Can you, I wonder, give these tragedies any meaning? Can there be even a spark of hope at all? Your response seems hardly a whisper! Do you 'close your eyes' because of your own sense of the pain? It feels as if the void of nothingness stretches out, erasing the hope that at least the death of these kids and the suffering of the injured may not have been in vain? There are those who still weep. Others look for the truth that will bring an inner solace. This still goes on, so long after that dreadful day.

I know you cannot be blamed for those deaths. The painful truth is that responsibility rests with us, including me. This feels so very uncomfortable. There is a sense that at times I feel the guilt within me. At one and the same time I am attempting to understand and to share what happened, whilst simultaneously I fear being implicated. Atrocities these days are not new. Right down history there are more examples than one cares to acknowledge. For instance it is hard to regard those parents who tenderly gave each of these children the potential life which belonged to them, only to see it destroyed, all in a swift unpremeditated moment. Many suffer the anguish of unanswered and maybe even unanswerable questions. Why? Why? Why? Mothers lost their most precious treasure, the very flesh of their flesh, and blood of their womb. It seems so meaningless. It was suggested by some that their bodies were broken, and their blood spilt 'for the sin of the world'. But this I cannot accept. We do not need, do we, any updating of the Eucharist? Could giving this tragedy a sacramental dimension give a new meaning to those who suffered and those who mourn? It is hard to see how 'the sin of the world' is redeemed in any way by this tragedy, except to hope that the terror of violence will persuade some to non-violence. But I wonder! There can be no assurance of this, but we can, and I do, hope. However I cannot be unaware that at the heart of this event there was a terrifying sense of 'the passion'. The sacrifice of untimely and unnecessary death, remains a constant reminder that suffering may be redemptive for some, whilst for others it remains nothing but an enigma.

Then there is the gun that killed. Many other guns are still hoarded away in homes, and sheds, and armouries across the land. Now I wish I could collect them all up, and all the toy guns too, and dump them at the bottom of Loch Ness, where they could remain for ever, with the Monster! Consigned to Hell! The Loch would swallow up these 'tools of Hell', and provide an evil burial place in the depths, where they would just rust away into oblivion. Then this would liberate us all from the fear of guns, initiating a new social era. What an achievement this would be! However, keeping my feet planted firmly on the ground I cannot help wondering whether this can become a reality or whether it has to remain a fantasy? The Snowdrop Petition was a good beginning. But now, ten years on, there is not much evidence that reducing firearms in our society has been successful. We need a new impetus, and this will not come until the dreadfulness of the Dunblane massacre is burnt into the very heart of society. As yet, I can see no evidence of this. Hence I can't help feeling that this struggle is unequal. The power of evil appears to be stronger than the power of goodness.

This tragedy has forced some people to face up to the increase of violence and especially the use of guns on TV. Could it be possible to have agreed days when programmes without guns are screened? The obsession with bullying and the spilling of blood on TV could be given a lower priority. We would need the gift of a peaceful imagination to promote a new style of entertainment which no longer needs the senseless predictability of macho men in the James Bond role. A new imaginative portfolio of programmes could be designed to provide entertainment of a co-operative vision, rather than the stupid greedy provoking scenarios like 'Who wants to be a millionaire?' Entertainment that affirms the non-violent and the co-operative, with the style of gentleness, would have its own intrinsic excitement. This would be a fitting memorial to the children of Dunblane. The removal of the gun and all that it has come to symbolise would be a powerful influence for the wellbeing of everyone – except the gun-makers! Hopefully, God, this would evoke your favour, and perhaps, for some at least, be an assurance that life without guns increases the possibility for a peaceable society.

What do you think about Thomas Hamilton? Is there any mercy for him? I hate what he did. It is not hard to hate him as well. I'm left feeling shocked that even after all this time I'm aware of my own hatred. It is, I suppose, a part of my confusion. There is a conflict between my desire to hate, and the need to express compassion of the heart. It is all too easy, I find, to allow my fear to drive my thinking. Quietly as I look over his life, as much as I know of it, I'm aware that in a sense he 'died' years ago, long before that fateful day in 1996. He lived with his own prospect of death long before his own self inflicted death. I can't escape the feelings of my own shame, knowing that the latter part of his life was penetrated with pain, bitterness, failure, and rejection. The evil net of bitterness entangled him with his secret fantasies based on unmerciful revenge. So he became a victim of sterile social exclusion. He knew little of love, warmth, regard and esteem. What he did not have, he took away from others, including those undefended school children and their teacher. The price of his social exclusion was the death of innocent victims. Sadly there still continue to be too many other examples repeated around the world. Those children in Dunblane were looking forward to a normal day – to an ordinary day, that never came. Most of us need to know as well as understand much more about the love that promotes justice, rather than revenge. Life is meant to be enjoyed, but no longer at the expense of the less fortunate people in society. Deep down, the bitterness of Thomas H still pains me, and no doubt many others too. The cultural 'food' of our society has to change so we can unconsciously imbibe a creativity that despises every vesture of violence, rather than condoning it. Society needs the virtues which I remember St. Paul wanted to promote in his own letter to his friends in Philippi, all those centuries ago. The virtues of honesty, purity, loveliness, and things of good report have been around a long time, and remain so relevant and contemporary. These virtues have the strength to move society forward to a new desire for equality, diminishing the number of the socially excluded.

Tenderly, in the privacy of my own self, I have 'kissed the memory' of Victoria, and Emma, Melissa, Charlotte, Kevin, Ross, David, Mhairi, Abigail, Emily, Sophie, John, Joanna, Hannah, Megan, and Gwen Taylor. God – have you 'kissed their memory' too? In your tender heart will you cherish them? Can you offer them a solace that brings with it a freedom from their pain? Are you able to guarantee for them entry into a new life, which humanity has speculated about beyond the constrictions of time and space? I cannot say I understand all this. But I hope your 'something else' will be real to them even if its reality has to be hidden from me. Sometimes I feel that the door to a fuller understanding of these things remains firmly closed. All I can do is to go on knocking. This is what Jesus advised, didn't he? In any case, I hope you will remain close to Dunblane, because it remains a citadel of suffering. Linger in the homes of those who still mourn, and encourage them to make a triumph of their broken lives. Your own secret knowledge could be a comforting benediction, hallowing this sacred memory with some indelible mark – perhaps symbolically in the memory, in the imagination, in the soul of our society 'sixteen modest crosses', with that other Cross, allied with its own symbol of power to heal.

The waiting vigil will go on – how hard this ministry of waiting feels. If your suffering and theirs could be more readily understood, then maybe a new sense of solidarity for all the afflicted, of every age, would spur a new hope. My only response now to tears, theirs, mine, or anyone else's has to be a silent yet lively AMEN! Returning today to this quiet Cathedral to write to you about my feelings and reflections has helped me to measure up to my own determination to keep probing the on-going mystery of suffering. In this I am gratified with the experience of Job, and his own journey, and with the oft repeated theme of the Psalms, along with the growing company of my contemporary fellow searchers. I now believe that the enigma of undeserved suffering will eventually give up its secret to humanity. But when? I cannot tell. This is why I have persisted in writing this letter. Can there still remain an unexplored avenue? Yes, maybe. So my ministry of waiting will continue as a day to day desire, grounded in my loyalty to the powerlessness of non-violent truth. My daily 'lived-in-action' will have its place diminishing the ever present threat of pain and anguish at every opportunity. So vouchsafe to all of us, who seek it, your assurance of hope, as a sign of your journeying with us. In the inner mystery of my own inner self, I need the grace to know that I remain open to the expectation of your yet to be experienced quiet revelation. You will see clearly, this letter comes from the depths – so I patiently wait. But for how long?

Letter 4: Is death an end or a beginning?

Dear God,

Today is All Saints' Day. Some of us use this occasion in the liturgical calendar to remember those whose memory we bless with thanksgiving and appreciation. Looking back and reviewing humanity's history, reveals how many women and men can be seen, to have been examples of how to live positively, with love and grace, fearless for truth and justice, yet with humility and openness. All Saints' Day in the Christian calendar encourages me to emulate them, in my personal living and in my professional work. For some this occasion has become a time for reflection, and memory of loved ones in their ordinariness, and others who have died in the year that has just passed. It's a time when I feel the need to reflect and recognise my sense of thankfulness.

Today, I think that awareness of death is gradually emerging from earlier taboos and superstitions. The media's reporting of death is capricious. The tendency is to report violent death almost avidly, whereas the quiet death of old age and illness is less likely to 'grab' the headlines. Obituaries are more common and have an established place in newspapers, implying I think that the lives of individual persons deserve to be marked and noted, and on occasion valued and honoured. This signifies a conscious acceptance that death is an integral part of the fabric of life and our shared experience of living.

The longer I live the more aware I am of the fact of death, with the accompanying flow of reflections, doubts, and hopes. Death appears to be a final ending. But then again, I wonder if it is? God, can you say how relevant my sense of time is to you? Your capacity to remember will be, at least different from mine. I know I am time limited, But you, I think, are not hemmed in by time. If it is the case that time doesn't exist for you God, then the human need to remember could be irrelevant. It would seem that your knowledge is for ever simultaneous perhaps? Humanly speaking people need to be remembered. Not being remembered feels very sad. Each of us has to do our own remembering. I know how buoyed up I feel when unexpectedly someone has remembered me. I wonder if and how you remember? Humanly speaking, recalling the trillions since the beginning of our world, do you remember in any accurate way? Because most of us want to be remembered, I think, especially by you. Is the notion of remembering everyone just stupid? Some clarity is needed I think, but at the moment I do not know how to go about it. All Saints' Tide is an act of remembering. For me it is a sad occasion, each year, because it is the anniversary of the death of Mark, our son. Over thirty years ago he was knocked off his cycle by a car on the main road near to the bungalow into which we were preparing to move. He was killed. I remember being driven by the police to the hospital mortuary to see his body. Strange how there seemed to be hardly a scratch on him. The mortuary attendant stood with me. I asked him to remove the cover from his body. Mark looked so young, strangely full of innocence with what could have been just the slightest glimmer of a smile. It seemed indelible on his young boyish face. I stood there alone with him. Just him and me. The attendant had left us alone. I felt I was in shock, but as I stood there looking and holding his hand, there was a strange sense of benediction. My eyes took in every detail of his young body – bone of my bone – flesh of my flesh – I thought. My son, my son, my son! And the words of King David from the scriptures seeped deeply into my stricken mind – "O Absalom my son, my son, would God that I had died for thee, O Absalom my son!".

Mark was dead. Mark is dead. His body lay there, and strangely all I could do was to adore it with kisses – beyond number. Standing there alone with him I found myself uttering quietly the blessed words – "Lord now lettest Thou they servant depart in peace, according to Thy word: for mine eyes have seen thy salvation, which thou hast prepared before the face of all thy people". And then the shout of "AMEN!". That was the last time I saw his face, his body. But his life, his person, that inner 'something' that was him, and still is him, has stayed close beside me over the long mourning years. But he is dead! At All Saints' Tide I celebrate his life.

Mark was no saint. But neither was there an inch of evil with him. I'm not romancing. He had his jokes, and his ribald version of various songs. I recall him singing a song he learned at Scout Camp, that goes to the tune 'She'll be coming round the mountain when she comes'. There's a verse he used to sing with cheeky glee

– 'she has a lovely bottom set of teeth, she has a lovely bottom set of teeth, Oh! She has a lovely bottom, she has a lovely bottom, she has a lovely bottom set of teeth!' How he giggled, out of his mind with fun, and a laugh, and sharing it with his rather sombre Dad! He loved music and played the recorder with finesse. His eyes sparkled, he was open, believed the best, and had no guile. He was quietly warm, with an attractive loving sense of dependence. He was only a child when he died but looking back now with a maturer insight and reflection I'm aware he had a spirit of uninhibited trust. As far as I know he never thought badly of anyone. This I suppose was his good fortune. In the play park he would play with any other children who wanted to play. Nonetheless I cannot imagine that in his young life he ever contemplated sainthood.

Yes each day – everyday, the question that goes through my being, repeatedly is "Where is he now?" No – I do not mean his body, precious though that was. He was cremated and on a cold Spring morning we scattered his ashes lovingly and in silence over the Pentland Hills. And since then I have a hunch that the ashes were not the real him, the real Mark. His life had been cut off in his buoyant tender years, still with some innocence 'behind his ears'. Now I wonder, where is he? The real Mark, is he anywhere at all? I used to think there was an answer to every question. Today I'm clear that this is not the case. Increasingly, as the web of life is spun, weaving its own pattern, I realise that there are more questions about life and death that remain unanswered. The important question for me is "Where is he?". My answer is that I do not know. I have no answer to this question. And it feels quite unpalatable. God I hoped for an answer from you. But your silence for me is an enigma I wish I could solve. Surely you will understand that this is not an unreasonable question for a loving father.

I recall that a psychiatrist friend in a letter to my wife and me, wrote that if you decide to have children then you open yourself up to the certainty of many risks, because children and adolescents do things which bring pain and regret. Mark loved cycling, and spent a lot of time looking after his bike. A motorist was driving a little behind him, and one of them, or perhaps both of them made a mistake. So he was killed. It seems straightforward. At the time I railed against you oh God. My anger overcame me. "Why, why was he killed?" "Bloody God!" I yelled with all my tears and bitter anger. I hated you and the whole human race. Many tried to sooth me. My wife upheld me, and how she did it I do not know. But now looking back – as I do at each All Saints' Tide, I know how human error and foolishness caused his death. I see now I can't blame you. You were not in control of him, and the car driver either. This accident, like unnumbered others was, and still is a part of our human life. But it remains hard to accept. Somehow or other it all feels so unfinished. I know he died because of an accident. So now the question is different – "where is he now?". I think you have the answer, but a strange quirk of our humanity prevents me from knowing the answer to my question. In my frailty I'm left weakly wondering when I will know, and whether it could be only when I too leave this 'weary soiled earth'?

The religion I have lived most of my life has fed me with the notion of what is called heaven. A place, a time, a state of being, which comes after death. It is beyond time and space, and in a sense because, if this is beyond the power of the imagination, what we are talking about is beyond description. I do not know its boundaries, and if it is not material in any way can there be a formula by which I will know what it is that is beyond? Presumably it is within what is called eternity. But I can not visualise this at all. Yet it remains important for me. Why? Because hopefully I might discover Mark there, and of course many other long lost loved ones. This longing is quite human isn't it? Can heaven be thought of as a temple, but without a building? Some tag this as paradise, which I take to mean a place of perfection. But this hardly satisfies my yearning spirit. It's hard being human trying to think in a way which is not human. I'm left wondering if this is a pointless exercise. Do I need to call off my search? Is my exploration just 'mission impossible'? To me this feels like the biggest question for theology and philosophy. It is the biggest question in my life, because if it is the case that each human life is of the greatest value, then it is not unreasonable to be concerned for each human life when their time here on Mother Earth is terminated. Does the value of each person lapse at the moment of their death? Are there only memories to which we can cling? My question is whether or not I will continue to be Ronald Beasley beyond my death? Dorothy Day, on one occasion said 'for the faithful, dying does not mean that life is taken away, but that it is changed'. But I wonder what kind of change? I'm thinking now of the vivid language used by St. Paul when he wrote a letter to his friends in Corinth. His use of language and the incisiveness of his poetic style leaves me shaken, yet strangely hopeful. 'This mortal must put on immortality' he says – I wonder what this means, and it looks as if I will have to go on wondering till my own dying day. If each person is to have a resurrection body my imagination does not know how to envisage it, and if it is all beyond the fertile imagination, then to me it feels as if we are getting into something that remains inaccessible. On death the body decomposes, and at the crematorium it becomes ash. This cannot be re-constituted. So I am left with a picture I cannot visualise. Dear God I'm having to accept that you still hold on to this mystery. I can only hope that as my life proceeds, and the nearer I come to my own death, I shall become more aware of what this mystery will ultimately mean.

But now, for a moment, I want to go back a bit. I can accept that you started off the whole process of life all those millions of years ago. I cannot see how it all started itself involuntarily. Presumably you knew what you were doing then? You created this boundary between living, and then not living. Could it be, I wonder, that at the world's beginning – you were, dare I say it – but an apprentice? Why not? In human experience apprenticeship has been a tested process of learning, acquiring skills and knowledge, and has served humanity well. So is it too daunting, too inquisitive to wonder if in the beginning, you found yourself an apprentice? To whom? Well, I have no idea. But beginnings are beginnings and we all go through the learning stages enabling us to come to mature experience, insights of knowledge, and perhaps most of all, learning in apprenticeship provides us with that deeper learning that comes from mistakes made and then understood. Since the beginning death has been the experience of every living person. We know that life here cannot go on forever. On the one hand I'm intrigued with the question as to whether you intended for us a life circumscribed by death? Of whether in what can only be mystery, the interplay of beginnings and endings has within it an ultimate meaning, which for the moment is shrouded so that the inner significance remains yet to be understood. What appears to be unplanned, has behind it a plan. But at the moment the missing pieces leave us only with what appears to be unplanned. I feel I am trying to describe what remains beyond description. In a sense all I can do is retreat to mystery vibrating with unknown potential. In this no man's land between you and me, between life and death, between heaven and earth, between reality and eternity, the notion of peering for the truth is rather like peering through opaque glass. We cannot see through it clearly. Our vision is curtailed, and yet there is some light, but the image beyond remains blurred. I'm left wondering what is this undefined, and blurred image? I try to come to terms with the unnumbered multitude of the dead, and I'm left wondering how can individual identity be safeguarded and cherished? After all it is on record that you do cherish every person who has 'come into the world'. I've read the pointers given by St. Paul, the vision and prophecy of Isaiah, the stories of 'the last days', and enigmatic writings of the Book of Revelation. And I am left still in a deep quandary. However, dear God, be sure that I do not know how to deal with it. And once again I come to 'the waiting game'!

I have friends who are responsible and who think and who try to live with creative purpose. They believe that this present life is all that we have. They say that this is our only chance of living, so grab life and get out of it as much as you can. Just enjoy it! There is nothing else, and all we have is here. It means when life is over and death comes then that is not just the end, it is for them, the final end. I suppose that if I knew with complete certainty that this really is the case then I might become used to it. But I doubt this, just as I am left in doubt about the notion of eternity beyond this present transitory life. I have a sense of inadequacy that is beginning to fuel a deeper sense of irritation, and maybe anger. I'd prefer to live without the constrictions of overwhelming doubt. I am not one who prefers not to know. I do not wish to conspire with evasion. For me truth matters. I am not forgetful that Jesus told his disciples that it was not given to them 'to know the day or the hour'. Part of me is aware of that aspect of worship that captures only momentarily that sense of not-knowing, and yet being able to stay with it, and trust it, so that these moments, are special and take me as near as it is possible to the spiritual, that for but a moment I can briefly bear. Ignorance is a lack of knowledge. But I have a sense that my comfort can only come from a spiritual incision into my day by day working world. And I think I feel that the spiritual has within it caution, not knowing, and the waiting that brings a mature gravitas of the soul. Could it be that this assumption is basic for attaining something of being 'a saint' – with a tiny and very small 's'?

This audit of my experience, dear God, tears out my soul, and feels like an agony of the mind. The issues are so big and in it all I feel so small. Maybe it is not so strange that so many will not face these difficult and ultimate questions. The story of Jesus is a perfect story. I cherish the notion that resurrection discloses a victory of good over evil. All around me I am all too much aware of the victory of evil over goodness. There's too much of this for comfort in these times.

I'm wondering what the difference is between 'Jesus is alive', and 'Christ is risen'? The boundary beyond these two assertions is unclear, and the repetition, like a never ending mantra, dilutes whatever meaning can be derived from either. On occasion the words seem empty, but on rarer occasions they may bring moments of ecstasy, when what can only be called 'presence' momentarily fills my being. Yet it can quickly vanish – too quickly. I have not met Jesus on any Emmaus Road, as far as I am aware. I can't say that I have had a real conversation with him. I hope I am open to the possibility. But I recognise I am just one of a great number who share a sense of doubt which arises from deep disappointment. As I read the conclusions of the four Gospels and turn to the opening chapters of the Acts of the Apostles, I have a tinge of jealousy of those who had a first hand experience of these things. Perhaps if I had been there, physically, I might feel and think very differently. From the record, clearly the lives of some were changed, and across the centuries others have followed suit. Jesus has influenced many, and he has influenced me. But I can't help but wonder why after two millennia his following today, is, statistically speaking, so small? I wonder God if this brings you disappointment? Did you think that his life on earth would have changed things more quickly? Certainly it seemed as if he had some success over his own death. No one else has achieved what he achieved. But to plumb the depths of the enigma of life, death, and then new life seems to take a whole life time of pilgrimage, and yet even then there is not much to be over certain about. I'm at the end of my life and I have the feeling that this whole exploration remains in its opening phase.

In my search for you, and in my questioning and stumbling before and since Mark died, I have found some comfort when I immerse myself in the music and words of Faure's Requiem. This music, for me, does something extraordinary to the words. The religious words at first hearing seem unrelated to me and to my life. I know that they are as old as the Church itself. But the language sounds remote and feels in some ways alien to my intellect. Nonetheless, the music translates the meaning into a vibration of the soul, too perfect almost for utterance, or evaluation. This work has within it a hidden revelation which for the brief moment is utterly transforming. It leaves a blessed brief memory of the transcendent, transmitting a whisper of a quality of life, bordering on the infinite, a treasure which I always treasure.

I am attempting to create a listening post of the Spirit where I might encounter you, God. Within the rich unseen truths, which on occasion lie buried in myths, metaphors, stories, parables, and poetry. The implicit and explicit vie with each other in the euphemistic art of painters, musicians, choreographers, as well as through the yoga tableau, along with the still-point circumscribed meditation. Can these bring a focus to my heart which will enable me to be in closer touch with you in the spiritual adventure? To communicate what appears to be beyond communication is such a tantalising frustration of the spirit and of the mind. It feels to me that much of my search for you is locked into what I can only describe as incognito occasions. Where the ethereal shutter comes down and the effort to grasp the moment is sadly lost. I'm trying to walk 'the space' between you and me, and I feel I'm having all too little success. This reminds me of an experience when I was driving on my own, at night, on an unknown minor road to an unknown destination. The icy surfaces were made worse by fog, and I felt I had all too little control. On occasion I was forced to stop, even though there was the danger that a vehicle following would smash into me. The map I had did not help, and the mobile phone was useless. I felt utterly on my own. I could hear other traffic but could not see it, and indeed was afraid of it. I was isolated behind the wheel of the car. And the recognition that others were going through this same experience helped not a whit. The senselessness of it all was mirrored in what I felt when Mark died. It wasn't that my tears blinded me in that mortuary, it was that he, the real Mark, was no longer there. Through all these intervening years there are moments when he feels 'close'. I feel it is more than just my fertile imagination. His life has ended, but who he was and now still is, can feel near. His identity is beyond sensory experience, but in the very private self of the citadel which is me, this actual relationship we still share. If I felt you God, as close, then there would be a double joy in my heart.

There are those who testify to visions, like the story of Mary in the Garden, where she thought she was talking to the gardener. The notion of an exchange within the imagination, between being faced with a gardener and realising a mistaken identity, is evocative. But is this all it was? A mistaken identity and nothing else? I have had my own occasions of mistaken identity, when I have been moved to tears and wonder in a conversation of rare pregnant insight from a piece of music or an evocative painting; a rare tender moment with a friend or lover; a newly discovered vista of a meadow backed by majestic mountains merging into a newly found horizon. The sharing of bread. Behind the unplanned, lies a plan. These are some of the insistent themes of mystery that have stopped me in my tracks. They are beyond my understanding of the human grasp. They hover uncertainly, and defy clarity with their clouded and uncertain description. Oh dear! I have tried to share some of my human experiences that still remain 'out of this world'. They do not solve the riddle of life or death, not even the strange riddles of the inter-relationship of yesterday and today, today and tomorrow. Nor have they yet given the clarity I seek about the relationship between me and Mark, an unscripted saint.

Dear God, please read this with care – I write with a struggle. I'm ready to expose my own experience for scrutiny. I'm ready to be probed about my passivity on the one hand, and my assertiveness and passion on the other. My sense of being open or closed, hopeful or depressed, lucid or confused, imaginative or pragmatic, is all a part of me. The exploration of the realm of unknowing, with the desire to push back the barriers out there, as well as within my inner self is a part of the day to day agony and yet wonder of living. The motivation force which drives me on is my desire to know if my love for Mark is with him wherever he may be. Whether Jesus is alive or not, and whether Mark is in any sense alive, beyond my own sight is my own quest, stretching into the future. My search is not hindered by the immensity of the enigma, but probably because of it.

All Saints' Tide helps us all to recall quietly and lovingly the fact of death. Though some may feel no reminder is necessary for them. The Remembrance Tide quietly follows on in the calendar with its own solemnity. With war and violence ever present I'm wondering if the actual circumstance of death itself makes a difference to the victim. A violent death, being murdered, or forcibly killed in one way or another, being killed in an accident, or coming to one's own death with a sense of agony and undeserved pain – how much does this matter facing death itself? Dying a good death, waiting for it in quiet confidence, feeling it is 'just right', full of years maybe, and 'ready to go'. Meeting one's new beginning, if this is what death is, is it, I wonder, of any consequence the way one died? Those who mourn are aware of the after-feelings according to the mode of death experienced by the deceased. Jesus died a horrific death. So have many others. But when the earth is left behind, is it all equitable? If Mark had died in a quiet way, without the violence of actually being killed, it would have felt better for me.

But is it an issue for him and others who have died violently? Loss by death is still loss. But the manner of the death is an important matter for mourners, and if it was known that this in no way alters the ultimate life beyond for the deceased, then I am sure the process of death itself would be understood as being just that little bit more humane. Probing the experience of death is a natural desire, motivated by perplexity and natural enquiry. I am sure I am not the only person tottering on the edge of this void. Sharing anxiety or hopes and feeling the comfort of others, who travel in hope, in a sense provides a grace to be enjoyed. Poets attempt to express the inexpressible, and this poem by Christina Rossetti helps to bring comfort and an increasing measure of grace.

Remember

Remember me when I am gone away,
Gone far into the silent land;
When you can no more hold me by the hand,

Nor I half turn to go yet turning stay.
Remember me when no more day by day
You tell me of our future that you planned:
Only remember me; you understand
It will be late to counsel then or pray.
Yet if you should forget me for a while
And afterwards remember, do not grieve;
For if the Darkness and corruption leave
A vestige of the thoughts that once I had,
Better by far you should forget and smile
Than that you should remember and be sad.

Coping with the mystery of grief, mourning him and valuing the past, his life, and yet not allowing the past, wonderful as it had been, to inhibit the present, and the new future with its promise, requires some integrity of spirit.

This letter, has cost me a good deal. I feel I have taken risks, because I want so much to understand whether or not you have any sense of the wilderness and the desolation where hope is hard to find. The loneliness of life after the loss of a precious relationship, the intimidating feel of death, as Christina Rossetti suggests, requires a bravery of the mourner that is not easily captured. As I struggle to pierce the uncertain meaning that lies behind the exploration of this letter, I hope that I can at least begin to regard death itself as an adventure which only in the short term is locked into the utterly unknowable. Sharing the pilgrimage with a much loved son or daughter, or with one's spouse and lover, with whom life's journey has been intimately shared in this world, for almost a lifetime, becomes more special when the moment of 'letting go' beckons, and in trust the insoluble human mystery, the last 'frontier', becomes the hardest task of all. Will the wilderness remain? Finding the mode and words to say goodbye would be that little bit easier if buried deep within there was the hope that all too soon they were superseded by the biggest surprise of all, by an unexpected 'hello'! Maybe this will even beat the notion of resurrection! In the waiting game no matter how long it takes, I'm hoping for the surprise of all surprises. All Saints' Tide could be a helpful directive. Could it?!

Letter 5: I want to be alive when I die

Dear God,

He was standing there, quietly. Facing the people with the wafer in his hand. "This is my body………" and lifting up the host, he placed it in his mouth. In the very next moment he collapsed and fell to the floor. Father Harold was a saintly priest. He gave assurance to everybody. He was always there. No one ever heard him angry or patronising. Day after day for nearly thirty years he exercised his ministry. It was the whole of his life. He died at the zenith of the holiest act of the Mass. The wafer still in his mouth, and the blessed words still on his lips. Everyone there was overcome with shock and confusion.

I think this confusion could well turn to anger. And why not? This saintly man died in the very act of the Eucharist. Father Harold in his death personified the baffling fact that many who are saintly, like him, live out their lives quietly, being their best, only to die an unanticipated death. His death to the bystander appears to be unjustified, certainly from a human point of view.

It was not just his death. It was the manner and circumstance of it. There does seem an irony about it. Is it expected to teach us something? If so what? The wicked prosper and the good perish? It looks like it, doesn't it? He was in his prime, with so much to give. He lived his life giving to others. He cared nothing for money or power , nor for comfort either. He was singularly, 'a man for others'. And he is, unexpectedly dead. Why? Has he died before his time? Is there, in fact, a right time to die? Was this the right time for him? How shall we ever know? Is there a 'divine arithmetic' in these matters? Yes, I know we all have to die, but the actual circumstances are not unimportant, are they? Father Harold will not be remembered because he died, but rather because of the manner and occasion of his death. To say that he just died of a heart attack might be true, but the deeper question is whether or not it could have been preordained or not? You will know the familiar words of the funeral service, "As it hath pleased Almighty God to call to Himself the soul of our brother / sister etc". I suppose this could be regarded just a form of words. On the other hand they might be regarded as something akin to the notion of pre-destination.

Traditions die hard, and even though the poetry of the words can be pleasing, the truth of the words is more important, and relevant to this incident which I am trying to explore. There are those who are prepared for their death, and for them the transition can be calm and peaceful. There can be no better way to die – in peace and at rest. To die a good death, clearly, is to be preferred to a death of pain and agony. But Father Harold's death was so harrowing for his congregation. As far as we know he had no particular preparation, unless of course we concede that the whole of his life was his preparation. Time to prepare for this most far reaching journey any of us will make, does seem important. Nonetheless I suppose large numbers of people only think about their death when it happens, with no preparation. With Father Harold no one had time to say 'goodbye'. Nor did he.

Life on this planet is full of the unexpected. This may be viewed as good, for the unexpected does not always have to be frightening. But with the frequency of accidents, on roads or the railways, with air disasters, and more recently with the increase of terrorism, we face the possibility that at the actual time it will not always be possible to be prepared for death. Yes, there is the reality of human error. But then with natural disasters, who or what is accountable for them? Some are accounted to be 'an act of God', according to some insurance policies. But clearly other disasters cannot be called natural, as they have a human origin, such as, the cutting down of many, many square miles of virgin forest, with a potential catastrophic environmental disaster. So the factors and conditions that bring death are multiple and indeed complex. Unexpected death these days is never far away. Life can feel tenuous. Clearly it was for Father Harold. If life has a meaning, and I believe it has, then so also death must have a meaning too. But what is it? With regard to both birth and death it could seem that none of us have much control over either. So it is understandable that one will feel vulnerable and anxious about what the future may hold. I hope it does not sound too primitive, but with the manifold cause of death, the more important question is whether or not you have a hand in our dying? I feel Father Harold, for instance died before his time. But did he? This exploration to me feels like knocking at the door of mystery, which seems reluctant to offer up its meaning.

There was a 'wake' for Father Harold. After the solemn Requiem Mass, in all its uplifting liturgy, his people wanted to celebrate his life. In effect they were saying 'thank goodness he lived'. And 'thank goodness we knew him and he knew us'. Afterwards his coffin was lowered into the grave, and there his body will rest. It was all over. Another ending. The people were left with their memories, and an aching void. – a gap of nothingness. I feel it too with them. To experience the sudden and unexpected death of a friend does bring its own gloom and disillusionment. I feel so alone. A sense of isolation seems to take 'the ground from under my feet'. I'm left feeling that involuntarily I'm clutching at my own one unrepeatable life. I say to myself, well, I'm still here! I'm not ready to let my life go. I want to live as fully as I can. So being more tenacious might help short term, but I guess that long term I'm faced with the fact that death will come to me too. But I'm left wondering, when?

When talking to a friend she suggested that it could be that when we are ready 'to go' we then live as fully as possible. Looking forward to living, on reflection I think I've learned that my life has been given meaning, not so much from its 'when' and 'where', but more significantly from the relationships I have acquired over the years. Without them my life would have been very barren. Father Harold had a large circle of people who felt they were important to him. His congregation was small, but that community had its own sense of closeness, even intimacy. The closeness brought comfort. But now it seems rather less than certain. This is evidence of the deep sense of loss.

I'm just thinking of that parable of Jesus and the rich man and the beggar Lazarus. It's a graphic story – too graphic really for some, I think. I'm left wondering whether or not the great gulf, fixed, is so ominous, that for myself I feel almost terrified. The pictures of hell are uncomfortable, and the insistence in the parable that there is no possible communication between there and here, leaves me feeling vulnerable, and yes, quite afraid. It's in the light of this that being born is so much simpler than dying. Although there can be complications at birth, there is only one process. With death – the ways of dying are multitudinous, and I can't help wondering if one dies on a battlefield, or in one's own bed, all alone or within a crowd – does it matter? My question would be, does the manner of death affect in any way the following 'journey'? The Bhagavad Gita said, "Invisible before birth are all beings, and after death invisible again. They are seen between two unseens. Why in this truth find sorrow?".

This meditation has, I think, two perspectives to it. Death can be approached as a part of the process of living. The whole creation is subject to death, sooner or later. So it might seem that it was part of your plan. Some think of life here on Earth as a prelude to heaven hereafter. So that in a sense death is as natural as living. It's the sense of sustained loss that gives death its bitter human edge. When death comes with old or older age then it feels more natural. But sudden and unexpected death in the young is experienced as a bitter blow. However to me this has been complicated by the notion of death being an enemy. This notion seems to be rooted in the death of Jesus. Death was his enemy, wasn't it? The notion of him being your Son, to say the least is for some surrounded by doubt and hesitation. To the 'man in the street' the Sonship of God is not straightforward. The teaching of the Church has always been that the death and the ensuing new life of Jesus has opened for us all, the 'gate of heaven'. The small matter of the relevance of this in all its mystery, to those who preceded the Jesus 'gift' – who lived in the preceding centuries, remains, to put it simply, unclear. Were they, are they, now included in the heavenly host?

When death comes savagely to any person, then it is not difficult to see death as 'the enemy'. However it also has to be said that for some sufferers, death itself has been a welcomed friend. It has brought the end of suffering when everything else had been tried, but unsuccessfully. The enigma of life and death, or earth and heaven, of beginnings and endings, with the on going struggle between good and evil remains for most of us a vista awaiting more extensive exploration. For scholars and academics books and philosophies about death and life have been written. But their insights and searching often are wrapped up in a language and idiom which are not always accessible to others. But the search for truth will go on, and I hope the sense of yearning of this letter will signal that new discoveries in understanding of the life and death cycle will be made, especially if the search is perceived as a valid interest and relevance for every human being.

For most of us death remains the ultimate ending. Endings are important. They have a special value. But the mystery contained in this ending – the ending of our life on Earth, will require a particular and sensitive ongoing research. Is there, in fact, any new truth to be perceived? Or is it rather that we have all that there is to know? There is nothing else to be discovered or researched; we can only be satisfied with what we have? The state of unknowing is the only state we have, and with it there is the space for grace and calm expectation, but this comes without any certainty. To put it simply, in your providence, God, we are secure. In my best moments I can be ready to rest my case, and tolerate my unsatisfied inquisitiveness.

For some time now I have resolved to, as it were live each day, as if it were my last day. I've found it a salutary exercise. When the vista of death arrives for me, I want to experience it fully. I don't want to miss anything. I want to be conscious when I die. I want to see what can be seen, to feel what can be felt, and to know it is for real. This is the journey I want to travel with expectation. Nonetheless I know I can't plan my death as I hope to plan my summer holiday. Living one day at a time, or perhaps more realistically one week at a time, does give me a more immediate perspective to my life, adding a sharper focus to the stewardship of my daily living. For me it is the 'human face' of existence that is so precious, and I would like in some way to take this with me. Like the rest of my life, I want to be a participant and not just a spectator. I hope this will add some sense of humility and wonder, assuring me that the process for each person will be a loving process. So for Father Harold's sake, enlarge my imagination, and keep me expectant, and hopeful for the miracle that will bring incandescent illumination. And if I flag a little or grow querulous, hold out a morsel of the hope that will satisfy my searching insatiability.

Clear thinking has not been my most outstanding achievement, but perhaps you'll acknowledge my tenacity by staying with the issue, the problem, and being ready to hold on 'to the end'. Writing letters I think facilitates the opportunity for deeper reflection, so that hopefully I'll embrace that, which at the moment, cannot yet be understood. Father Harold, without knowing it, I suppose, by his death has projected me forward, and has enabled me to grow, so that I can be even hopeful that my letter on this occasion, to you God, will bring something that gives peace, greater certainty about you, and your purposes, which I hope will grow into a deeper sense of 'being known' mutually. Thank you for reading this letter. Perhaps without my knowing you have been at my elbow, as the typewriter rattled away!?

Letter 6: Asking questions

Dear God,

I've just come back from visiting Mrs. Browning. My conversation with her has sparked off some reflections, as well as dredging up some deeper questions from my occasional meanderings. She is a lady of ninety-three. I always enjoy talking with her, and I know she likes having a visitor. She can't walk far, but mentally she is alert. Sometimes I admit, I'm astonished how up to date she is. She always has her questions, and she is not backward in making me aware of her views. She can be a little intimidating, though I'm sure she is unaware of her occasional brusque manner. It is a cold day, and the wind is chilly, with a draught from under her kitchen door. She was huddled close to her gas fire. She had on layers of clothes, and her hair was combed and tidy, and everything around her kitchen looked spic and span. She lives modestly, and depends on a neighbour to collect her weekly pension from the Post Office. She does not complain much. She has her few pot plants, and she's an avid reader of the newspaper. She is sitting in her rather unsteady arm chair which has a straight back to it. She had a hot water bottle on her lap, which is a great comfort to her.

Over the years since I started visiting her, we have got to know each other, and it is a good friendship. Sometimes she surprises me. When I arrived this morning she was chuckling away. In *The Scotsman* there was some sensational reporting on a sexual caper of some kids in Fife. She threw the paper over to me for me to read for myself.

Ten or so years ago her husband died. They had had a long marriage, and it had been a good love affair. As well as the difficulties, she remembered the times when they had had fun, sexual happiness, parties, and lots of friends. Her husband's photo was on the shelf, and she speaks of him by his nickname, 'Tiny', even though in his prime he was a little over six feet tall. She was saying that in her younger days condoms were not much use. They were unreliable. But, she said this did not dampen their enthusiasm. She talked casually as she made a pot of tea. She felt the newspaper was being stingy in its editorial, and decrying the fact that these days kids spent too much time 'messing around'. She quipped that newspapers had sex on the brain – not a good place to have sex! And I tended to agree with her. She had flipped though the pages, the regular features of fashion, clothes, and the gossip of stars and personalities, who, she thought spent too much time having affairs. She wasn't one to criticise the young much, though she did not like the continuous focus in the papers on drink, drugs and fags. She reckoned that if questionable behaviour was okay for adults, then it's okay too for kids. She loathed hypocrisy and the 'holier than thou' attitude. All this time she was sipping her tea and enjoying her digestive biscuit. There was a quiet moment, and then she reflected that she hoped that when they got to her age they would be lucky enough to be as satisfied as she was with life and its achievements. She went on to say that she and Tiny had an open relationship with no secrets. We enjoyed having our children with all the ups and downs. But as we went on talking I became aware that she was beginning to ponder, and I had a strange feeling that perhaps I was in the way.

I had a picture of her, energised and vivacious, with a racy marriage, and lots of involvement in the community where she lived. For her, fun had a deep and mutual satisfaction, and I detected no selfishness. Not being well-off, they lived modestly with few mod-cons, and her husband working long hours. Her philosophy was that life was for living, and for living today. They worked hard and played hard. For them there was no glitz. They learned to defer pleasures, and to wait, and yet to enjoy the intimacies of family life. As she talked away I became aware that she was not living just 'on the outside'. Rather, she had her own inner perceptions which had freed them both from pretending to be anything other than what they wanted to be. I reflected that this felt like genuine integrity.

I was rinsing the cups a little later when she was getting up from her chair, to show me a book she had been reading. Without any warning she let out a yell of pain, followed by a deep, deep sigh. She then flopped back on to the bare settee. Her voice was trembling. She looked uncomfortable, and she sounded tired out and dead weary. "Why doesn't God call me?" I was a little taken aback by her question. This all seemed a rather long march away from our recent conversation. I caught sight of her face, as a wisp of sunshine poked though her curtain. It was deeply lined. I had not noticed it much before. She had quivering lips and steel grey wisps of unruly hair. I noticed just the suggestion of a tear, which she quickly padded with her hanky. "I go hopefully to sleep" she yearned with a sigh. "But I still wake up each morning". "Why doesn't he call me?". In that moment I had what felt like a flash of astonishing insight – in her soul I could see that she was already 'on her journey'. She was ready to leave – but to where? Well, I'm not feeling very sure. I was sensing some uncertainty, and yet it was mixed with eagerness, an urge, to get going. This was a precious moment of realisation for her, but also for me. Sitting quietly she conceded that she wanted 'to get on with it' – as she said, she was ready. I then listened quietly as she talked about being ready to leave her home, her friends, her grown up family, some in Nantwich, and others just north of Oban. She said she was sure that she'd miss what she called her grand-adolescents – all three of them – because each of them had given her lots of happiness. Somehow or other she had always had a sense of living purposefully. She wanted to die purposefully too, and clearly, she thought the time was ripe. She had few regrets, and she was ready for the next step of her journey, and she recognised that journey's end was near at hand, but perhaps not near enough. As I reflect now, it was her question that has remained with me – "Why doesn't he call me?". So, dear God, you can see why I'm wanting to share this experience with you.

I stayed a little longer. Sitting beside her with my hand on hers, and looking straight into the orange glow of the gas fire, I said quietly to her, tongue in cheek, "Well, maybe he's too scared to let you in". "Why?" she asked. "Well because of the complaints you might make, almost as soon as you are over the threshold". She chuckled. She'd got her breath back. With some composure she looked me in the eye as only she could, "Well you know me – you know that when I get there, if I do, I'll be so relieved its more likely, I think, that I'll not have a question in my head. I'll have forgotten it all". Then an after thought, "Somehow I reckon there'll be no need for questions in heaven". She had some certainties, and some expectations which left me pondering.

Her insight disturbed me. And I want to explore with you now some of the implications for me, as I try to take seriously Mrs. Browning's perception. I'm not forgetting that there have been for me moments when I felt at one with everything. But what, I wonder would existence be like without questions? Life here on earth is full of questions. I pondered again – no politics, no education, no exams, no quizzes, no dilemmas, no laws – because in all these facets of life questions throb and tease the mind and the heart. No searching, no wondering, no questions?! Life I reflected without questions would be sterile. This prospect challenges and disturbs me. My mind shot away to the General Assembly of the Church of Scotland, where 'questions are always in order'. And of course I reflected on the other times when the Church has discouraged questions, usually because there are those who interpret questions as being almost tantamount to disloyalty. For some questions are a nuisance. But for me questions have always been a tool for living. Questions signal openness, facing facts, with an intention to understand what is not readily understood. In classes, workshops, and groups where I have been teaching, and with counselling clients questions have always been important – their questions and my questions. Wrestling with a serious and unpalatable issue stirs up in me the desire to get to the nub of the issue, and this remains impossible without the tool of quiet reflective questions. It is exhilarating to enable others to articulate their questions and accompany them, as it were, in the search for authentic answers. Being in the grip of an unspeakable question is a hard and unpleasant experience. Looking back, bringing up children in the family was full of questions – most of which I think I appreciated and even enjoyed. Questions are the basis of democracy, free speech, and the search for justice. I can think of little that gives so much satisfaction as a good and full answer to a hard heavyweight question.

Questions precede discovery. Questions fertilise the mind and the imagination. Questions stimulate the artist, the poet, and the musician. Questions threaten dogma and political correctness, as well as the arrogance of those who think 'they know everything'. Here on Planet Earth there are still many unanswered questions. For most of us questions probe the here and now, but they also probe the territory of the spirit and the world of transcendence. Questions freshen intimate and personal relationships, so that boundaries can be recognised and probably crossed, and horizons scanned.

So my neighbour's startling outburst still sticks in my mind. I'm left wondering if it could be a clue to what might be expected in heaven? Paul wrote, 'then shall I know, even as also I am known' – fully open, and nothing hidden. I'm wondering if this implies nothing will need to be posed, asked, or explored? For my neighbour the prospect of no further questions seemed to her like a long awaited promise. I suppose some school teachers, and maybe some politicians might fully sympathise with her! It is not easy trying to imagine a state of all-knowing which might make questions so incongruent. Could there ever be a condition for mortals where there is no further need for exploration? Could it mean that in heaven there is no questing and no searching – no fulfilment in the wonder of discovery? The possibility of no questions, only fuels my imagination with more and more questions. For me heaven, as a zone where questions are welcome would be more comfortable than a zone where questions would be unnecessary. Preparation for this transition from Earth to Heaven would entail a cosmic and spiritual re-orientation, and might be better achieved with the services of an 'entrepreneur of bridging courses'! I feel a little self conscious, and I hope you are not laughing at me! But you can understand my hesitations? I want to pitch my concerns as honestly as I can. I want to be honest and yet not so hesitant that I cannot explore my own doubt and the incredulity of experiencing life without questions. At the same time I recognise that for my neighbour the prospect of no further questions seemed to her like a long awaited promise. I imagine that school teachers and others who face consistent questioning, may have a similar yearning as my neighbour. But if heaven is the prospect of life with no questions, this means for me an absence of the sense of exploration which only multiplies my anxiety. Can there ever be a sense of living where there is complete understanding? For me I fear this might turn a heaven into purgatory. So, for me, the issue of whether or not heaven is a question-free zone is fundamental.

My neighbour touched me with her sense of readiness, and her wanting 'to be called'. Her face fell into a quiet repose and as I got my coat on prior to leaving I felt I had been privileged to be at hand in her moment of unfulfilled anticipation. I'm hoping that I will mellow into something akin to her sense of reality – to be ready – to have something of her imagination – and to feel free enough like her to leave life here, ready for some other life, even though its definition is hard to express. And I've been surprised how her sharpness about the importance of questions has embedded itself inside my own thinking and reflection. I'm left wondering if questions are a given part of the new life that some hope will succeed this life on Earth? When I feel I am travelling a desolate road, when the sun does not shine, and confusion comes upon confusion, then the heart cries aloud with its hard edged questions, searching and questioning, for my experience has taught me that to question is to prove the very reality of the life I've been given. But in heaven? Well, I'm open to something new, which for now I cannot even comprehend. Desolation is eclipsed, and after a life time of wanting you, dear God, you will then be known to her, my friend, and to me? This is the knowing that is loving. Even now, I hardly feel safe saying it! But I can, and I will. I hope I'm a ready and eager learner. So, I'll keep writing, if for no other reason than it fertilises my imagination, and reveals new aspects of myself to myself. Illuminating!

Letter 7: Hope for the hopeless?

Dear God,

I wonder if you know this couple? Earlier this morning they sat here in this room, small as it is. Yet they were as far away from each other as possible. Their faces were cold, hard, vacant yet lined with trouble and anger. As they sat there it seemed that each was trying to avoid everything and everyone. They each had worn out trainers, and patched jeans, but still with many holes. They were dirty, and each had lank hair. Mary has a small shining stone stud in her nose, and a variety of rings on her eight fingers. Hamish has ear rings, pointing out under his long hair, which looked as if it had been bleached. They looked uncared for - tense – suspicious, with no vestige of self esteem. They had neither dignity nor joy. Oh dear, I thought, where do I begin?

They were referred recently by someone who knew their plight, but felt helpless to do anything. This couple had been living together, in a fashion, on and off for a few years. Now in their mid twenties they were at the end of their tether. Each of them had had 'anonymous childhoods of rejection, abuse, and pain. They grew up trusting no one, not even each other. As teenagers they appeared to cling to each other. They found a mutual sexual satisfaction together, but sadly it was crude, and it was their attempt to escape hard reality. For them life was only short term. But now all that the lies, deceit, and selfishness has provided them with is the terror of nothingness. For them everyday brings the fear of tomorrow, as well as the fear of the pimps to whom they owe money, the money they do not have. They fear the police, and in fact they fear everyone. And worst of all they have a hunch, as sure as day follows night, that what lies ahead is endless questioning, interrogation, and there could be the easy seduction of suicide. Except though, that they are afraid to die. But, they are also afraid to live!

The shared life of this couple has broken down. They live in their own wilderness. There are many others like them. You see, for them their wilderness seems big and endless. They have never known anything of beauty, positive purpose, or affection. For them truth and love have no meaning. The lives of each of them have just been one exploitation after another. The noble virtues have found no lodging at all in their consciousness.

These two have been violated since their earliest days. They've had experiences they will never forget, etched for ever on their memory. They have been kicked around, and now an apparently compassionless society can only offer them the same 'vile medicine'. They are at the end of the road!

My coming up against them, made me feel in an uncanny way that I've had to come up against all the others who they seem to represent. It's not a nice feeling. Mary and Hamish are not alone. I'm attempting, you might say, to love them both. But in such a way so as not to diminish them. I do not want to take away from them any sense of responsibility that remains. For me, they are 'the tip of the iceberg'. They are just below the surface of the icy waters of hard and friendless, self-satisfied Scotland. They are inhabiting the wilderness of today's uncaring society. For me, writing all this is a discharge and relief. I have a sense of urgency to commend them to you. Whether this helps them, or not, I do not know. But in a strange way I think it does help me.

When they left here earlier, I was reminded of Jesus being called the Shepherd of the sheep. Mary and Hamish have no Shepherd. They may not have much idea about what it means to be a Shepherd, and no one is looking for this job. Their mood swings from being insatiable for attention, and then to being completely withdrawn into the abyss of their own silent world. Not for them money, clothes, friends, good times. They've had little food. As I sit here writing it could seem that they do not exist. I suppose it's my fantasy. But they do exist! They were here with me this morning, for about thirty minutes. It felt like eternity. And I feel guilty because I realised that eventually I just wanted them to go away.

They said little, other than a few verbal obscenities. They had no questions. For them the time for questions had run out. By now they had grown immune to endless questioning from the police and social workers. I had a hunch there was the slightest sign that they wanted to be listened to. Trying to piece together a coherent story of their plight felt like 'drawing teeth'. To have given them money, though difficult, would not have been the solution. Finding a small caring community that would feed them, put up with their dirt and smell, as well as their negative attitude, would take some time. An open and non-judgemental group, the very few that exist, find it hard to survive for more than a few months. Stress in these 'therapeutic communities' can be destructive. On the other hand few groups can handle such difficult people, and at the same time offer them a new sense of responsibility. It's not practical for me to have them here. It would be a difficult challenge and I doubt if I would be up to it, and my wife would be genuinely ambivalent – it's a real dilemma. But their plight is desperate – and I'd welcome a 'divine intervention'. No such luck I suppose? You see it's because I feel so low about them, that I thought a letter might help, and in a strange way it has.

I know that they need to accept some responsibility for how they are. The chance of them coming to terms, even with themselves, seems a thousand miles away. As things stand I could more readily fry an egg on the top of a volcano than be able to guarantee anything of good, for them. I feel it's all so unfair for them, and for me! Even though I'm feeling rather impotent. I do want to love them, though I'm unsure of how to show it. Buzzing in my head is that bit about Jesus 'having nowhere to lay his head'. This often repeated rhetoric clashes with my practical mind and all my other responsibilities. So I'm perplexed, what does it mean for me to make a real sacrifice?

I know that being a therapist and counsellor, a caring person, I should be on the 'side of the poor'. This is a slogan heard too easily these days. I want to be ready to go 'the second mile', even though in a sense 'the first mile' for me has hardly started. Sacrificial solidarity is utterly compelling, and I know some who have gone the whole distance. I admire them and support them when I can. But I feel it's not for me to give up family, as its coming nearer to my end than I would sometimes like to admit! Solidarity with the poor is very tough. I'm feeling the sharp edge of my own guilt, and frankly I'm not feeling 'very tough'. I will try to keep in touch with them. I'll find some clothes, and will see that they have some food tokens. I'll search around yet again to see if there is anyone else who might have something to offer, that would be acceptable to them. I'll talk to the community police officer, and the minister at the local Church. But deep down I know that this is not enough. I've heard it said that our society is a victim of compassion exhaustion. I feel my own inadequacies. I've heard too the comments about 'the nanny state' – but to help, one does not need to be 'a nanny'!

All this bites into my soul, and it chews up my stomach. Here I am at the end of a long day, feeling exhausted – as someone said 'Virtue has gone out of me'! Mary and Hamish have been failed by the education system, their families, the political system, and I can hardly face myself.

Some will say to me, well, you've done your best. But clearly, this is not enough. I've tried to keep in front of me the image of the Good Samaritan. But to change the world of these unfortunates, the marginalised, and the numberless poor, nothing less than a revolution will be required. The new Parliament here in Scotland is trying, gentle step by gentle step, but held back by political inexperience, and timidity. Few people have any sense of urgency when it comes to redressing the need of the poor. Underneath the latent frustration lie seeds of anger and violence. Society feels brittle and dry, readily inflammable. As a pacifist I'm unsure, though I acknowledge the sense of perpetual tyranny that prevails. For the oppressed, violence seems to be the only weapon that can help them. Our ghettoised society builds the invisible walls of separation.

Some friends on the basis of their understanding of the scriptures believe the poor will be rewarded in heaven. This is not convincing me, and of course it brings us back again and again to what we believe about heaven, about which I think there is a shortage of information available! For me the caring Christian has the task to change the world with whoever else is ready to join her and him. But the longer I live the more I am inclined to believe that this task is bigger than any of us. It is clear in scripture that you 'love the world' – then if this is so your intervening power is required. But in spite of the stories in the Old Testament – the epic occasions of biblical history – the Israelites and the Red Sea and all that, I'm wondering yet again how impotent you are? In a way I can understand my own impotence, but it is not easy to recognise that in your own nature, when it comes to issues like 'the poor', then this is entirely in the hands of humanity. Once again, I'm recalling Mary's Song, and those vibrant words 'he hath put down the mighty from their seat' – how I yearn that this could happen – but now from experience it is I think, quite unlikely. Any intervention from you is 'not on the cards'! But were it to be, I'm wondering would this curtail humanity's freedom? Were you to intervene, say to take charge of situations requiring a reservoir of wisdom and intention at which women and men would baulk, would we then just become your 'robots'? On the other hand could this incur for us a greater readiness to accept our own inadequacies as well as our impotence, rather than to go on grumbling at what we think is our impotence?

So maybe now you'll see afresh why I am able to liken life here to something of a wilderness – and without a compass! The agony of hopelessness is real – I see it in the glazed eyes of Hamish and Mary. The shared fog of impotence is also without a map or compass. I want to believe that love will never be defeated. But St. Paul wrote of 'being workers together with God'. But it is hard to feel existentially that you, God, and humanity can be working partners. The evidence is not overwhelming!

The cameo of Mary and Hamish raises hard and urgent issues, and the outlook does not seem promising for them. Poverty is growing across the face of the Earth. But some visionaries think it could become history! Sometimes I feel that perhaps you might have washed your hands of this struggle. I hope not. But the feeling is in my guts, and it's difficult to dislodge it. I'm aware that perhaps I'm not exactly sure of what I'm asking for, or of what I'm expecting of you. I'm feeling washed out, but its hard to even think of you being washed out too! Maybe I'm in need of a new revelation – a new perspective and yes, a new hope. It's just that the world you caringly made, will be beautiful even for the oppressed, the marginalised, and all who have nothing but the dregs of deep disappointment. Writing this letter has hurt. But the hurt will not matter if from it springs up a new chapter – a new beginning. Is this possible? Well?

Letter 8: Discoveries on the erotic journey

Dear God,

I need to write to you. Yes, again! It's because I've made what feels like a rich discovery. It's scintillating, so special, beautiful and over powering. I'm unsure as to whether I can share it with others, but I do want to share it with you. I hope I can be coherent. As you'll see it's not easily described in words. This experience has proved to be a living, nutritious oasis in my desert. It feels so precious and fulfilling it has made my heart sing! It has helped me to confront the stark existence of wilderness living with a more fertile experience arising from the healing power of personal creative love. Strangely I am tempted to keep this a secret. I'm afraid of losing it. I'm also afraid it could be tarnished by ugly cheap innuendo and bawdiness. I feel I have pierced a horizon, and that now I can see further than ever before. This sense of vision is a new mode of seeing, for me.

I'll try to describe it. Yesterday, by and large, had been a good day. My wife and I had a pleasant meal together in the evening. After clearing up we chatted over coffee. I felt mellow and clearly she was relaxed. The day was ending well. No rough edges, no blank silences, no anxieties that I could detect. For us the ending of the day – each day – has a speciality about it. We had a bath together, and we were drying ourselves, just chattering, laughing, and catching a glimpse of each other's reflection in the mirror. It was a lovely warm feeling – relaxed – comfortable cool in the head. But I was aware that something else was happening. I wondered if this might be a 'turn on'? I wondered if an act of love was forming itself inside each of us. We had a drink, sitting on the settee. I put on some music, and there was a remainder of a bar of chocolate, which we shared.

Our eyes met. Our hands touched. It was clear now that a mutual feeling was enfolding us, without resistance. It was lovely! I'm feeling right now, that it's not easy to find the right words to describe what happened. It was inside each of us, and there was an outside aura too. Two bodies, two minds, two hearts, which must have embraced each other thousands of times over the years, came closely together with a sense of the powerful urge of intimacy. This was not new to us, yet in a strange way it was new, and this sense of newness was altogether exciting. We kissed. We stroked. We looked. We whispered. It was all so gentle and so rhythmical, with a pulse and a throb, as if one led quietly to another. One word led to another. Yes, the gradual sense of anticipation had a power of its own. You'll remember, I hope, in another letter when I was trying to explore the practice of prayer, when I said that for me it was a means of 'paying close attention'. Well, here was another example – we were paying close attention to each other, in body, in mind, and in the secret places of the heart. We were soon firmly on the road where the need for control was ebbing away, into a free and wonderful abandonment. She was so adorable. She was so malleable in my tender hands. My finger tips were delicate searching for the touch that goes straight to the heart of the ecstasy. I was also enjoying her search, as her hands glided over my body. Dare I feel as if I were a new man? Surely I had been lifted out of myself. I felt the arrival of her touch in those places that slowly ignited a fire of intensity that was both beautiful and yet so hard to bear. The music intertwined our feelings, our thoughts, our bodies, leading through this searching to a deep, mind-blowing discovery.

The immediate and the ultimate were compressed. We found the space to lie down, and claimed the liberating posture of love, and making love, pursuing the adventure to a mutual and satisfying consummation. This seemed to be an endless moment, as it were, suspended from time into timelessness. Eventually we shuffled off to the bedroom, dimmed the light to a low glow, and became aware of the music mode. We took oils and anointed each other carefully, slowly, as if time had ceased to exist – from head to toe and into every crevice – such a tender exploration. The intimate words of love flowed – the gem-like words of entry and response, of delight, words shaped for this sacred moment of penetration and shattering welcome. Our bodies throbbed and control was thrown away and with wonderful abandon we were now one – just one! It was all we needed. The consuming pleasure of her was me, and for me it was her. And after a lingering time of utter and supreme pleasure I entered her with all my functions so wonderfully intact. Her juices were a joy, with a soft tender welcome dancing in her eyes. We both experienced a wonderful and mutual climax – orgasms of supreme delight, spending ourselves on each other with no other consideration, even a thousand miles near. Gradually, carefully naturally, we cooled. Alex Comfort imaginatively said, "Orgasm is the most religious moment in our lives, of which all other mystical experiences are a mere translation". Quietly, we mutually were still feeling each other, as if the molten juices of love had generously overflowed and we discovered ourselves freely in an embrace that would hold us secure for ever and a day. As we lay there, at one, in the depths and at peace, both of us felt touched to the core. We relished the delight that had no control. On reflection, it seems as if there was something of a paradox here. This miracle of love only flourishes when control and the desire for control evaporate, and the freedom of letting go allows an ecstasy otherwise quite unknown. However, I know that this is a far cry from my normal urge of will to be and remain in control of my whims and desires, along with my own egotistic self-satisfaction. My usual struggle to be in more control of me only leaves me feeling impotent and diminishes my effectiveness as a lover. Making love shows me that the impossible becomes possible when two lovers seek only the pleasure of each other. Letting go, provides a naked experience of the wonder of actually being out of control within the open mutuality of 'making love'. I now know that true love cannot be understood without giving up control, so as to give the profoundest pleasure to one's beloved. Many times I have wished that you dear God were in more control of this uncontrollable world.

But perhaps my hunch that you may have given up control, not in despair, but in order to be an inspiration to us mortals so we too could anticipate our own readiness to give up the selfishness of preferential status, choosing rather the way of implicit trust. This truth I believe lies partially hidden within the lovers' relationship. Whether as lovers, or as stewards of the sanctity of creation, it seems to me that the giving up of self is the kernel of a truth that is more far reaching than I had originally understood.

Underneath the practice of our intimacy there is the validation given by years of trust, and service, with all the ordinariness which has filled our years, since we started on the journey of living together, and loving the joyful creativeness, of living and loving. Trials and pains, losses and failures, with disappointments scattered on the way have been mutually experienced and at times have come near to breaking us. Nonetheless it might not be too bold to say that the down side of our relationship could have been consumed, it seems, by the availability of the ecstasy of actually 'making love' - yes, making it a love of depth enabling us to give up our individual selves for the other, in the sure knowledge that neither of us will be extinguished. It seems to me that this in itself, for women and men within a mutual and loving partnership remains an unspeakable gift.

As you know, God, it is not easy to describe the indescribable. Words remain inadequate to express the wonder and the joy of this act of loving, as it fertilises the normal ordinary day. I feel that this part of our mysterious humanity is so gracious and rewarding. So it must not remain a secret. Rather, with quiet satisfaction it has to be celebrated without inhibition - yes, even from the housetops, if you like!

I've tried to paint an intimate portrait of the love which is accessible to humanity, which tastes in some measure, something, if I dare to say so, of your own perfection, and your ingenious creativity; as well as the truth, that you rejoice in its vivacious spirit. However this may be, this letter cannot be complete without recalling, sadly, the shadow side of our sexuality, from earliest times until now. A chasm exists between the sexuality that is embedded in spiritually aware love, and on the other hand the widespread gratuitous exploitation of sex. I acknowledge that I feel uncomfortable and at times distressed with the pre-occupation in our society with sexual extravagance and indulgence, to the point of obsession. Having sex has become a social pastime, an item on the social calendar. It has become a selfish mode of enjoying 'yourself', and too frequently exploiting casual partners in a way which has now resulted in a big increase in sexually transmitted diseases. I can remember when the subject of sex was taboo. Thank goodness those days are over. But now the change in attitude, behaviour, and morality itself has conferred on people a sense of liberation from restraint. At one level this does not have to be bad in itself. However, it has also brought with it a sense of disregard for the sacredness of the intimacy which has its own mystery and meaning. Sadly, I'm left thinking that sexual gratification and the pursuit of it, without any sense of boundaries, has become an ersatz industry, employing thousands of women and men all over the world. I can't help feeling that something very precious is being tarnished and misused. The delicate and intimate erotic resources of the human spirit designed for good are being turned into a nightmare of unbridled indulgence leading to great sadness, pain, disease, depression, and despair.

Some of my friends have difficulty knowing how to handle the treasure and the pleasure. Sex itself has become good business and is readily exploited for selfish gain. Searching for personal satisfaction, ironically, indicates a deeper desire to be loved and cherished for one's own sake. Not just for 'tonight', but for a lifetime. I'm anxious not to be a spoil sport, with a sense of any moral superiority. And as for puritan elitism, then perish the thought!

My hope is that sexual love with undimmed shared erotic pleasure, experienced as a gift, generously made, and located with a sense of enduring delight, from its spiritual foundation, might be increasingly accessible to couples who desire to confer on their own partnership a seal of hope that will serve them well for their mutual lifetime. Achieving this goal might eventually mean the gradual death of pornography and all that demeans the splendour of sex and sexuality. I am not advocating a moral crusade with a dangerous judgemental core. A revolution of change much deeper than just in attitudes which entwines the mysterious with the erotic, would make accessible a mellow sexuality devoid of exploitation. My experiences as a therapist and counsellor have persuaded me that partners who are able to avail themselves of psychotherapeutic support are more likely to discover a mature satisfaction in their relationship.

I recognise the deep hurt of personal disaster experienced within marriage. Marriage itself, as we have learned can cover a wide range of experiences, including domination, manipulation, isolation and a daily dict of bitterness, fear, and uncertainty. Sadly, too often marriage has demeaned women, encouraging men to cling to their macho role, perceived as monsters. This has fostered a culture of abuse, which has been responsible for crippling the lives of wives and children. Some see their partners primarily as possessions. Home becomes a cell of fear with no escape. The supportive notion of the complementariness of women and men melts away. It is not uncommon for me to listen to women who tell me that all men are bastards. And men say in despair all women are bitches!

Neither gender was designed, was it, for domination? Did you, dear God intend the equality of women and men? If so, we will still have to discover the mutual comfort that can celebrate the joy of sexuality. We will bury for ever the notion of sex as a commodity to be purchased, within a competitive market that sets men against women, and women against men.

Of course each one of us has a choice when it comes to the sexuality of our own person. I'd want to affirm those who choose to remain chaste and celibate. Women and men can discover and enjoy the relationships of mutual acceptance expressed non-sexually, and feel fulfilled.

A sense of growing selfhood, integrity, satisfaction with quiet confidence and fulfilment are gifts both for the celibate, and the chaste, as well as those who enjoy the sexuality of a partnership. These life styles, I believe are designed for co-operation and not for any competitive role. This tolerance will enhance us all, so that any pejorative feelings between 'the married' and 'the singles' will not find any support of those who discover for themselves a spirit which is the sure foundation for a compassionate society.

I started this letter, sharing with you something of the inter spiritual/sexual contour of my marriage, rejoicing in its long term fulfilment, shared with my wife and the other members of my family. To put it succinctly, our partnership in all its facets has been a gift. Just more recently, facing the fact of ageing, I've been wondering what might be in store for us as stamina declines, and physical and mental agility diminish? I'd like to acknowledge that fifty years or so making love to the same partner has not been boring! Though the familiarity has had its down side. Practising together, lovemaking needs a special grace, so that this 'jewel' does not became tarnished by deadening habit and unthinking custom. This is delicate territory, but I believe we have explored it in such a way that the regular pleasure of making love does not have 'its spark' dimmed, but leaves us both unfettered and able to continue to be a part of the essential, tactile, erotic and mutual exchange, both of us growing in maturity and mutual respect. If long term marriage is to be revered and valued, then hopefully more will need to be done to ensure it validates itself, quietly, and its everyday practice enhanced with tenderness.

Dear God, if you have 'up your sleeve' anything more intrinsically wonderful than the miracle of sex, I'm thinking it's well that you have kept it to yourself! The sexual experience has within it the integrated joy and responsibility which when yoked together pass human understanding. Nevertheless, defeating the wilderness of hedonistic selfishness remains a hard nut to crack. Fertilise my imagination; restore rigour to my thinking and feeling. Enable me to grow sensitively, so that more of us will glimpse the essence of undimmed wonder with lives where purity yoked with fun and orgasmic profundity can be understood as the 'pearl of great price'. Then we will search knowing that we can discover it for ourselves, and all our brothers and our sisters.

In this regard I hope that when 'I come' - this is none other than your special touch.

Letter 9: The dilemma of prayer

Dear God,

Since I was a child, from my Sunday School days. I have been intrigued with "saying my prayers". My parents never insisted on me saying them. When I was quite small, about three or four years of age. I think, I learned to say "Gentle Jesus meek and mild, look upon a little child - God bless Mummy and Daddy". My mother sat on the edge of the bed while I went through this nightly ritual. I think this performance was short lived. Soon I was left to my own devices. Going to bed became a solitary experience. I had my own feelings and fantasies, and some confusion in my young and uninformed mind. I recall lying in bed talking to myself quietly under the bedcovers, chattering away to myself about my disappointments, hopes, and what I'd like to do, and be - thinking all the time that 'someone' was hearing me. Occasionally I felt my parents didn't listen to me enough. But gradually, like other children, I lost interest in prayers. I suppose this may have been because I could not feel or see anything actually happening. But I did begin to learn that talking to myself was not a waste of time. I could have imaginary conversations, which in a way helped me to be aware of myself, and to sort out a little what I might do, or say, if the right chance came by. In a way I still feel that this private process is not a hundred miles away from the dimensions of prayer.

I think I might have had a rather vague picture of you, God. though I cannot recall now what it was. I was fond of pictures and my imagination had a childlike fertility about it. Sometimes my pictures inside my head were shadowy, enveloped in a mist, and usually seemingly far away. I felt puzzled most of the time. My Sunday School teacher talked a lot about 'talking to God', so I wondered why should I not be able to do the same? At Sunday School I learned about Jesus, and there were Elsie Anna Wood pictures of him on the wall. I listened to stories about him as well, and because I could see him in the pictures he seemed to be more real, and so I started talking to him. I told him about the things that worried me. I imagined him standing there in his strange clothes, listening to me. But, he never said anything. Then I began to wonder if he was really there? On and off this continued to be, in retrospect a bewildering experience to my young questing mind. I did feel mixed up. I never seemed able to sort it out. And I suppose that in a way I'm still trying to sort it out, all these decades later, and it's why I'm writing this letter.

Later at Grammar School we had Morning Assembly, when the Rector said prayers, from the platform. It was a daily performance. I used to peep out to see who was listening. Clearly some boys thought it was 'a joke', whilst the masters just stood rigid. I joined the Boys' Brigade and went to church. There were vespers, but they seemed to me like a blind alley - they did not get anywhere. None of us talked about prayers, and none of us asked any questions either. Later on I took on the job of manually pumping the organ at church, for the Sunday Services. I did this each Sunday and was paid a few shillings. From behind the organ screen I could peep out and see the minister and the choir. During his prayers I watched the choir. His language was strange and seemed to me different from normal language. It did not seem like a conversation. The business of praying seemed like a coded game. But I never discovered the code, so I never cracked it! My question now is: not different from my question then. 'Who is listening?' Because it remains my question I have this deep urge to write this letter to see if I can convey to you God my sense of bewilderment as well as my desire to understand. On occasion when I listen to the radio or at church there can be a sense of a 'beyond mystery', which so far I have been unable to articulate. Some ministers seem obsessed with the need to tell you of all the bad things in the world, as if you don't already know about it all. They imply, I think, that you are out of touch This may be an oversimplification. I'm not sure. However, for me there remains an underlying importance, which motivates me to pursue what praying actually is. And this must be relevant to my question, 'who is listening?'. Clear thinking is necessary.

I seem to pray in fits and starts. Occasionally I might feel better for it. It depends on the occasion and the circumstance. If it is the funeral of a beloved friend then somehow or other the prayers are charged with a special intention. This prayer 'touches' me. But I have an increasing intensity to probe this mystery - the 'flat' prayers - the prayers that 'touch' - with an adult mind and with a vague sense of my own spirituality. However so far I have found no helpful map, compass, nor rulebook that makes contemporary sense. I am aware that messages go from mind to heart - it feels like a long stretch, to stay in touch with what I am thinking, as well as feeling. If prayer is just a one way conversation with you God, then for me it feels a waste of time. In a conversation there are agreed criteria about listening and responding. Body language from a human perspective is also indicative of the feelings of mutual response. In a way, the praying conversation in my imagination has a kind of 'non-verbal knowing' about it. If this is real and intimate, then the two way exchange stands a chance of being creative. Again, for me, prayer might feel like an ever repeating desire, or hope, or commitment. But this can be laced with my inner anger, or disappointment, and even bewilderment. But all of this comes from the depths of me, and is validated by a passion that melts into something which I feel to be akin to prayer. But can I use my prayers to discharge my anger, my disappointment, my anxiety, or even my zest and exuberance when I'm feeling good? Somehow or other I can't really. Because I feel I'm not in a relationship with you. I'd like my prayers to hold together the deepest feelings and desires. They may not be polite, for when the heart is laid bare, and the mind is incisive, politeness is irrelevant. When my flesh is in turmoil, and my spirit is caught desiring a meaning that assures me that 'all is well' - which of course is what I want to know. But sadly prayer for me can hardly have this therapeutic outcome, which is disappointing, and once again, I think, underlines the fear that God and me have yet to find the necessary pre-requisite, a real and vibrant relationship. Because your attention feels so hard to secure, I'm left feeling abandoned to my own silence.

Today's world with communication technology is a changing world. Communications are almost instantaneous. Our culture is unsatisfied with anything that cannot give instantaneous results. This desire for instant gratification means there can be 'no waiting' time allowed. This does contrast with my experience with you God, inasmuch, as far as I can see, my prayers, or my attempt to pray seem to face a long waiting time. In this transcendental arena the perceptions of my heart and brain can be so different. When I recall from the biblical stories that Moses, Abraham, and others 'talked with God', then clearly there was an immediacy. Did you give them preferential attention? To be honest; if this were to be my own experience today, it would 'blow my mind'. But I'd like to be ready for the experience.

I'm now recalling the hymn which is insistent, 'the voice of prayer is never silent, nor dies the strain of praise away'. Do you, I wonder actually hear the barrage of words - holy words if you prefer, from every island and continent? Could there be a sense in which these words are a help to you? I'm wondering how much care and pity from you actually touches the countless thousands who are on their knees? Humanly speaking the dynamics and logistics can hardly be conceptualised. Perhaps this can lead me only to a conclusion that prayers with you can never be measured or evaluated, because it is contained in spiritual mystery. Of course I am aware of the great prayers of the saints and the mystics, and I'm not devaluing them. The spiritual elevation of the Prayer Book and the wisdom of the disciplined monastic communities, and the Desert Fathers provide a quality of contemplation that cannot be bettered. But I feel rather inadequate, and hardly able to embrace such a life style, for fear of my own possible failure. Others are able to live a life with a single focus of continuous prayer, and no one, I guess, can evaluate how this quiet and unseen ministry has a significance even for those who consciously are unaware of it. But I'm aware of others who in their loveless lives, and perhaps demented by fear and guilt can only 'rage at the dying of the light'. In the agony of their today, they can only strike out at you God in all their impotence. I find this frightening and perplexing. Can their rage be their prayers? And if so, how would you respond?

I'm left wondering whether the majority of people who pray have a picture of you in their minds as they pray? I'm wondering if it is possible to pray without a visualisation of you? To pray to an 'oblong blur' hardly gives the insight and the sense of expectancy which I would think is in part something of the essence of prayer. To explore the visualisations would be a fascinating research project. They would tell us something about the 'pictures' prayers have of you. I'm sure there would be much to learn, not only about you, but also about the process of prayer itself.

I've always felt that prayer has a dimension of listening about it. When I sit quietly listening the effect is therapeutic. Listening is an awareness skill, though many of us do not score very highly from its practice. When I try to pray, I try to listen, but I'm unsure what it is I will hear. Will I hear you? Then, I'm wondering how you score in the skill of listening? When people make their prayers they are anticipating that you will actually listen. But when I consider how many are praying to you, your listening ear may be faced with 'task impossible'? From my own experience I know how reassuring it is to know that in a moment of crisis I have someone's listening ear. Are there log jams of your prayer internet? Is there what might feel like a worldwide babel - out of control and competitive noise? This brings me back to my own question. Are you really listening to me? Really listening? And how do I know?

There is a particular scenario that spells the dilemma of prayer for many people. It is customary to pray for persons who are ill. In churches there are intercessory prayer lists. Some on the prayer list recover, but others do not. Some assume that prayer will help recovery from illness. But to what extent? Are there any useful guidelines? Are there unanswered prayers? Can prayer be used therapeutically to heal? Experience reflects that the outcomes appear to be varied, yet without a pattern. I'm left wondering if there are limitations to prayer? It is not a divine slot machine! There will be no ready made answers. But this can be bewildering. If prayer can be described as a precious process, then I feel we need deeper insight into its nature and purpose. At the same time any sense of measuring the effectiveness of prayer does feel crass.

I readily acknowledge there have been moments when I have been moved 'to take off my shoes' and the ground of my being, and my peace of mind has sensed a sacred moment. I feel though, this vanishes before I can clutch it. Praying to you on occasion can feel like the poet endeavouring to express the inexpressible - the infinite within this finite world. So I'm not overlooking that on occasion prayer can appear like a pipedream. The poet and the psalmist appear to be aware of what has been called 'the garment of prayer'. Somewhere, somehow I sense a paradox here, though I'm not able to be as explicit as I would wish. I suppose I have to keep trying?

In the Gospels we read that Jesus prayed regularly. This I find is not surprising. It would be part of your bond with him, and his with you. What is called The Lord's Prayer does have about it a shape and ethos that seems to give it a special place in the lives of many people. It's useful when one feels lost for words. For those out of their depth, when praying the Lord's Prayer provides a solace and a sense of benediction. But then the prayer of Jesus in Gethsemane - and his cry 'Let this cup pass from me' is wrung through with agony. And I know of others who in their own hour of dereliction pray the same prayer and sweat the same terror. And they like Him then confront the moment of apparent betrayal 'My God, my God, why have you forsaken me?'. This sounds like the prelude to defeat. I know of the moments when I feel, in a crisis, and you have not responded to my own cry of agony. Others too feel abandoned by you in their moment of torture. Jesus was betrayed - in my life too I have been betrayed. And no help has been forthcoming from you or anyone else. This comes near to 'the dark night of the soul'. The utter aloneness with the crippling sense of abandonment. There is nothing harder to bear in this human life of ours.

For me this overwhelming scenario requires a depth of maturity which I do not possess. Yet I still want to stay with this ultimate dilemma. The Cross was a reality to Jesus, and to an untold number of others, who have borne their own 'crucifixion'. You allowed him to suffer this sense of dereliction and defeat, and his prayer was not answered. And yet you loved him? Beyond doubt? This is a circle I am unable to square. In my mind it takes me back to that other story of Abraham and his son Isaac and of how the record tells of you telling Abraham to abort your previous request for his physical sacrifice. This does sow the seed of suspicion, pushing me a little with the question 'what kind of God are you?' So at this deep level of exploration, it is hard to know how to address the quandary. Maybe, again, the essence is within the perimeters of paradox. I'm reminded of those insightful words by T.S.Eliot, 'doing the right thing for the wrong reason, is the greatest treason'. I wonder what you make of that?

When I reflect on these profound issues within my own pilgrimage, somehow or other the Church in all its plethora of formality, with its doctrine, creeds, courts, hierarchy and bureaucracy, leaves me feeling quite alone. Feeling unsupported and facing what for me is the Church's doctrinaire portfolio, it seems so out of touch with contemporary life, and quite unable to pilot me, as it were, through the quandary of prayer and the pragmatic dilemmas to which I have already referred. The earlier portion of this letter is littered, it might be said, with questions and with doubts. However, in the Church I have perceived that the asking of questions, with any notion of persistency is regarded as weakness. But simultaneously I'm aware that the world is alive with questions, both seen and unseen. In the world, questions are regarded as avenues to new understanding and truth. Yes, questions may be motivated as troublesome and even mischievous, but they fulfil a necessary purpose. My worldly companions tend to hold a perspective of healthy doubt about prayer and the spiritual life. They have a healthy creative approach which too frequently I do not find in the citadels of formal and official religion. These companions have a knack of being able 'to leave doors open' rather than be in a hurry to close down on what are difficult and complex concerns, such as those I have been trying to explore with you. Some are free enough to be able to live with uncertainty, without bitterness, and quietly knowing that they do not know. Sharing doubts has its own fellowship of searchers. This contrasts with the 'pious elite' who on occasion are quick to display what they think is their spiritual superiority. The companionship of fellow doubters and searchers is a blessing. Doubting is not a sin, is it? Rather I see it as a probing of reality.

There is another dimension of prayer which I think deserves a parallel exploration. It's an approach that appears to have a more earthy and practical image. I first came across it when I was introduced to the Iona Community. 'To pray is to work'. It was at the core of the Worker Priest movement in France, with its Latin tag 'Laborare est orare'. For me it restores the image of prayer into a practicality which I think some spiritual groups have lost. When I have found myself unable to find the right words for the prayer that is struggling for expression from my inner being, the only satisfying response is to do something, which in some way or other no matter how small brings a satisfaction that has within it a potential to change what needs to be changed, for the better. Prayer may be about being, but I've discovered also that it is about doing. I think this can in itself widen the circle of prayer, and bring an accessibility which enables a practical sense of participation. So to stand in silence at a vigil, or to hand out a leaflet which has a clear message, or to write a letter of protest - these come very near to the essential essence of prayer, which is to give birth to change for the good. This is why for me, letters can be the wings of a prayer!

To pursue this more practical image of prayer, I am grateful that I came across the words of W.H. Auden, who in 1970 wrote - "To pray is to pay attention to something or someone other than oneself. Whenever a man so concentrates his attention on a landscape, poem, a geometrical problem an idol or his god, and he completely forgets his own ego and desires, he is praying". What a bold assertion! It is strange how we discover truth in unexpected places. In the traditional sense Auden was no saint. But his words come very near to my own experience. For me they are an encouragement. There is a sense in which for me, living my life is and has been a cavalcade of paying attention. Being alert emotionally and intellectually, both to myself, and to my world, formulates my stance at prayer. I have a choice about what I attend to. But the exciting implication for me is that I feel I can do something. Even to be aware of someone, something, some issue or dilemma, in the very giving of my attention to it creates the opportunity for change, growth, love and for understanding. If the whole human race gave attention to the issues of survival and for justice, what a mighty prayer this would be! Auden went on, "The primary task of the school teacher is to teach children in a secular context the technique of prayer". This message needs to be sent vibrating around the world. His sentiment is charged with a practability, popular no doubt with children. If this is followed through it has the potential to evoke deeper feelings of worship, and perhaps even adoration. It could also instil a sense of guilt because the purposeful unevenness of life refuses the opportunity to millions to escape the daily grind of starvation and poverty. Paying attention has within it the potential for looking deeper within oneself and simultaneously looking out to where there is a need for sharing love, and creating a world that is not solely pre-occupied with self and the pursuit of fun and wealth. From my perspective this model of prayer, as paying individual and corporate attention, could revolutionise congregations of the churches across the land. If in services of worship the person leading the prayers said – "Let us pray - let us give our attention to....." Maybe more could be persuaded that prayer in itself is a life of practice, and motivation, rather than just a vague unthought out desire. This paying attention I expect will give a 'result' that is commensurate to the attention actually given, and which will go on being given. Paying attention will harness new knowledge and at the same time keep our feet firmly in the reality of the world.

It was back in the '60s that Albert van den Heuvel suggested at a Youth Conference in Edinburgh, that if the Church was serious about widespread hunger in the world, it would be ready to forgo the daily celebration of Holy Communion – 'The body and blood of Christ for you in the costume of Bread and Wine' until the day dawned when everyone had their own bread and wine. Clearly this image of paying attention has been rejected, and we still have the hungry with us across continents, even now. To work is to pray - to pay attention is to pray - to forgo the most blessed of sacraments for the hungry of humanity is to pray. It was Abraham Heschel, dear God, a Jewish Rabbi who a couple of decades ago declared - "Prayer is meaningless unless it is subversive, unless it seeks to overthrow and to ruin the pyramids of callousness, hatred, opportunism, and falsehoods". The liturgical movement must become a revolutionary movement, seeking to overthrow the forces that continue to destroy the hope and the vision". So dear God, what, I wonder, do you think about this? Is it music to your ears? These thoughts shatter the image of prayer as a flaccid act devoid of stringency. Prayer as subversion gives intention a sharp cutting edge. It echoes the thundering declaration of the late George Macleod - "Everything - and prayer too - ends in politics". Prayer is participation as well as an inner discipline of reflection and examination. These secular 'gems' of attention giving and subversive designs, will vibrate with passion and commitment. They will confront the silence of agony and the discrimination of injustice. So dear God, hear me in this letter. Quietly, now I know that my heart is open - my hands are open - and my mind is open - expecting a new awareness of you, and dare I say it, of you with me. We can share, I hope, a new fertile image of the prayer that will be the crux of my life from today. So - please – be present in my going out, and in my coming in! I'm waiting, for however long it takes.

Letter 10: Engaging with the silence - authentic worship?

Dear God,

If I could, I'd like to escape the wilderness of my daily experience. I am uncomfortable being caught up in the banal jargon of self-centred living. You know what I mean? Contriving one 'buzz' after another with an unhealthy appetite for more and more shallow pleasure. So I am writing today from this quiet place. It is very quiet! It's a retreat, and for me it is a haven. Quakers and Friends have gathered in this Meeting House for a very long time. The stones of this sacred place are saturated with silence. Sitting here, I feel strangely open to the past of this House, and I'm caught up in the habit of quiet and reflection. The quiet and intimate feel of the furnishings are simple and give witness to a history of devotion. I have a sense of utter well being and a deep calm. This deep relaxation of my whole self feels perfect. I'm being nurtured by the personal silence which emanates around the worn stools used by worshippers over many generations. I feel I can stay here with my own silence, and knowing that a precious part of me has now come to life. Someone, I remember, has suggested that this insight is the perceptive code of mindfulness. The door of the house remains open and unlocked, so one may come and go at will. This is a haven, away from the over-verbal world of language and babble. Here I feel secure from the assault of jargon, arrogant speech, the gabble of 'internet and text deformed' speech, where words and dots and slashes riot together, leaving me confused with messages of doubtful meaning, with their ever present noise.

As well as this personal sense of therapeutic solitude, I also recall the social silence. This is the shared silence of those together in a group enfolded by the safety of quietness and reverence. I sense that those who are familiar with this place readily find themselves in a mode of shared at-one-ness, with no dependence on language at all. This shared silence tastes of something deep and spiritual, and mutually understood. This may last for moments, minutes, or hours. If I never come this way again I will not forget how I have been strangely changed, challenged, and nourished here. This is not easy to explain because the sense of it all feels quietly 'hidden'. This quiet encounter is precious, rich, supportive and greatly valued. For some this would have been a turning point, and this has been true for me. But as well as being the experience of a few, I'm told that on occasion there is nothing more powerful and impressive than the united and self imposed silence of the crowd. Within it, I am told, the gathered people are able to acknowledge the mystery of 'being one', and to know the power of oneness.

There are many of these Meeting Houses of modesty where Quakers gather together regularly for the quiet mode of silent worship. In this mode, I can't help wondering whether you, God, visit occasionally, or even frequently? The religious question would be, 'Do you dwell there, in this Meeting House? The reflection that is welling up for me, almost instinctively, has a soft but pregnant tone which allows me, what I can only call, uninhibited and quiet confrontation. This confrontation with myself, with the objective of knowing who I am! Beyond the silence, and yet within it, I have an awareness that for me the sacredness does expose me to a deeper knowing of myself, and with it the paradox that the silence and the meeting assure me that I will never be isolated and shut off from truth, beauty, and love, along with the other rich gifts of human existence. To know this is so refreshing. Can there be anything more personal and yet more confrontational than this? I think not. I'm tempted to linger here, but I'm quietly moving forward to surrendering my anxiety and my fear of both boredom and frustration so that I can fully enter the meditation that becomes worship. Simultaneously I can be alone and yet feel secure. Yes, it's a mystery, perhaps disturbing but never threatening.

This benison of silence in its depths and its breadth promises further discoveries. For instance I'm recalling 'the high' of an art gallery where as a visitor I may revel in the beauty or the candour of the canvas, with what feels like an interior view. This feeling replenishes my hunger and thirst for the integrity of insightful experience. Alternatively in the wide out-doors, by stream, or perched high on the lee of a summit, or again just savouring the rhythm of the lap, lap, lap of the returning tide on the beach. When I gaze across the boundless ocean, lift my eyes to the night sky, shimmering and alert, I'm taken in by the sparkling revelation of that which is beyond human creation, yet cradled in the silence of another realm. Well! This may feel like a trance, because I'm relieved of the hard, sordid and unexplainable other world with its inescapable frustration.

There are other silences which on occasion also minister to me. The silence of the bedroom, and the bed itself; the silence of the gradual awakening from sleep; the shared silence of a relaxed breakfast; the silence surrounding the reading of a searching text; and also the silence of the Board meeting, which anticipates a struggle to discover perhaps a verbal agreement which then emerges but with surprise and relief. Even the silences of the examination hall, or the funeral parlour can be therapeutic. As well as the sense of solitude awaiting the train that never seems to want to arrive at the small isolated station well after the world seems to have gone to sleep These silences - gaps of reflection – are scattered across my experience, and each has its own potent insight and revelation. They can, as it were, 'open a window', and give me breath to overcome the stress that otherwise would choke me. I'm recalling Abraham Heschel's words, 'Just to be is a blessing - just to live is holy'. To be is to know, and to know is also to be known. I feel that this private part of me can discover gracious support to what feels like my outer self - that more public bit of me; resulting in a joyous integration. Perhaps this is what maturity is about? I am aware of it. This idiosyncratic insight leaves me in a state of inner peace, and I am free to enjoy it.

The secret of living revealed from this exploration reminds me, yet again, that my deep desire is to come closer to you, dear God. My time at the Quaker Meeting House has propelled me into a state of anticipatory enquiry. In my mind, and from my therapeutic practice I'm thinking of 'a tool' which is known as the one-way mirror. This is used for personal consultation purposes. While a doctor and patient cannot see the on-looking student group, the student group can freely and confidentially observe the encounter between the patient and the doctor. This is an enlightening way of observational learning. However, this has urged me to ask you if there is a one-way mirror between you and humanity? You can 'see' how we are, our behaviour, mistakes, the good and the not so good bits of us, and even perhaps our motives and our desires. Many people are not aware of this 'mirror' with its one way perspective that appears to be to your advantage. This focuses on what seems to be 'the hiddenness' of you. And we can feel exposed in the light of your all seeing freedom. There seems to be a huge silence in which our own experience is played out. I'm recalling a story told which I hope you will agree is pertinent to this discussion. It is lightly told of a man who wanted to cross the road. Unthinkingly he stepped off the kerb to cross to the other side. He had not seen a man on a cycle approaching from his right hand. As he stepped out he collided with the cycle and its rider. In sheer terror he cried "Oh Christ!" – "Shush!" retorted the cyclist. "Incognito!" I hope you enjoyed the story. But you see it is this sense of being 'incognito' - there but unseen, unheard, and unrecognised that creates for me – and others - a sense of deep anxiety. So we are left with no picture of you. On occasion I may have a sense of presence, but it's not easily described, and I wonder if it could be your 'presence'?

With Jesus, at least we can have a picture of him, even if it is 2,000 or so years old. Your being incognito perhaps means that 'the silence' is the only route to you? My own journey into silence will continue my exploration. And the evidence of my seriousness will be seen by the intellectual rigour I am able to muster and yoked to it will be emotional integrity which will honour the feelings that have, and still do shape the experiences of my life. My approach to you has to be a two-pronged strategy - that is via the mind and via the heart. These two strands complement each other. Of course language will facilitate my expressions and yearnings, as also my searchings and longings. So this on-going dialogue will be progressed by unambiguous communication - by talking and writing, as well as the hidden approaches which go beyond language.

But now I'm wondering if there is a shadow side to this exploration? Words can be exploited and misused. Language itself is continually in danger of being prostituted. This mars the image of words, with overtones of manipulation of the truth, the soiling of beauty, with other values and virtues being tarnished. Sadly this is commonplace in the media, with its printed word as well as in the surfeit of television programmes. But lest you think I am being unduly hard on human institutions, I can only observe that the Church, worldwide, has not been able to model its own communication, copying from the artistic language of the Psalms, for instance, or for that matter having an ear to the poetic rhetoric of the Prophets. Or again, after all this time we have much to learn from the profound economy of language as used by Jesus in his parables. Even St. Paul had his moments of virginal clarity!

Sometimes when I go to Church, worship can feel like a verbal extravaganza. I feel like pleading with the preacher for quiet. The sanctuary itself can evoke its own message, paying attention to what is seen, rather than just what is to be heard. It is difficult to find silence in the week by week public worship in the majority of our churches. I'm not arguing that there is no place for preaching. Of course not. But to preach with a sense of humility might in itself be more persuasive. I suppose it is not surprising that anyone might feel that perhaps the worship of the Church has become somewhat dog eared. Much of the worship in both Reformed and Catholic churches misses the quiet insight of the Quakers. The opportunity for silent reflection and meditation would enrich our worship. Within the modes of worship across the ecumenical range the Eucharist should be allowed to refresh the human spirit by the sense of its mystery. My feeling is that the Churches have to be aware of the danger of their obsession with words, and the battle for words and wordiness intruding even into the inexplicable of the Eucharist. On occasion the churches can give the impression that they are engaged in a battle of words. Where they are engaged in 'selling religion', and sometimes with the promises of 'free gifts'! Quaker Worship benefits from the input of the laity. An occupational hazard for the clergy is to assume that they think that they alone are the architects of worship. Worship is the domain of clergy and laity alike. This transformation would ensure a greater sense of silence, creating with it a sense of your presence. Hopefully you will concur with this?

However there are those Christians who believe that they are experts in mission. For them faith is not entangled with doubt. This implies for them a special relationship with you. A relationship which others do not have! I wonder if you agree? These Christians hold no attraction for me. Their obsession with 'holy words' and their extrovert religious confidence evoke in me some suspicion. Some years ago there was 'A Decade of Evangelism' in the U.K. The purpose was to 'save lives for Christ'. This was a verbal assault on society. Whereas for me, a 'Decade of Silence' might have been more effective. It might have enabled the Church to be a listening

Church - a Church open to questions. Silence facilitates listening - deep listening! Women and men need to know that they are being listened to. Don't we all feel that 'out there' someone, somewhere, near or far, is 'paying attention'. When the tragedies of life and unfair conditions impose themselves, many feel that their own initiative is sapped. For me this can be an abject moment, and I hope that in it you are listening.

I'm remembering that there are, what might be called, other silent territories of the Church. I'm thinking of communities of priests, nuns, and others sharing lives dedicated to silence and contemplation. They live in retreat and appear to negate the world. They have few worldly pursuits. Their focus is inward and not outward. Some of these silent communities are to be found in the geographical desert, with uncomfortable living conditions, and a hostile climate. In a way, I covert their life of retreat and silence, but I suppose I'm not so keen on the accompanying discomforts! Yes, I suppose I'm being ambivalent! But clearly I can be left in no doubt that this life style is a direct challenge to me and to our world which is bent on spin, chat, and the pursuit of money, wealth, and the obsessional search for pleasure. However, I need to remind myself that what I have alluded to as 'the religious life' has its social aspects – cooking meals, gardening, perhaps nursing and teaching. But everything is done as an intention towards you God. In a real sense they too live in the world. I sense that many people are not fully aware that there is a choice of life style. If they did, some might be attracted to a pursuit in which silence would assume a greater importance in their lives.

For me, the Meeting House remains a symbol of hope. On occasion I have wondered if our cathedrals might be perceived as 'cathedrals of silence'? I'm tempted sometimes to question whether some cathedrals are in danger of becoming extensions of a commercial market? Cathedrals on occasion can appear to be filled with the traffic of visitors - some of them wandering around and idly gaping, 'shutter happy' with their cameras. People are easily 'sucked into' the tourist role. It's not easy for this to be conducive to the spirit of silence and worship. Cathedrals have their shops and their cafes, and of course they provide a service. However simultaneously they also provide a traffic of commerce. I have experienced the babble of a busy cathedral, and I find it unpalatable. Clearly there is a conflict between being a place of worship, and a sightseeing venue on the other. Instinctively my wish is for the cathedral to be safeguarded from the babble of the High Street. Nonetheless, the openness of a cathedral is an invitation to a visitor to imbibe the atmosphere where quietness is expected, and where the secret of the sacred can be perceived. Cathedrals and other sacred sites are precious. They need to be open, and accessible. Hopefully, this priority will ensure that pilgrims and searchers will then make their own discoveries.

For myself I doubt whether more expertise in management and marketing will help greatly in the near future as economic downturns beset ecclesiastical sites. Policies in these matters are not easy to shape. But a way has yet to be discovered, so that when a person leaves the outside world outside, then they readily recognise that they are entering into a sanctuary which has its own secrets to share. Hopefully the visitor becomes aware, and from this their 'inner life' will be nourished. This quiet purposing of cathedrals will be of greater importance that any other commercial consideration.

This letter must be brought to a conclusion. Just for now! I've rambled through the mysteries of silence and worship, and I'm grateful to writers like Thomas Binney, a 19th. century hymn writer. At a time of Victorian religiosity, he attempted to find words to express what perhaps is inexpressible. He has a verse in which he attempts to fuse poetry with the hope that can take people like me to the heart of a delicate and precious question:

O how shall I, whose native sphere
Is dark, whose mind is dim,
Before the Ineffable appear,
And on my naked spirit bear
The uncreated beam?

One sage is reputed to have sighed 'You are nearer than breathing, and closer than hands and feet'. My own language is inadequate. But my search for silence, though with hesitation, projects me forward, little by little, even if it is with stops and starts. It leaves me with the faintest hope that there is a way of being closer to you. But I'm hoping you will engage with me. This is the depth of my desire. So I will wait expectantly. This letter, I hope gives you an entry into my own inner self. My door will remain open - wide open!

Letter 11: Struggling families

Dear God,

I want to tell you about a girl who though so young, is already seen by her parents as a failure. This afternoon she sat here in my room, looking fresh and turbulent. Her baggy clothes disguised her sparse figure underneath. The cigarette was perched between her lips, and her shiny hair was proudly spilling over her new rimless spectacles. She was humming some tune or other. She stretched out her long legs, and gave a yawn. Somehow I felt as if she was putting me mentally into one of her 'boxes'. She had a question. It would not go away. It had been around for weeks, perhaps months, but no one at home wanted to hear it.

Pippa is in her sixth year at school. She has been a normal student. She liked most subjects but hated P.E. and Sports. She is a good talker, and she likes an audience. But for her, listening is something else - something she is not good at: She likes to talk! Her life has been lovingly cradled by her parents, right from the beginning. When her brother came along afterwards, to be followed by a younger sister, somehow or other Pippa began to turn in on herself. As the years went by, as she grew up, gradually she withdrew and seemed to take more pleasure in her alone-ness. The shine of her earlier sparkling self gradually rubbed off. As she grew into adolescence she became more concerned about her feelings and her friends. It seemed to me that she was becoming too introspective, and I was unsure how healthy this was for her. School lost its interest for her. She stopped visiting her Granny who lived at the other end of the town. She withdrew from the youth group at the Church. She spent more time in her room, tiny though it was, playing her PC, her discs, and surfing the web for the world 'out there'. I gained the impression that she was thirsty for excitement. She clicked on to the hundreds of seductive adverts about clothes, holidays, clubs, and sex. She was discovering her real self - she thought! But it was scary too. With her new group of friends she did not want to 'miss a trick', as they say.

As far as the question was concerned, her Dad said a firm 'No!!' No matter how frequently she repeated her question, his answer was the same. As he filled his pipe once more, he would say "Your place is here with us. Besides I can't afford to pay out extra rent, when there is a perfectly good room here for you. You don't know how lucky you are". Of course Pippa was quite clear that he could afford it, if he wanted to. She certainly did not feel she was 'lucky'. He was just being difficult. He was always difficult. And of course, Mum always agreed with him. So the three of them did not talk much. Pippa got into the habit of coming home later from school, and ignoring her homework. She never helped in the kitchen with the dishes or the cooking. And she left her room looking like a tip! If Mum attempted to tidy it, all she got from Pippa were screams of protest. She spent endless time on the phone, just talking and giggling - not the kind of language mother liked to hear, as she eavesdropped from behind the kitchen door. Then one day her Mum felt quite anxious, suddenly wondering if Pippa spent too much time surfing 'the net'. She had heard dreadful stories of the things people can get up to on 'the net'. But she didn't breathe a word about her worries to anyone else. Pippa seemed to have become a 'closed book' – she was afraid for her. Pippa now had a mind of her own, and was seldom biddable. She was usually argumentative. Mum was afraid that the two younger children would eventually follow suit. "Oh God", she sighed.

Well, one day Pippa did not return home from school. She just didn't arrive. At ten o'clock in the evening the 'phone rang. "Mum, I'm at Jackie's flat. She says I can stay here. So that's what I'm going to do. It's much better here. Don't worry, I'll be okay – really! I've got a job, filling shelves at Tesco, four evenings a week - so I'll manage. Bye for now". Her Mum was stunned. Her tears just flowed. Dad would be furious. Thank goodness, she thought, that the other two were in bed, and her husband was away. If he'd answered the phone, he would have lost his rag. But throbbing through her head was the question – "Why?, Why?, Why? What have I done to deserve this?" She went on to herself –"I thought I was a good Mum - God knows I've tried". The thought went through her mind. Was this, she wondered, the beginning of the end? Or perhaps it was the end of the beginning? Either way, the future looked stark. In spite of the ITV advert on 'the box', her future was not 'bright', and it clearly wasn't 'orange' She wished so much that she could clear it all out of her head, as if it had not happened. But this seemed impossible.

Dear God, all I have written here is for real. I feel sorry for Pippa and for her Mum. As for her Dad I just don't know what to think about him. Sadly this circumstance happens a lot in families. So now I'm wondering if you can appreciate this situation? Do you know what it feels like? I'm wondering too whether you know about adolescence? It can be such a turbulent time. Is it stupid of me to wonder if you know what it is like to be growing up so quickly in our fast moving society, when your whole being just craves to be free to enjoy yourself and not have to worry about boring things like school, parents, exams, so that you just can get on doing what all your friends are doing - and above all enjoy yourself? Since seeing her this afternoon, I've been remembering back to my own adolescence. Some of it was boring, I didn't fare well at school. I wasn't a high achiever, and I never had enough money. But my parents gave me quite a loose rein really. Things were different then. Quietly in what now seems a strange way, teenagers then seemed to accept their lot. Today it is different, and growing up is far from easy. These reflections raise for me two important questions. Firstly, can I ask you if you do understand how Pippa feels, and do you think she'll survive? And secondly I'd like to have a clue as to what you think can be done, if anything, for her disillusioned parents? This whole business of growing up seems to become more complex as life goes on. I used to think that growing up was part of a straightforward, almost pre-ordained process. Now I'm thinking this has been an illusion. Growing up is fraught with dilemmas. Clear and unambiguous guidelines appear to have melted away. Growing up seems to involve so much conflict and compromise. Being parents and having children and looking after a family seems to be increasingly difficult too. Sometimes I think about it all romantically, and I get a buzz, out of the expected excitement of facing the world, but only if you are lucky enough to live in the right situation. But in a way, that's the rub, really, isn't it? What are the right circumstances for growing up? What is the right circumstance for being parents, trying their best, working hard, and taking care? The sad truth is that for far too many families it is all falling apart, and all that is left is disappointment and frequently despair. High hopes crumble. Over a long process, from the beginning of history, birth itself, and loving relationships which nourish the family have become the very fabric of our society. We would not know our society without the structure and ethos of families, or without the hassles of growing up, following in our parents' footsteps, leaving childhood behind for adolescence and the journey into adulthood. But I feel that as we move forward into and through the twenty-first century, more complexity lies ahead, with parent/child/adolescent relationships becoming more fragile. This does seem the pattern written of our Western society though it may be different in other cultures. Fewer people are choosing marriage, and fewer are choosing to have children here. And there is a feeling that our culture is caught in a trap of sexual chaos. In Scotland the birth rate is in decline. Well, dear God how does this seem to you? I hope it's not irreverent to suggest that you have, after all been around a long time, and you must have seen it all for yourself. When you think about your original great design for the world - how do you feel today? This is not to overlook the good experiences of living - it would be foolish to do so. But you are a realist, I suspect. I assume you are in touch continually with your creation - cherishing the outcome of your own intimate creative power. If you do still deeply care, then in the nitty-gritty what do you think may be some answers for the likes of Pippa and her parents?

Time was, when Pippa and her Mum and Dad got on well. She wanted them to love her, and they did. And she did love them. Then she started to want things which they did not want. Then she faced a dilemma deep inside herself. If she did what she wanted, when they did not approve, would they stop loving her? Gradually it became more important for Pippa to do what she wanted, even if it meant the risk of losing their love, as well as them losing her love. Sadness has engulfed this home and something precious appears to have been lost. Mum and Dad feel failures, and on occasion blame each other. It's hard when the child you birthed, mothered, fathered, loved and cherished then becomes the one who rejects you. When you know your family is being overtaken by something that feels bigger than you, you find yourself feeling deeply impotent. This is the crisis faced by many families. Parents hate admitting failure, and to make it worse they know this cannot be kept under wraps. Non-judgemental supporters are hard to find. The 'wisdom of Solomon' is hard to find too. Ironically this dilemma is the substance of the plot of novels, 'soaps on the box', films, videos, and some poetry.

But there is not much that offers possible solutions to family crisis. Recently, I was looking at a painting 'Abraham's sacrifice' by the 17th. Century artist Rembrandt van Rijn. It is a large graphic and sombre work, frightening in its detail. The painter shows Abraham's left hand covering the face of the boy Isaac, so that we cannot see the real horror in the boy's face. You'll know this incident, recorded in Genesis. Traditionally it is about your requirement of Abraham to sacrifice his son. Usually for the sacrifice a lamb would have been used, but on this occasion the story says you required Abraham to sacrifice his son. Presumably this was to be understood as a test for Abraham? However you stopped him, at the last moment because you could see clearly that Abraham, for whatever reason was willing to comply with your wish. His predicament was horrendous, and I can't help but wonder why you set this 'test' for Abraham? Was it meant to prove something? This is an ancient story and I'm left wondering if it has relevance for life today? Has it anything helpful to say about families in today's society? I'm left wondering what may have happened if Abraham had ignored your wishes? I remember the painting - the image is embossed on my mind - it is so graphic, and it troubles me. I'm left wondering what this incident has to say about you and your motivation? Can you help me to understand it? I'm wondering, do you cherish the family and its key importance in our society? Is this story saying something about testing the love of parents? Or is it to do with the sacrifice parents make for their children, or even perhaps the sacrifice that some children are required to make for their parents? To get back to Pippa and her parents, what value does this story have for them? Your demand of Abraham may not be irrelevant when I think of the demands made by Pippa on her Mum and Dad. The pain is hard to bear. Parents' can be astonished and driven to near despair by the demands of their children. It feels as if the family is something of a cauldron for testing out and determining how far its members can go. Perhaps somewhere within this testing out (just as you tested out Abraham) there may be a secret of harmonious living to be discovered. But for the moment there is a sense of tormented mystification in Pippa's family, with counter concerns competing for control. I'm wondering if in the very intensity of barren relationships within families your influence could be more readily recognised in achieving longed for conciliation?

I'm intrigued with the questions arising from my own reflection about Pippa and her Mum and Dad. As they fondled her in her early cradling; as they responded to her childish tantrums; as she grew away from her parents, have you in any sense been able 'to speak' to her, or to them? How is your presence mediated? Is it by way of mediating by either friends or colleagues? Or is there another process? Successfully piloting parents and children into supportive and complementary relationships so they learn the disciplines of control, is almost a life time's occupation. It might help if we were to give attention to that story which is credited being the best known in the western world - the story of two sons told by Jesus. It's a fertile tale, but for me a significant factor within it is that no mention is made of their mother. I'm wondering if this is an omission on purpose or not? Mothers are important aren't they? Surely the mother of these two brothers must have had some loving influence in their lives? In this imaginary family could it have been that one brother was favoured more than the other? Was there a 'mother's boy?' Or a 'Daddy's boy?' That this wonderful story leaves out the mother, for me, has to be of some significance. The Church is 'heavy' on teaching that you are 'God the Father'. How significant is this to families today? From the Church we learn that Mary is regarded as 'the Mother of God' - Quite a difficult notion to understand. Mothering and fathering are equally significant in families today. So for instance, can the ideals of heavenly fathering and mothering provide any guidance to today's families, and especially those that are lost in acrimony and isolation? To be a little more graphic, does the 'wilderness of family brokenness', with its overwhelming experience of betrayal and disappointment, rooted in obsessional behaviour, dissipate these ideals? Do you think each child has a right to have a father and a mother? I ask because more children are being born into single parent households. But again, I'm not forgetting either, how tyrannical the family can be. Infidelity, selfishness, possessiveness, can all threaten the wellbeing of family life. Children can grow up happily within a single parent family. The fact is that fewer adults are marrying, and thereby increasing the number of single parent families. Relationship disintegration touches every part of the fabric of our society. The earliest story of Adam and Eve has modelled the experience of relationship breakdown. From this are we to draw the conclusion that life on earth in families will primarily be about struggle and risk, and only after pain, which appears to be an integral part of the human experience of love and loving, can we find a vestige of some happiness that has a healthy, and satisfying purity about it. I wonder?

As you can see my time with Pippa has stirred up concerns which raised questions from my own anxiety, along with ultimate issues which bring into question the basic foundation of the family. Pippa and her parents have made me aware of the basic need for hope, even in what looks like a hopeless situation. Their sense of lostness is not unusual, and it leaves them, and me, feeling that humanity is really on its own. From where else can help appear? They - we, have to get on with it. I'm unsure whether I or we can look to you for much insight and constructive inspiration? You have provided what you have provided. Now humanity has to get on with it! This feels to me like having no other option than to pull on our shoestrings even though they may be frayed or even snapped. It's impossible. This is the feeling I have about Pippa and her parents, and others like them. I'm having to face the hard truth that in spite of knowledge, insight, and a will to goodness, the flaws in families can appear to be without achievable solution. To be blunt, this is hard to accept. Pippa seems rather like an Icon of Despair, and perhaps her parents may be even deeper into their own disillusionment. Yet for me there is a counter hope, and this is for a new 'Epiphany'. An epiphany which will ensure a seamless piloting through the intractable agony, which will diminish the feared prospect of catastrophe. Dear God your first-hand touch could help me to express with finite words something that has an infinite power, enabling us to see ourselves as we truly are without the stupid manipulation of focussing the blame on the other - be it daughter, mother, or father. My plea is that you break your silence, so that our intimate imagination becomes vibrant with a new perspective. Your breath could melt the despair of their relational wilderness. This is but a pictorial metaphor to try to express what feels like the unexpressible. At the moment this gift remains hidden. I've tried to bring it to view, so that it is revealed to human eyes, demolishing the weariness of our human minds. I admit I'm struggling. So please don't allow this struggling to go on and on. This will sap basic hope, and that would not be very loving, would it? I hope this letter has rescued some clarity out of confusion - so I'm expectant. What else could I be? And again, yes, again, I'm waiting.

Letter 12: The choice — violence or non-violence?

Dear God,

This is not going to be an easy letter to write, but I need to write it. My heart is full of the deepest sadness because the world is dominated by the deep pain that violence brings. This drives me into a deep depression of impotence- the feeling that very little can be done to eradicate it. By violence I mean over-powering physical force destructively injuring another, and the tyranny of military weapons, nuclear and biological weapons that cause indiscriminate hurt, the suffering and loss of life. We now know that humanity could be destroyed by its own inventions. Violence itself is an intense and furious force, driven by a passion of fury with total disregard for anything or anyone. Violence desecrates! It bubbles away, incessantly. It's all around me. In the streets. In bedrooms and kitchens. In school bike sheds. It's featured on television. It's the subject of numerous films, videos and DVDs. It rears its head in the play of children. Every newspaper features it daily, along with the majority of journals and magazines. Sadly though, this is not the whole story. Violence infiltrates the politics and economics of nations, cultures, tribes, and religions so that war itself has been present in the world for as long as can be remembered, and not least in the 20th and our own 21st century. Controversy still dominates the question as to whether or not there can be what is called 'a Just War'. Nonetheless war devastates Chechnya, Tibet, Afghanistan, Iraq, as well as many countries in the African continent. It has wounded the very heart of Israel; and the Palestinians go on and on suffering the intended violence of those who themselves experienced the most vile violence in the notorious German concentration camps. War is a brutalising process bringing in its wake starvation, poverty and utter despair. Sadly, humanity has not yet learned how to banish violence. Indeed in these recent days a different model of violence has spread across the globe. It's called terrorism. No one, nowhere, is safe. Life has never, ever, been so dangerous and insecure.

Nonetheless this is not the whole story. There are those who consider violence as a viable tool in what they consider to be the important struggle for liberation by those who are oppressed. They consider it the only way forward to gain freedom. They would maintain that they use violence for a good end, and that liberation only comes at the price of violence in their struggle. Some terrorists consider themselves liberators, and the liberated. They are persuaded that it is the only way to gain their freedom. It is expensive, requiring huge investment of funds, and this leaves others resigned to the worsening of relations, and feeling quite powerless. There have been many examples, and for many - here at home we bear the scars and pain of the extended 'war' in Ireland between the Unionists and the I.R.A. Here, even after all the long struggle, the outcome remains very fragile. There are regional terrorists spread across the globe, each spending incalculable sums of money for the arms needed. What a waste! The fragility of life brings with it the daily anxiety of 'walking on egg shells', with endemic uncertainty.

Perhaps the saddest reflection has to be that you God cannot be blamed for this overwhelming scenario of violence! You'll be glad to hear! In all this chaos, truth is always a casualty. But like the violence itself humanity has become adjusted to this situation. To live in a world unsullied by violence and falsehoods - some might want to call it heaven. But I suppose this may be 'jumping the gun' as they say!

However, to complicate matters there is another violence experienced, in today's world. It's the violence of what we call natural disasters. It might appear that humanity has no control over this brand of violence - though this has to be questioned. I'm thinking of the severe extremities of the weather which brings flooding and considerable damage to life and property from gales. It is frightening to be caught up in a hurricane and typhoon. Earthquakes rock the very foundation of cities, villages and the vast expanse of wild countryside. The tsunami in December 2004 caused the largest national disaster in recent times. Hundreds of thousands died and others were so traumatised that they cannot face their own future. In this extreme situation some have even blamed you for not taking control. Of course, now we know that some natural disasters are being exacerbated by the way humanity treats our planet Earth. Global warming and other environmental trends, together with our misuse of natural resources including our greed for more short term fuels, threatens the very environment we know we need to conserve. So, it could be argued that humanity is an accomplice as it were, to what appear to be natural disasters. So in brief, humanity experiences this as a 'breed' of violence - all such a far cry from the traditional quiet and placid summers evening! In earlier times humanity seemed to be the victim of natural disasters, while today now we have more insight, and knowledge and have learned how to respond to the plight of these disasters which are beyond our control. But the question remains, that here in the basic work of your creation there seems to be something of violence in its very heart. Why is this so, and can humanity ever be given the insight to understand why such disasters are an important segment of the life of our planet Earth?

Across the centuries many natural disasters have brought much suffering. For example, take the year 1783/84. In France there was a long winter. No summer, with endless dark rainless days with low temperatures. The countryside was left with a widespread scum of grey penetrating dust. Natural forces were operating beyond human control. This remains an event that has been much studied by scientists and meteorologists. The people who lived through this experience must have been quite dumbfounded, frightened and realising that life on Earth was not predictable and the unexpected could bring fear of the unknown. Today scientists tell us of major eruptions, for instance the collision of a meteor with our planet 23,000 years ago, which killed at that time all living things. So afterwards, in a sense, the whole story of creation had to be re-enacted.

Was this a flaw in your creation? Or does it have another meaning? Again, we are told that scientists have recently discovered immense quantities of frozen methane under the ocean bed. They think this occurred in a catastrophe, it is said, 80,000 years ago, which also at that time blighted the entire creation. Ironically, if I understand it rightly, it is now estimated that this frozen methane could be a new source of energy for tomorrow's world! If you like, a kind of contemporary act of creation! I'm reciting these ad hoc fragments of history because they alert me to an uncertain past, and I'm wondering if this may be indicating that the future of our planet Earth may yet be subjected to further overwhelming disasters? Nothing appears to be certain. Humanity itself is not in control. And I am feeling very, very small! These matters raise important questions about beginnings and endings, with the part that apparently, violence has to play within what we call the natural order. The longitude of time within the fabric of creation has taken its course, but it appears to be beyond the comprehension of many. We now have to accept that in the millions of years that have passed, creation itself has gone through many phases - the Ice age, the Palaeolithic period, the Cro-magon M173 marker as it has been called by scientists, and the Neanderthals, just to mention but a few - leaving my mind just reeling! Gigantic continents have moved - seas displaced - disappearing and then re-appearing moved by gigantic power beyond human imagining, but wearing the face of unpreventable violence. This staggers my mind. To put it simply, if I can, how is it that you have been around all of this staggering chunk of time? It is almost beyond my comprehension. And here I am - little me, daring to pose my own inadequate questions - yes, again! Even though I've lived less than a paltry one hundred years!

But I can't dismiss a deep sense of conviction that all life is sacred. Yet whatever may be the inner secrets of creation's birth - or births - notwithstanding the violent birth pangs, far reaching and terrible, it evokes a spontaneity of absolute awe and wonder, though sadly tinged with fear, apprehension, and most importantly, out with control. Because for me there is a credible urge to interpret the violence which I feel is at the heart of all creation, a rather far cry from the idyllic picture in the opening chapters of the Book of Genesis. I would not, in any way, wish to suggest that this in itself gives credibility to the reasons and purposes of humanity's own urge to violence. But at the same time, I'm left wondering whether you have sown within 'the frame' of every woman and man the seeds of potential yet terrifying human violence? Perhaps this is a secret hidden still, within a sense of a yet to be achieved maturity - which then will be able to discern the causes of violence both from within and without the human psyche. After all, if violence itself has been one of your own tools, then could it be also the case that at times of extremity, humanity will be faced with the same dilemma - to be seduced by violence, of whatever magnitude, but to recognise that the goal will be more important than the actual process of achieving it? Yet, if it is the case that all life is precious, how is the circle to be squared? Maybe our enlightenment has yet still to be discovered or revealed? To put it pictorially, I'm left looking for 'a star' - probably a 'distant star' that will shine and bring this longed for and needed illumination, to show us what up to now has remained a secret, perhaps born of inexplicable ignorance?

I need to move on now to the domestic scene, where the sad truth is that violence is endemic. Interpersonal violence has become responsible for the decline of happiness in a large number of families. It has also infiltrated much of the social and business arena. Children, women and men have all been affected by the bitterness and anger that only feels itself expressed when it erupts in physical assault, with the intention to hurt and on occasion to kill. You will know, I assume, how seductive and manipulative personal violence is. It destroys integrity. If I submit to personal violence myself, I find myself its prisoner. Today, kids playing in the park or on the beach can be exposed to unexpected violence. On the other hand, for adults, the intimacy of love, the sexual act itself can become the tool of inter-personal violence. There is the frightening realisation that the incidence of violence in discordant and fragmented personal relations threatens the wellbeing of marriage. Increasingly, the family instead of being a citadel of security, for some has become a cauldron of deep unhappiness and anxiety. I find this so frightening. Sometimes I catch myself even cowering against some imagined and unexpected personalised violence, such is the power it has over my own imagination. These moments can feel strangely charged with fear, but I know I'm not paranoid!

There are public occasions - sports rallies, games, tournaments, community events, including public holidays where it almost seems as if the crowds, or sections of the crowds go mad and individuals fall foul of bullying, and personal injury. Communal violence with its recriminations against ethnic minorities, by protestors on the one hand, and by the police on the other can be responsible for the formation of ghettos. Ghettos sow seeds of isolation and fear. Too frequently I think, and sadly, the police seen to come off worst. Though it would seem that even the police on occasion appear to be infiltrated with those who nurse a personal or professional violence, in so doing rob the police force of necessary integrity. Road rage is increasing. It is another social example of the spilling over of anger that is out of control. Zero tolerance campaigns have been promoted in an attempt to reduce forms of personal abuse and violence, but it seems only to have had limited success. From all this evidence I think there are deeply embedded traits of violence within the human psyche. Women and children, and on occasion the elderly appear to be most endangered. So I'm wondering how are we to understand this pre-disposition to violent behaviour? I know, from my own experience that frustration from deep feelings of insatiable and yet uninhibited anger do, as it were, spill over without warning, and my behaviour can feel as if it almost out with my control.

Understanding violence depends on insight into the acting out of anger. Part of being human assumes the necessity of expressing angry behaviour in daily life. The crux is about allowing your anger to remain devoid of violent expression – commonly a difficult boundary.

In the diversity of behavioural traits, the challenge is to isolate those traits which are expressed violently. This acting out is motivated from insatiable frustration. Psychiatrists and psychologists are probing the deeper issues that have formulated some treatments in anger management which enables those who feel trapped in violent behaviours to be more aware of alternative strategies which will lead to more fulfilling and positive controls.

However, progress in transforming violent behaviour both in private and public life still has far to go, before society can be complacent. The Book of Genesis tells the story of Cain and his brother Abel. It sheds some light on the inner understanding which led one man to kill his brother in his rage and jealousy – something not uncommon in today's society. Whilst research provides encouragement to some, there are others who remain frustrated at the tedious slowness of change in attitudes as well as limited effectiveness in research – both in personal and in public violence.

However, can you God begin to identify with the fears and hopes of humanity, facing what appears to be such an intractable situation? Will you share this increasing sense of deep insecurity that is felt right across the globe? Not a few are terrified as they contemplate their future. The sense of 'ingrained' violence erodes the purity of the soul, and assails the sanctity of one's personal hopes for the future. People are left feeling quite desperate when they care to recognise that to all intents and purposes today's violence is widespread, and outwith effective control. Yes. You are right, this is sobering and bewildering. Sadly, for many, all they can do in response is to try to shut it all out of their mind, and anaesthetise their feelings. Others just immerse themselves in a continuing roundabout of indulgent and obsessive pleasure. To be sober about the future, I doubt that increased legislation, or for that matter injecting further funding into the common purse will bring about the mature behaviour which alone will be able to modify violent living. Something more radical and deeper is required, but what this may be precisely remains for the moment unknown, we have to stay with the research. A deep sense of dedication will certainly be a pre-requisite for finding a ready antidote to violence. Of course there are those who either because of dejection or exasperation will cry "What the hell - we'll be a long time dead!" Sadly this compounds the depression of others, and snidely one begins to wonder whether we are caught up in a search for the unattainable - a violent-free society?

Recently I wrote a letter to the Radio Times, asking if it would be possible for the programme planners of Radio and TV, to arrange for one day a week, or even one day a month, when there would be no violent programmes broadcast or screened. I received neither reply nor acknowledgement. So my fantasy is that the Editor's department thought I was an 'oddball'. The implication being that if she went along with my suggestion, then the programme stock would have to be halved. I have not researched the matter because I think the implications are clear. Anyone scanning the pages of the Radio Times will see the situation, starkly for what it is.

Removing violent programmes out of the daily schedule would be like removing the traditional cup of tea from the habitual menu of society! It may be worth noting that the nearest competitor to violence in programmes, particularly on television is sex! But that's another story. Or is it I wonder? Nonetheless I'll not be diverted!

Personal violence, relational violence, community violence, and military violence, and the influence of a psychology of violence, all together provide an overwhelming scenario which defies human understanding. Some in response say this is clear evidence of sin in the world - our world. But this does not add one whit to the hope of any realistic solution to the status quo. There are plenty of those who use this scenario of violence to create a culture asserting that enemies can only be overcome by violence and the tools of violence. They assert that no other method is effective. There are passionate feelings, and the boundary between passion and violence may be paper thin. Can you - will you, in spite of all I've written, fertilise my insight, and enlarge my understanding? I'm listening - I'm hoping!

Now I want to move on. I feel I need to rescue something positive which in spite of everything still sticks in my mind, and infiltrates my experience. In my better moments I feel there are some initiatives that could have within them vestiges of hope. For instance I'm thinking of the World Council of Churches and its Campaign to combat violence. This has followed an earlier initiative, the Campaign to Combat Racism. Clearly these two initiatives are closely linked. Elsewhere, there is the Zero Tolerance Campaign directed against the violence particularly towards women and children. These have been promoted by visionary women and men, some with Christian conviction. On a human level I am sure they have made a difference, individually even though the term 'success' might be a bit over the top On the other hand it has to be admitted that the focus of these two campaigns has been directed to the people of Europe, the USA, Australia and New Zealand. In other words the people of Africa, Asia, and the oppressed elsewhere have not had the full impact and benefits of these Campaigns. It reminds me of the reputed daunting words of Jesus, 'To those who have, shall be given, and to those who have not, shall be taken away even that which they have'. Is this too harsh an assessment?

Today there is a divide across the world. On the one hand there are those who struggle to create a peaceful world by peaceful means. On the other hand there are the military powers who have only one mind set, and this is that weapons and the means to use them will alone safeguard the world. The sales of armaments spiral, and there appear to be endless financial resources for weapons research. In fact some universities balance their books with the assistance of military research income. However the Peace Movement, and groups and organisations committed to a genuine strategy for peace are without the kind of income that could perhaps then give them an equal chance to have 'clout' in this depressing struggle. Historically I think it is true to say that more children, women, as well as men, have died from the violence of war than any other single cause. The implications of this remain to be learned and understood.

Again, I am aware and feel apprehensive at the thought of you not being in control if even it would be only to ensure the preservation of our world, and the prospect of peace and justice. But it seems as if humanity has its own unfettered control of the future of our planet Earth. For myself I just quake with fear, and I admit to some anger, should it be clear that humanity in all its totality is finally responsible for the future of the world. I feel a deep sense of helplessness. As if we are being left 'to stew in our own juice'. It's as if the truth is, that there cannot be life without violence. And this prospect I find quite frightening. Were you to devolve control of the universe to humanity this would be presumably because we were adequate for the task. On the other hand if you are to retain control then we are 'let off the hook' as it were, and we would then continue to wallow in our negative culture which continues to blame you. So how is this hiatus to be resolved?

To return to the record of the Old Testament you are seen as the God of Battles by the People of Israel. And this may not be far from the truth as far as the present government of Israel is concerned today! They believe you 'are on their side! But much about this also contradicts the caring, wounded, and loving image of other passages of scripture, and supremely I suppose of the style and thrust of the life of Jesus, My own perception leads me to believe that there is only one thing to do with enemies, and that is to love them! However my guess is that the majority would maintain that this is nothing but folly. The present mood is that the only response is to kill, and to do so with any means to hand. This ensures that violence escalates, with the fear it will all get out of hand. 'An eye for an eye', does have its own rationale, but it makes no sense in an age of nuclear and biological weapons. Military strategists go on about a 'relative response', but it is not clear to me what it is that is relative. Could it be a just cause? A just peace? A last resort? If the sting of modern weaponry is the sting of ultimate death and decay, can they ever be endorsed, with integrity? We face the possibility of a nuclear blackout - and does this move you to cry out when this precious universe could end in a moment, and undo all your work of love? Not being 'in charge' for you must be so full of utter frustration so that your anger is kindled? Anger is the fruit of inexpressible frustration.

Underneath the themes of this letter I'm becoming aware of the need for me to have a clear understanding of the notion of power, power does not need to be violent, nor destructive. It is present in a multitude of ways within our universe. It can be creative or destructive. As a Boeing 737 climbs up after take off, it has the power force to over ride gravity and to fly in the open sky. Or again, an athlete coming into the final straight of the marathon, is as fast as the power force within her body and her will. The launch of a great liner as she slides down to her mooring is a symbol of great power and force. Or again, tellingly I've seen the power of determination as an elderly crippled woman, determined not to be chair bound, moves to the sink to wash her teacup. And this reminds me of the power and force of image and symbol - the naked Cross - the flying Dove which evoke dedication and even reverence. Nor can I forget the power and inner tenacity of those who have not capitulated to torture and bullying. I 'm aware that these examples do have the power to lift us up - even the most timid - as we are able to celebrate such achievements, occasionally against overwhelming odds. This creative force has the power to transform apparent defeat, and offer hope, when previously only despair was present. The liberating act of love with its quiet insight has power and force of its own which will breed the confidence so that the ground under our feet will feel the firmer, offering a new sense of security. So I'm caught up in this sense of mystery, which seeks to understand how to practise power force, without any violent component present. It is the practising that is difficult!

This brings me to an issue that has further complexity for me. For most of my life I have tried to live non-violently. It's been a commitment, though on occasion it has been more than difficult to uphold. There have been many examples of non-violent living, and wherever there is crisis there will be women and men who quietly demonstrate the authority of a non-violent approach. This approach however, for some, means that it becomes an absolute. Absolute non-violence it is argued is the only relevant response to absolute violence. So I'm wondering, dear God, do you think that there are absolutes? By this I mean a strategy, belief, approach that is always right in every situation? I'm thinking that any concept of an absolute, dilutes the importance of on-going critique - critical appraisal. For me the danger is of falling foul of our own arrogance, as if we 'know everything' with unlimited certitude. Some have been edged out of the movement for non-violence because though non-violence was central to their life, they were not sure that it was the best approach in every situation. I'm still of the view that non-violence as a life style is of ultimate importance, and has proved its power time and again. But, an absolute? I'm far from sure! I'm recalling the example of a young Jewish woman prisoner in a Nazi concentration camp, awaiting the gas chamber. She was young and beautiful. The commandant took a fancy to her. He arranged for her to have little treats, and eventually seduced her, but not without her willingness. One evening he gave a party to a small group of colleagues and, friends. He wanted, as it were, to show her off! She was admired by the guests, and naturally, gossip and questions were hovering around! There was music and dancing. She was a clever, graceful and sensuous dancer. So in the gaiety of the moment she partnered him, and they glided around the dance floor. She 'draped' her right arm loosely around his shoulder, as he held her close to him. In the rhythm of the dance, on a limited but crowded floor, she quickly drew a knife from the fold of her dress and stabbed him in the heart through his back, to a quick death. He collapsed and medical help was too late. The other dancers stood fixed with rigid astonishment, unable to move. But quickly an on looking guard shot her dead with a single shot. Hers was an act of contemplated violence, deliberately chosen. She had perceived that non-violence would not do what she thought was needing to be done. Was she doing the right thing for the wrong reason, or the wrong thing for the right reason? Many have died in the non-violent struggle, just as many - probably many, many more have died in the violent struggle. This Jewish woman knew her days were numbered anyway, as were the days of thousands of others. None in the camp would escape their fate. The commandant's grisly role was abruptly interrupted, and for her this was her single objective, which could not be achieved non-violently. These choices are ambiguous, but for some it will be an imperative that cannot be evaded. Death violently or in the cause of non-violence is still death and can never be an easy choice. But the choice will always be present. I know dear God that you will see this with a heart of compassion, and the memory of this woman will always be a blessed memory. But I'm left wondering if you have a greater clarity about the guidelines, and do you have now any new insight into the unending dialogue between means and ends? Clear thinking is needed, but it may not be enough. The dilemma remains. I'm remembering those lines even though I do not remember the author, 'The Lord has yet more light and truth to break forth from his Word'. In this stark quandary we desperately need new light and truth. How long have we to wait?

The image of Jesus on his Cross intrudes my thoughts. His too was a violent death. If it is the case that humanity is to be redeemed by a violent death, can it not be argued that all violence can be effective? One act of violence is but a part of the total violence. The tradition is that you chose a violent death for Jesus, to redeem humanity. And over the course of the centuries the violence of many martyrs has endorsed again and again that violence can redeem. The dividing line between violence and non-violence is blurred and requires a new sense of humility if we are to perceive this complex paradox. This has much to do with the emerging insight of the power of powerlessness. It's within the shadow of servanthood. And the enigma for me, and others, is that you have given up your power, and your existence perhaps will be better understood when we recognise that your model of powerlessness, is the style that is calling humanity today.

I need your grace to keep me alert. You'll see from this letter I still have a great deal of learning to do! Perhaps you'll use this letter to enlighten me, beyond my understanding? I do want it!

Letter 13: Christmas? What's new?

Dear God,

It's Christmas Eve. For me there's an air of anticipation, even excitement! Something is going to happen. I'm in a wondering and expectant mood. There is to be broadcast from King's College Chapel in Cambridge, a Festival of Nine Lessons & Carols. This will present a wonderful kaleidoscope of stories, myths, and hopes with music and silence, holding together the anticipation of Christmas. Many thousands, are tuned in to listen. In my mind's eye I can picture the glorious Chapel wrapped in a reverence of mellow candlelight. Children, women and men sit quietly as the organ evokes the expectancy of the choristers and the congregation. This sanctuary, hushed and sacred, reflects an iconic stillness, which stretches back into sacred history. Music and language provide a symphony of beauty and peace. It is as if an eternal word is to be offered to those who have come expectantly and who are anxious to hear it and revere it. All of this is grounded now in this present and significant moment. Within the walls of this Chapel worship pervades. But outside in the busy street the commercial tinsel invites others to a 'good time'. The inside and the outside fail to meet. The two dimensions of life being lived cheek by jowl remain far from each other. This symbolic difference is deep, and the boundary is clear as one crosses from the street to the threshold of the Chapel itself. From out there, into here, feels like moving from chaos to peace. It is no actual distance, but paradoxically the two worlds appear widely apart. Though both, in their way, are within the parameters of the Christmas event. Thank goodness!

I feel fully engrossed. The impact of the Lessons, the language of the prayers and the poetry, the pauses and silences, and the well loved Advent and Christmas carols, together generate a feeling of benediction, whilst my mind is already grappling with the enigma of the meaning of it all. In my study here where I sit with a small lit Christmas Tree, the cards, and the wrapped presents ready, I'm immersed in the mystery of this worship., But simultaneously I'm aware of some discomfort of contradiction and confusion as I struggle to accept the 'old story', just as it is. It all feels real, I tell myself. But sitting now reflecting afterwards, the struggle of the heart and mind leaves me feeling ambivalent - wanting, and wondering. I'm feeling less secure, and I'm confronted with the reflection that perhaps after all these years I have to face the discomfort of knowing and yet of not knowing. This shakes my sense of security and I feel 'wobbly'. I know I still have something to learn. In a sense I can move from the warm comforting 'womb' of the Chapel, to the world which has grown cold and seems too frequently inhospitable. The Lessons and Carols point the way to the emerging Babe of Bethlehem, who in a unique way has 'touched' me. There's no other way of describing it. This experience has been stripped of the encumbrances imposed by time and history. The Service has helped me to realise how contemporary the experience and the message is, despite the garish religious glamour we have come to associate with the simple stable.

In my imaginings I've been led to wonder whether or not, had I been there on that night I would have understood any better than any of the Shepherds? I'm ambivalent! But for this moment the story of Bethlehem as recorded for me, with the emotion of this afternoon's music, and the verbal drama, has left me, could I say, spellbound! Yes, I think so. The variation of detail within the synoptic differences only adds, in a way, the poetic pattern which has its own ethereal attraction. I find myself repeating the story, word for word, line for line, indelible on my memory, all with a sense of quiet awe. In a sense the story is deep inside me. I'm in the stable of that Inn. The cold draught is sharp, but the warm breath of the animals brings comfort, while the tenderness of the baby enfolded in straw with swaddling shawl draws all my attention. The silent father and mother astonished by the baby who from the moment of his appearance is the epitome of gentle strength. The arrival of the surprised shepherds, with the brilliant star above, tuned into the echo of a heavenly anthem, yet at that moment unaware of the rarity and the significance of that humble stable scene. Did Mary feel alone in herself at this conjunction - the glory of the baby with the absence of normal maternal comforts? The short stay with the uncertainty of when to move on? Then the deep questions in the mind of Joseph, pondering the uncertainty with Mary, but tied in with their own love for each other, and the speciality of their bond which had safely delivered to the world a new Heir of Creation and

Humanity- the Special one. I'm ready to bet that those shepherds surprised Mary and Joseph. Just think of it, I'm saying to myself, friendly shepherds from the nearby familiar hills uncomfortably looking on in a strange but busy inn. I'd give my back teeth to have an inkling of what they were thinking, feeling, as they stood gazing there. They were real witnesses to an incredible occasion. A tiny lamb or two, probably newly born themselves, too fragile to be left on the bleak hillside - became an integral part of the occasion. The angels were in full forte, though the stable was smelly for an unexpected birth. I would bet that the eyes of those shepherds almost fell out of their heads as they gazed on the unimagined scene. But I wonder, did they believe what they saw?

This story has been repeated numberless times, and it looks as if the re-telling will go on forever. Being 2,000 or so years old, has its own power and its own persuasion. But has it yet to reach its zenith? For how long does an event of this antiquity have to go on to capture a contemporary relevance? For ever - however long this may be? And yet? Where is the secret that can cast a shadow over my doubts as well as the doubts of others? Doesn't the passing of time blur the event, and doesn't history diminish the potency of any happening as it recedes with its immediacy diluted? I'm looking for the secret that will engulf my doubts as to the meaning of this mystery. Is there an awaiting revelation that maybe prevented by a panic of pragmatism? This letter is my fragmented search, the search for a wonder that is not saturated with doubt. Can I put a ringed fence round my doubts? Words and thoughts pinch my mind and questions evoke uncertainty. I feel so deeply split. Yet I acknowledge the story still has an essence of power to move me on occasion to worship and wonder. But I 'seesaw' to and fro, and I know that tomorrow I will awaken to strange doubts that struggle for their own meaning. At one moment they feel deeply uncomfortable. But at another disturbed by my spiky impatience. This dialogue of meaning will not allow me to rest. Hence God, my searching assures me that the truth that I feel still needs to be 'discovered', could take more time than what may still remain of my life. There is an urge to go beyond what are the 'facts', to a meaning which if it is sublime and compelling in its liberating force might then allow some firmer ground for those who along with me, and after me, will venture on this pilgrimage. Hopefully to find, and to be found. In a strange way the words of this letter, for me, and the words of the actual Christmas story, be they divine or human, have an actual unmistakable inter-mingling. So I'm wondering if I have to learn to tolerate the silence of the centuries - to be speechless - to listen with patience, and then to know I do not know. I'm feeling vulnerable and maybe I have to learn that in my vulnerability insight may dawn.

I'm lingering in this quiet study. My brain begins to tick over, and gradually quickens. Questions stir again and my momentary sense of wonder is quietened by a sense of explicit doubt with its hesitation. The Book that tells the story still lies open - I have not closed it. I'd not wish this examination of traditional exposition to close down the special sense of wonder. This is precious in itself. But I suppose this could be tantamount to 'having my cake, yet at the same time needing to eat it'. But I'm aware that the truth is that I'll need another's hand to hold mine, and I suppose I'll have to acknowledge that perhaps your hand will not be near enough to hold mine.

Mary, by name, we are told was a virgin, sexually. I'm not wishing to read our present into the past. But for her to have a male partner - espoused we are told - and recognising their relationship, with her remaining sexually aware, to say the least, raises questions which for me still remain unanswered. These are not cheeky questions. They are questions about human behaviour, the personal behaviour between a particular woman and a particular man, in the culture of their day. In this important matter no one wishes to be hoodwinked. She had a baby, and we are told it was 'by the Holy Ghost'. So did you, God, impregnate Mary yourself? How? Why? It's difficult to get my mind round this. I'm reflecting, is not every birth of every baby sacred? When the human process of intimate sexual encounter - a part of your creative plan I think - is enfolded with love and with longing, then the birth of a baby is a welcomed gift. This is the mystery of the wonder of creation, in which women and men have desire as well as control. The process of human birth can never just be regarded as ordinary, initiated as it is in the foreplay of intimate love, sublime, and intended as one of those 'high spots' which cradle forever in the memory what has to be unforgettable. This is a process that can be understood as physical, biological, but with another dimension, even those words cannot articulate it.

I think my own question now is becoming clearer. It is about you, yourself impregnating Mary, and I pose it with ultra seriousness, honouring its natural privacy for you and her. This special birth - this one off occasion - for me clearly signifies that Jesus has to be divine - he is, as it were, of your seed. He is, as it were, without our common humanity. So the assertion that he remains both human and divine can only be a conundrum, defying human logic, and taking us into a realm clearly beyond the human. When you decided to have 'a son' were you anxious that the process should be put into Mary's hands? For her your decision to choose her must have felt like an accolade! Mary was chosen, but no one knows why. Nonetheless for her it was more than an accolade. And I readily bow my head in the deepest regard for her. My sense of confusion however does not inhibit my desire to offer my own worship and adoration to Jesus, recognising that Mary and Jesus enjoyed a relationship not available to any other mother and son. And lest it seem an after thought, I'm struggling to ensure that Joseph is not left out, though so little is known about him, it is not easy to discern the true nature of his place and part in this one off and once and forever incarnation.

Jesus is now known as the Saviour of the World. Some believe that you God are present in each human being. I cannot state this with great confidence because proof varies so much as the study of the human species grows and develops. There can be no physical proof, and the notion of a spiritual proof is hard to construct. But it is hard to dismiss the claim of Quakers that 'there is that of God in every person'. This does give some comfort. But I can't deny that whatever this presence is, it lies within to be pondered, recognising that its effect comes and goes. For myself I can testify to feeling something of you God, in me, on what I might call special occasions, of uplift and inspiration. But, as I have said, there are those times I need to 'feel' you, but alas you appear to be absent. And as far as Jesus goes, well I think, in a sense, I'd feel more comfortable if he were human, like me. Yes, I know this is a sweeping statement, but my quandary remains, as to how his divinity can in any sense coincide with my humanity. Does being divine allow him to fully understand me? Or for that matter me to understand him? Being divine leaves him an 'exit' not accessible to human beings. I hanker after the notion that because you were in Jesus in a special though undefined way, this has enabled humanity to 'taste' something of your divinity in a way that remains a mystery. I feel that on the imaginary ladder from humanity to divinity I'm on the very lowest rung! My climbing of this ladder is slower than slow! But I'm not forgetting some rare occasions when I have felt a strange upward mobility, though I know too, it is short lived. And this has no connection to the 'up' and to the 'down' of spatial sense. I'm unclear as to whether I have ever sensed the divine, maybe unknowingly. How would I know? When I tuned in this afternoon to the radio broadcast of the Christmas Eve service? This leaves a lot to ponder. I am still wondering whether the hard edge of my own day to day reality will be infiltrated by the sublime revelation of a birth which I have yet to understand, and in some way or other also experience? If I had been with the shepherds it might have all been so much easier!

As I meditated today I found myself venturing further into an unknown area. In recent months some exploration has been made which has placed us on the edge of discovering new insights, relating to the human body and the human mind, which have the potential perhaps to diversify the traditional roles of women and men. Since the discovery of DNA, there has been an upsurge motivated by enthusiastic scientists to advance knowledge and experience, in such a way, that the previously tested boundaries between right and wrong, good and bad, become less clear. This is perhaps exemplified in the field of human fertilisation and embryological discoveries. We now have the opportunity for male sperm and female eggs to be donated for the benefit of those who have found themselves to be dysfunctional or infertile. This new process has the possibility of bringing some joy to otherwise childless couples. The 'right' to have a baby is climbing higher up the public ladder of 'rights'. It is now possible to use this newly discovered process, even though it is open to misuse. There is the possibility that the profile of parenting could undergo important changes. Recently Reproductive Genetics Institutes have been established in some countries. They hope to develop the technical possibility of creating 'artificial' sperm' from the cell in a woman's body which can then be used to fertilise another woman's egg. Human and therapeutic cloning seems to be more likely in the not too distant future, though there remains a good deal of anxiety and heart searching about what might be called "the morality" of this whole process,

The need for ethical boundaries which might give greater assurances that such research will abide by regulation which ensures greater integrity, will be welcomed by all those who stand in awe and wonder of the original embryonic process. I'm trying to share with you issues and developments where human exploration might appear to be invading a province hitherto wholly yours. The birth of Jesus in that stable, on any ground, was a miracle of yours - very special. But humanly speaking I have been unable, like others down the ages, to probe the process and the mystery of it all. Human birth is a most wonderful gift. But the birth of One 'outside' the human process, relished as divine, continues to probe the human mind beyond human understanding. You did what you thought was necessary when Jesus came to earth. But the onward march today in the field of genetics and embryology does, I think, raise questions as to whether they could be 'biting off more that they will eventually be able to chew'. Could this insatiable human search just be a deep scated latent desire for the embryology scientists and researchers to be 'as God?' Is this process nothing more than the full blooded desire to become co-creators, and to share the exciting discoveries which come with the growth of knowledge and experience? This leaves me anxious, to put it mildly. But an adventurous spirit could be of you, couldn't it?

On the one hand I'm reminded of the dilemma which faced 'The sorcerer's apprentice'. But on the other I'm trying to focus on the notion of being fully human! By this I'm imagining the gifting of rare insight where experience is opened up by the disappearance of 'scales from our eyes'. To wear a new skin, and to have insight into a greater reality, which might, and perhaps indeed would lcad us to a greater understanding of you God. St. Paul talks about us being "co-workers with God". Would this then bequeath on human beings new tasks, with added responsibility, which might include new engagement in the complex questions about enabling embryology to become more versatile for the varied support of those who have a particular need?

There's just one more concern that springs to mind in the fertility of the Advent and Christmas season. As I listened to the prayers of intercession towards the end of the Service of Lessons & Carols, I was struck by the focus given by the priest on the homeless, the poor, and the hungry. Jesus was born in a stable. He was homeless. It's astonishing that you chose for Jesus a homeless birth. But this has struck a chord in the minds of many who struggle for justice. The homeless and the poor can identify with Jesus in a special way. I'm aware too of the image of Mary Mother, homeless too, representing the untold millions of mothers who struggle with their children to find a place where they belong. In many countries women are still the 'drawers of water', and 'the tillers of the sod'. In all the centuries that have past since they found that hovel in Bethlehem, today still there are millions who do not know where they will lodge tonight. They have no security, no food, and are abandoned. I can't help recalling Mary's Song, where she yearns, 'He hath put down the mighty from their seat'. I relish the words, coming from the mouth of a homeless mother. This sharpens my own sense of irony, remembering her terse cry. Now I'm feeling invaded by a fresh sense of immediacy, and inclusiveness. Sadly 'the mighty' have not yet been put down from their seat. In this day and age they can look impregnable! So when will it happen? Can it happen? My guess is that your response will remind us that liberation comes when people engage and initiate it for themselves. It's up to us! It will not come from heaven. I'm quietly pondering the words of her Song, and whether they still vibrated in her breast when thirty years or so later she gazed on her Son as he hung there on his Cross?

So to conclude, I now am convinced that our traditional Festival of Christmas has to be changed, and if you like, shifted into a 21st Century gear. For myself, even at this moment, I'm still in the frame of the Lessons and Carols from King's College Chapel. The sacredness of the Season has to remain. I am both sad and angry that this Festival has become a shopping extravaganza along with excessive eating and drinking. I'm advocating now that Christmas as well as being the recognition of Christ's birth, important though this is, simultaneously this needs to become a Festival for Homeless Mothers - across the world beyond religious and political boundaries. The time has come for Christmas to break the shackles of extravagant self indulgence. The world needs to be mobilised so that every homeless mother finds a home, and a home that belongs to her, her child, and her partner. Christmas is the Festival of the Gift of Homes for the Homeless. Dear God, you know the homeless in Bangladesh, in the Sudan, in Zimbabwe, Palestine, Iraq, in the slums of cities in the United States, Mexico, Brazil, and Europe. There is a long litany of places. Christmas is the occasion 'par excellence' to put the economic spotlight on the homeless - this has to become an integral part of 'celebrating Christmas'. So when I pose the question, 'Christmas? What's New?' - this is what could be new – very new! Deep within the soul of our society a sense of creative peace, the peace that has the power to make a new life for the homeless, now needs to have the seal of your own affirmation,

In this Advent season, my prayer is 'paying attention' to those who bear the sorrow of the world. In my imagination I lower myself, yes, I suppose reluctantly, on to the unkempt floor of The Stable, before the Baby of God, where I discern that within the midst of His radiant glory there is the inescapable pain of the excluded.

I hope this letter will touch you - and you will touch me.

Letter 14: An unpopular notion — Servanthood

Dear God,

In a bygone age, well-to-do families had servants, and some had a plethora of them. It was an age when 'class' mattered, and you found yourself in either the upper class or in the lower class. Servants were in the lower class. Today from some perspectives this difference is less clear. There are fewer households with servants, as such. Though this image is not absent from the workshop floor, the office, the Department store, and even in universities. 'Cleaning ladies' are servants, and servanthood in the mind of the majority is about undertaking menial tasks, and to find oneself devoid of authority.

However there is another level of servanthood, described pithily by St. Paul in his second letter to the Church at Corinith, verse 5 in chapter four. "Ourselves your servants for Jesus' sake". Maybe this was provoked by the recorded words of Jesus himself, as written in the Gospel of St. Matthew at the end of Chapter 20, "And whosoever will be chief among you, let him be your servant". So the notion of servanthood has a religious as well as a social connotation. We live in a time when promotion is regarded as a step up in the hierarchy, by which you expect to have more authority over others. In today's society there are ladders of promotion in commerce and industry, in education, and the media and also in the church as well as in the world of entertainment. This is regarded as the way of the world. Authority is a 'slippery' concept the more so when it is based solely on wealth and the accumulation of money. Most of us, I guess, can remember when we were expected 'to know our place' and to keep a low profile.

In spite of the indications from Jesus and the guidance from the letter of St. Paul, with further clues from other prophets recorded in the Old Testament, the notion of a servanthood ministry has had little credibility within the Church itself. The servanthood style, clearly is inclusive rather than setting out to be exclusive. Elitism is a feature of our society, as it has been I suppose since dim days of ancient history. In the Church today elitism is alive and well, and servanthood itself is not conspicuous. Dare I remind you of the functionaries, each with their authority – ministers, priests, clergy, pastors, bishops, archbishops, canons, deans, sub deans, moderators, Presbytery Clerks, Metroplitans, and Popes. They each occupy a particular level of authority. In contrast to this the Quakers have a minimal structure of hierarchy, where the mode of membership is quietistic recognising a corporate identity shared throughout each Meeting House. In the Church of Scotland, the model of the Church is recognised primarily as a Supreme Court in its General Assembly with lower courts. This is built on the practice of ordination whereby ministers and elders are set apart for their ministry. Some understand this as the conferring of a function, but others prefer to recognise it as conferring a status. Status implies the establishing of an elite – it is exclusive rather than inclusive. For hundreds of years it has been a domain for men, though in recent times women have been admitted, and last year the Moderator of the General Assembly was a woman – a real breakthrough which indicates that some long held restrictions are crumbling. Ordination seems to me to be a man made process, designed to create an elite. Jesus was not a priest. I prefer to recognise him as 'the Man for others'. Elites in themselves can be divisive, and tend to encourage self-gratification. When Jesus had his group of men there was no sense of hierarchy. The tasks and the learning were shared. This becomes clear when we look at what happened when James and John were looking for a special place within the group. Yet it can be argued that 'holy things' need management and perhaps discipline too. So there is a dilemma, how to explore objectively how much 'non-structure' would be sufficient for the Church in our times, rather than hanging on to modes of authority which frustrate the desire for unilateral fellowship, where 'the gifts' of all can be recognised and enjoyed. From history and from the experience of recent time clearly church structures have inhibited the wellbeing of the Church, and perhaps the price paid has been too high. If we could let go of much of the Church's hierarchical structures, we might feel a little 'naked', but this in itself could lead us into a new arena of openness with a corresponding freedom.

Søren Kierkegaard in his writings offers what I think is an apt and refreshing model that helps us in understanding the practicalities of a Servanthood Ministry. Theatrically, he describes the congregation which thinks of the minister as 'the performer', with the congregation as 'the audience', and then with you God as 'the prompter'. Not so, says Kierkegaard. Rather the truth is that the people of the congregation are 'the performers'. You God, he asserts are 'the audience', and then it is the clergy who are 'the prompters'. Two quite different pictures of the Church, both in its worship and its life. One of the reasons why I find it difficult to attend public worship is that generally it is the worship of the clergy rather than the worship of the people. If we believe that the Church is 'The body of Christ', then in the dispensing of the Eucharist, the laity will have an integral part in playing out this most solemn of sacraments. In a servanthood Church those who sit 'at the Table' are to share the benefits of the Sacrament, where Christ alone is supreme. There was a time when ministers in the Church of Scotland were recognised as the Teaching Elders. But alas the teaching offered by the Clergy in this role has not served the Church well. The Church contains too many members who are sadly ignorant of much of the substance of the faith, and more sad too is the fact that too few are aware of this, and for the clergy it has become a matter of less importance. I can recall, twenty or so years ago when the Laity were referred to as 'God's Frozen People'. Today, by and large they remain 'frozen'. The eldership of the Church resembles a 'sleeping giant'. One day it will wake up, and I look forward to this with relish.

Sadly in some countries there are what are known as 'national churches'. In England there is the Anglican Church, and in Scotland, the Church of Scotland. This safeguards the role and status of the Church in the national affairs of the country concerned. In many countries this is the state of ecclesiastical affairs. However, for me the notion of a 'national Church' is a contradiction in terms. "National" Churches have arisen from anxieties and fears motivated by desires to safeguard the national statute of religion in particular countries but the Church is a worldwide fellowship, the significance of national identity for me will come very low in the various 'signs' of the Church. In many cases the concept of the national Church is relished because it gives a sign of authority, and opens up ways in which the Church can infiltrate into the task of government. The notion of a national Church is that it confers a status rather than a function, but neither status nor function can be reconciled with the image of Servanthood. When I reflect on the life and teaching of

Jesus, 'the Man for others', there are no indications at all that he was looking for any national status. He was essentially a Man of the People, without any discrimination.

Belief in the Servanthood Church brings with it difficulty. This, for me, has taken the form of being judged to be a 'troublemaker', or a 'thorn in the flesh' of the establishment. This is not a label I enjoy, and neither do I desire it. But when you go out 'on a limb', my experience is that you will be 'daubed' and the essence of your belief and practice will be ridiculed. When the Catholic Church was called by Pope John XXIII to a Vatican Council, there were those who were quick to denounce radical changes as examples of disloyalty to the Church itself. It was then that the notion of 'loyal dissent' was offered, which sought to clarify that because one might not agree with radical changes, nonetheless ones loyalty to the Church was not to be called into question. Radicals as well as traditionalists are both able to claim that they are loyal – so loyal dissent provided a free passage for both the traditionalist and the radicals. To dissent does not imply disloyalty. In fact dissent may be loyalty infused with integrity. Nonetheless, for me, the accusation of disloyalty has brought its pain, and this has caused me great agony of spirit. I'm wondering dear God how you view all this? The occasions do come when to speak out one has to sacrifice popularity. I've noted on many occasions, how an article, an essay, or a book is judged not by what it is proposing, but rather by who has written it.In today's world we have created a prima donna culture where importance is given to who said what, rather than what has been said.

Human life faces in two directions. One is the way of acceptance and inclusion. The other is the quite different way of intended exclusion. Yes, of course I prefer to be included. But I know that too frequently I find myself being excluded. And the truth is that I do not like it! This experience is a painful split which goes right through the core of me. I find that acceptance is blocked, relationships damaged, and I'm left with anxiety and uncertainty. So my belief is that the essence of the Servanthood Church will provide a reputable place for the principle of loyal dissent, and unseemly patronage will dissolve leaving the Church with greater integrity.

I suppose one aspect of the Church and its role in your world is to unravel the implications of membership. In the Servanthood

Church the ideal is for a mutuality of membership. Gush advertising and publicity campaigns are not seen as intrinsic for a Servanthood Church. By its very nature it will be 'quiet', though also intent on being inclusive of introverts and extroverts – a difficult objective. Membership in itself is unlike the membership of other institutions and organisations, because it will not be primarily associated with gains or rewards, which are the sign of membership of many of society's other organisations. I know there are those who feel that, being a member of the Church have what might be called 'a closed television link' with you God. I mean a kind of priority of your care and your readiness to provide what some might consider a 'sacred insurance policy'. But essentially membership of the Servanthood Church provides no 'benefits' as such. Rather it is an association of women and men who are committed to being there primarily for others. To stand by those in need, the lonely, the misunderstood, and those who see themselves as rejected. The Servanthood Church is not an association of 'the saved'. Its openness is a key feature, and intrinsically this provides its core values.

However, when pursuing this reflection recently I was left wondering whether You will be completely comfortable with what I am calling the signs of the Servanthood Church? Why? Well, because I'm aware that scripture discloses that a very long time ago you entered into a special relationship with the Hebrews. They became what are known as your 'Chosen People'. I'm left wondering if this still stands? Is it still effective? Do you still think and feel that the Hebrews are your Chosen People – maybe in a sense, your 'favourites'? Or is it that the Jews were chosen by you to carry a special burden of suffering pain, and responsibility on behalf of the rest of humanity? The scriptures of the Old Testament hold the record of your relationship with the Hebrews, through thick and thin. To read it, is to be aware that it is a remarkable story. It raises many questions. On occasion it is difficult to distinguish the fact and the fantasy. However, my Jewish friends tell me that as far as they are concerned they believe you have a primary regard for them. Nonetheless the Nazi tyranny against the Jews has caused much pain and sore disillusionment. Some indeed lost their faith in You because they felt you were absent from the gas chambers and the concentration camps. On the other hand I know that in retrospect some Jews feel that now, as they seek to establish their nation You have given them well needed encouragement. This leads on to the tense dilemma currently in Israel and Palestine, where it appears to many that the policy, attitude, and actions of the Israelis are quite contrary to all your teaching. So why do You have a chosen people? Why out of the entire universe have you chosen the Hebrews? Does this mean some preferential regard for them on your behalf? Or is there a deeper dilemma the nature of which, thus far, neither the Jews nor the rest of humanity have been able to discern or understand? Certainly, it seems to me that your relationship with the Hebrews seems a thousand miles away from what I imagine to be your relationship with those who would embrace the notion of the Servanthood Church. The tentacles of limitless violence in the Israeli / Palestinian conflict present humanity with, perhaps, its most serious predicament – and so far as I know, there has been no intimation of guidance from You as to the possible root solution and still less of any peaceful agreement, which alone will staunch the endless flow of precious blood. I believe that the model of a Servanthood Church provides a prototype for the world of nations, so how would You see this same Servanthood model being advocated for the Hebrews (your people) as well as for the Palestinians?

Yes, I agree these are huge issues. But today we have to learn to think big in the Servanthood Church, but only in the sense that service itself has within it the seeds of reconciliation and a new openness of purpose.

This letter is about an aspect of the wilderness of today – abandoning the hope for peace, reconciliation and justice. Violence is in the ascendant. The most profitable industry, across the entire world is in the sale and the promotion of weapons designed to kill. The Armament Cartels are netting high profits. Poor nations are becoming poorer because they submit to the pressure to arm and re-arm. Increased military weaponry gives the impression of greater security, but the price paid is very high, and for many nations this is beyond their resources, with huge accruing debts. Can these pressures, do you think, dear God be successfully and finally overcome with the gentle model of Servanthood in the world, and modelled by the Church? A Servanthood society – a vision? Or is it, if you like, unrealistic – like pie in the sky?

My aim is to find a new route whereby the teaching of Jesus might penetrate the citadels of power, arrogance, money and investment, along with the fallible political structures which are in danger of complete disintegration. Because the prospect of worldwide chaos is not in any way a fantasy, but rather an all too threatening reality, my belief is that the basic notion of a Servanthood Church would act as a prototype for a Servanthood society. I'm not yet able to map it all out, but I am restless for You to come near and take the scales from my eyes. The 'devil will be in the detail', but with a vibrant imagination, fuelled with dynamic hope, I might at least come to the hilltop and look over the horizon and see the beginnings of the coming Servanthood age. I hope my feet are on solid ground. The blessed notion of Servanthood is as fragile as it is gentle. But even though it is based on values derided as ineffective by some, they do have the power to point to a new scenario of hope. The lines are drawn. Your enlightening touch is needed. Will You come face to face with humanity, choosing it in its entirety rather than just the Hebrews alone? If this letter has had a critical dimension, then the criticism itself resembles for me an imaginative attempt to tattoo soap bubbles on 'the body' of our world – they will rise and float out across our blessed Earth and hopefully be found eventually in surprising places. Then the Servanthood Church will float and not sink!

Letter 15: The risk of opening my mind

Dear God,

It's late! Before I go to bed I want to share with you something that struck me recently. I was watching the final concert of the Proms on BBC 1. For many years this final concert of the season has been something of a party as well as a concert. There's lots of audience participation. The orchestra, artists, conductor, and the entire audience were 'high as kites'. There's a tradition too, that much of the music is patriotic, with the waving of flags, the Union Jack, raucous singing and irrepressible fun 'noises' across the Hall. In particular there is the enthusiastic rendering of an Edwardian piece of music by Edward Elgar, 'Pomp & Circumstance No.1', which subsequently was set to words. It's full of sentiment reminiscent of the end of World War I - 'Land of hope & glory'. This piece of music and the song itself has become a kind of theme song of the once superior British Empire. The words go like this – "Land of Hope and Glory - Wider still and wider may thy bounds be set - God who made thee mighty, make thee mightier yet!" For me there is a troubling time warp. But sadly this does not seem to diminish the irrational enthusiasm of the audience. I'm left puzzling, and wondering whether the people of the audience really mean these words?

However, you will see that your name is well to the fore in this song. Apparently, the majority in the hall cherish the notion that you made the British mighty in the days of the Empire. And further, those people also share the hope that there will be wider bounds of power still for the British - and we'll be 'mightier yet!' Sitting here in front of my TV, struggling with the spectacle and the music I was aware of a feeling of deep distaste with this exhibition of such repugnant and blatant imperialism and nationalism, garnished with what I can only call polluted arrogance, left over from a bygone age. I loathe the way in which this closing concert has been turned into a patriotic extravaganza which bears no reality to the world in which we all live today. The empire has gone. Britain's power and influence in today's world is not what it was. At the present time I'm told that our Government can hardly afford to pay the gardeners who tend the upkeep of the expensive War Cemeteries of the dead of World Wars 1 and 2, sited in Flanders Fields and nearby in Northern France. This is just one valid illustration of an impoverished, integrity. The rhetoric of the concert reveals a poverty of our corporate imagination, a reluctance to acknowledge the diminished role of Britain today.

It's now morning. I managed to sleep a little. But in the cold light of day I'm left wondering if You can recognise any truth at all in the words of the Song? I do not believe that You had anything to do with establishing the British Empire in the 19th and 20th centuries. Am I right? I know that the Empire was won if You like, because of both brave acts of sacrifice, as well as by acts of war and treachery. However it's a dangerous step to believe that You give victory in battles, or are responsible for defeats. I see this as an abdication of humanity's own responsibility for the outcome of any war. I'm hoping that victory or defeat cannot be accredited to You. I know that there have been Army Chaplains who led their platoons in prayer before they went into the thick of the fighting. I'm left wondering whether or not this implies that You will be expected, in some imperceptible way, to look after these troops, whatever happens? For victories God be praised! But when there is only defeat, then the' God talk' has to be hushed and even muffled. All that is left is an unpalatable silence. In the Old Testament there are many bloody stories which suggest that the victories of the Hebrew people in their struggles and battles were due to your influence. The popular story of David and Goliath is a good illustration. You were with David and not with Goliath, and hence David's unlikely victory. I wonder what You think about this now? Isn't the interpretation, as we say, 'too near the bone?' This is what I think feels like primitive thinking, and therefore has little relevance at all to our day and age. On the other hand perhaps the message could be that You were wishing well for the underdog?

But then I'm also remembering that not many years ago the British fought a war in the Falkland Islands. Some believed that You were on the side of the British because they thought our cause was just. Many prayers were said. Then afterwards when the war was over, and the British appeared to have been vindicated, there was a Service of Thanksgiving in St. Paul's Cathedral, led by the then

Archbishop of Canterberry, Dr. Runcie. In his sermon he attempted a critique, evoking reconciliation and a mood of forgiveness. He was sharply rebuked by the then Prime Minister because he was not thankful enough to You for the victory! But it seemed to me that he wanted to assist the people to question this thinking – a brave intention at that time.

Reflecting on more recent years with wars in Iraq, Cambodia, Viet Nam, the Middle East, Sierra Leone, Serbia and Kosovo, is there any shred of reliable evidence at all, that You were on any one side? But then I'd have to say that if You did have the power to interfere, I would have found this quite upsetting, to say the least. But then again, I would expect You to have, how shall I say, sympathy at least, with a 'just cause'. Not that this would in itself affect the outcome of a particular war. So I'm left feeling, uncomfortable, wondering whether in the event of war, in all its terribleness, You can only be a non-active onlooker? Is this hard on You? Finding yourself, as it were, purposefully limited. It is reminiscent of the passion of Christ, posing the dilemma between what is apparent and what is real? Humanly speaking this sense of ambivalence is hard to bear. This will continue until humanity learns to order its affairs without resorting to war. Though this prospect seems far from promising. I'm wondering whether You think a world without war will ever be achieved? I'm fearful. That at sometime or other the overwhelming arsenal of nuclear and biological weapons will be let loose, bringing about nothing short of the destruction of the world. Could You, would You interfere then? To save your beloved Earth? Clearly, in the here and now, responsibility for war and injustice lies where it belongs, with us. Humanity cannot evade its responsibility. And I'm now quietly reflective - shaking a little, but in my head the poignant memory of Elijah who discerned 'the still small voice' - its mystery illustrates, I think the apparent power of the powerless. Quite a radical contrast to 'Land of Hope & Glory'!

For a long time I have been uncertain of how to understand or interpret the scriptures. There are differing views - literal, inspirational, metaphorical, and sometimes all three inter-penetrating each other. But I have to confess to my inborn anxiety of confusion and perhaps ignorance. I have friends who talk about 'the simple gospel'. However, as far as I am concerned the Gospel is far from simple and the scriptures in particular have a complexity of their own. In terms of everyday life there are portions of scripture which, to say the least, do not appear credible. For instance, the scripture that tells that you promised land to the Hebrews, i.e. Abraham. The implication is that You have favourites (Genesis 12; Acts 7.3; & Hebrews 11.8.) It would seem that you promised to the tribe of Abraham some land that was to be their very own, forever. This piece of land today is part of Israel. As far as I am aware, no other people have been promised land by you. Why were they chosen out of all the other tribes? So this belief by the Jews does go back a long way - at least five thousand years or more. More recently the political Balfour Declaration was enacted to ensure that the Jews had a validated homeland. But it also had regard for the Palestinians so that they too had a homeland. Now the world holds its breath while these two peoples who are different, and yet who have similarities, are deeply immersed in a life and death struggle, occasioned with the bitterest fighting and bloodshed. The Palestinians are the heirs of the Amalekites, Canaanites and the Jebusites who over long ages have struggled to find a territory of their own. Nonetheless the Jews too believe they have a God given right to their land. So now we have the most contentious rights of land issue of our day. The dilemma feels insoluble. What do you think can be done about it? I'd like to suggest, that if the scripture is accurate and is to be taken literally, then You become a key participant in the struggle. You are part of the problem, and have to be part of the solution. The solution has to find a way of shortening the blood-letting between the Jews and the Palestinians. I have a strange sense that makes me feel that in this matter it is not fair for humanity, on its own, to be left with what feels like an insoluble problem. There are landless people around the world. There are the Kurds. The aborigines in Australia, and the American Indian people of the USA who have suffered by having their land taken from them. The unwise carve-up of land in various parts of the world is a sad fact. In the Middle East in particular we are left with a simmering cauldron. Every person needs a place of their own, and today this is increasingly regarded as a basic human right. So how do you think this can cohere with the question that remains, whether you wish to give privileges to the Jews? Neither should we forget the plight of the Kurds. In a shrinking world, with the intensifying struggle between religions as well as between nations, I would suggest that the United Nations has a mandate to bring about the values of its founders which would then ensure a new sense of security for all races and all religions.

It may be a wicked thought but sometimes I can't help but imagine Zionists proudly tempted to sing with deep sentiment those words, re-written for them, 'Land of Hope & Glory'! Any military elite might be tempted to claim these words, and sing them with gusto. If the Zionists believe you are on their side then the words will be pertinent to Jews and other self chosen national groups. Perish the thought! The record of the story of the flight of the Jews from Egypt is nothing if not miraculous. You, it is said in the text, divided the Red Sea, so the Jews could cross over to their freedom, without loss. Whereas the chasing Egyptians were drowned, sealing their defeat. Even to this day some Jews believe that you were responsible for that journey to 'the promised land'. And they still teach their children this historical text with zeal. There are those who are content to call certain events 'acts of God'. But I find myself reluctant to agree. There are some historical occasions when I think it is wise to be agnostic! If it is the case that You have broken into history, why is it that in the twentieth century this has not been the case? Unless perhaps the miracle of Dunkirk in 1940 was an exception? Some felt they were rescued by a force or power that was not human. Have there been other occasions?

I can readily identify with those who still live oppressed lives, including those for whom Amnesty International ceaselessly campaigns. Is there a key to any of the possible interventions by You in recent times, or is it that as I inferred earlier in the real world You do not now intervene? We live today only in the human domain? If this is the case does the responsibility for the right dealing between nations and religions belong to humanity alone and not to You? If this is so, then to be blunt 'Land of Hope & Glory' is 'out of the window'!

Justice and equity, compassion, and the spirit of co-operation are the gifts that human beings are able to give to each other. This needs to be elevated to a rule for life, for every human being. At the same time I do not perceive You, God, being some kind of automated robot. You are not here in this world of ours to, as we say, 'dot our 'i's', nor to 'cross our 't's'. Nor do I believe that manipulation is the name of your 'divine game'. But the mystery of 'knowing You' and sometimes the enlightenment that shines through from You leaves me feeling that my own insight, my limited knowledge, and my experience is more shallow than I had realised. I'm left in sadness, and I'm wondering, what am I to do?

I do not fully understand 'your action' on that first Easter Day. Two thousand or so years further on, for some it still has great potency. Is it important to maintain the distinction between this unique event, from all those other 'happenings' that others have interpreted as your intervention in history? There remain those moments of horror when here in our world new diabolical acts of evil have reared their head. Evil is on-going and present in the world. Who could doubt it? If the power of the Resurrection has not prevented innumerable atrocities since the first Easter Day, then I am one of those who is left in doubt about its true power and significance of the words of Mary in her song The Magnificat, 'he has put down the mighty from their seat' - words which still remain to be implemented. When God, when? I seek to learn of you. Yet the death and despair of undeserved pain, screws me up, knots my stomach, almost stops my heart from beating. This is why in my confusion, in what appears an endless wilderness, I have to write these letters - they are necessary for my survival. This letter started from listening to a concert in the Royal Albert Hall, and after many circlings I still feel locked into confusion, so to get these matters to some extent, off my chest is for me therapeutic. Someone has said that before you make up your mind, open it first! My mind is not closed, as I hope you will have observed. This letter for me has been a mind opening experience. And not just my mind; but my imagination, my hopes, my heart, my whole being, for even my body feels that bit more relaxed and calm. You have my word for it, my commitment to persist with unanswered questions, and searching for new truth will not be abandoned. My resolve is sure. Help me to feel, to know, to hope, and to find solace and energy to pursue my search. I'm waiting.

P.S.

By a strange coincidence, later, when I was re-reading this letter, this coincided with the first of another series of concerts. I don't wish to give the impression that Elgar only composed what might be called imperialistic music. Because on this occasion the orchestra was playing his 'THE MUSIC MAKERS', a setting of the poem by the Victorian poet Arthur William Edgar O'Shaughnessy. The mood is so different, and here is a brief quote;

We are the music makers,
And we are the dreamer of dreams,
Yet we are the movers and shakers,
Of the world for ever it seems.
We in the ages lying,
In the buried past of the earth,
For each age is a dream that is dying,
Or one that is coming to birth.

I suppose this leaves me wondering how much of today's 'dream', for millions is dying, and how much, for the young, is a new dream coming to birth?

Dear God – Can I assume that you prefer to be understood as 'a music maker', rather than the 'God who made thee mighty'?

Letter 16: Differences and similarities

Dear God,

A couple of years ago some new people moved into a flat next door. Nothing strange about that. In our fast moving world people are coming and going continually. I like to think there is an embryonic community in our flats which quietly welcomes new arrivals. However, at the same time some of the residents who live alone tend to keep themselves to themselves and guard their own privacy. Others just seem unaware of their neighbours. Well, there is something different and particular about these new neighbours. They have come from Nigeria. They are black, Mum and Dad, young daughter and son, and a baby. Mum and the children tend to wear colourful clothes - I like them! Frequently I see them coming and going, usually with wide smiles across their faces. Their smiles are infectious. When I see them I can't help smiling back. The kids have lots of energy. Father looks rather a little more serious, and has a strong looking physique. He's a doctor at a local hospital.

They are not lonely. I don't know why, but I think I find this surprising. They have lots of friends who visit them. It seems like a continual stream sometimes, and because they tend to leave their windows open, I hear a lot of the talking, chattering, and laughter. The children play on the back green with other children, and they go to the local Primary School. After they had been here for a year or so they all went back to Nigeria for a holiday. Probably this meant for the younger children that they saw their homeland for the first time. It must have been exciting for them. Clearly now they have got used to living in Edinburgh. They are used to TV, computers, cars, and the trappings of western culture. I feel, in a sense, that the children are seedlings in a foreign soil. They have known little else since living here, and now take it all in their stride. They seem to have settled in without much bother. The paraphernalia of our fast secular culture has quietly wrapped itself round them. No doubt however, they must have noticed that everyone else here is white. They are black. So I've been wondering how it feels 'inside' for them? I mean, how do they feel within their own privacy - in that intimate bit which each of us keeps to ourselves? This private bit is theirs alone, and it is very personal. They are the only black people in this street. So I'm wondering what they feel and what they think, and how comfortable are they? For a moment or two I tried standing in their shoes. I cannot help thinking, and feeling that being 'different' will be significant for them. We and they are different. They know it. I know it. I'm left wondering, in myself, if this difference can be a shared positive realisation, for them and for me? Or should I dare to explore the possibility that it is negative? Maybe for them? Maybe for me? You can see how uncertain I am. I find it all a searching issue, and at the moment I'm not able to let it go.

I suppose most folk around here do not wish this family any harm in any way. Some might not wish to be bothered about them. Live and let live will be the view of quite a number of neighbours. But again, this I suppose, could be a kind of complacency which could hide discrimination. After all, discrimination does not have to be strident - it can be deceptively muted. Sadly, I think, the dangers of discrimination, hatred and intolerant victimisation bordering on the fanatical could be 'just round the corner'. Nevertheless, by and large, Edinburgh so far, could not be labelled a racist city. Occasionally racism and bigotry flare up. The situation could be worse than it is, and I'd guess that quite a number of citizens live with a shallow sense of hopeful satisfaction. This black family is in a very small minority. In a football crowd they would be invisible. However, at a deeper level within any community there can be no place for complacency if the ideal of integrated living in a modern western city is to be achieved.

But in quiet moments of reflection I'm aware of feeling uncomfortable. I've been to other parts of the country, only to find that when walking through the streets I was the one who was in a minority! I was shocked! I felt uneasy being the only white person within sight in a British city. It would seem that some suburbs in some of our cities have been 'taken over' by people from other countries, and religions from different parts of the world. In this situation I feel 'tables have been turned on me'. I have felt uneasy in such a tiny minority. I'm no saint! I feel somewhat ashamed to admit that though I have travelled widely and enjoyed much foreign hospitality, I'm feeling badly about my 'minority status' in some towns and cities in my own country. As I walked through those streets, feeling like a foreigner on my own turf I guess there was some muted anger bubbling inside me. Not a nice feeling! It makes me feel guilty. It's not as if the others were just visitors. Oh no, they were residents, which made me feel like a visitor. I'm uneasy with this reversed role and ambivalence hoping these feelings will go away, and quickly. I've always quietly prided myself on being an internationalist. For much of my life I've not felt threatened when I've been in a racial minority at a conference, or for a short stay trip to various countries across the globe. But to walk a street in a city suburb here in my own country where it is difficult to find a white person, I have to admit I feel threatened. I suppose then that the feeling inside me, of being afraid, is then projected out of me on to the 'alien' community in which I find myself. I loathe this feeling, and how I loathe myself. Looking at myself in this 'racial mirror' is not a pretty sight!

So I'm left wondering what is the value of nationality and culture and race? I hope it is not an impossible question. I'm remembering those words which have sunk deep into the liturgy of christendom, of all races 'made to dwell together on the face of the earth'. I want to distinguish between the natural difference of race, on the one hand, and the different distinctions of political and religious differences. It would be comfortable to assume that different races could live together, but are the political and religious differences to be so easily accommodated, I wonder? I'm remembering the biblical story of the Tower of Babel - quite a foul story, I think. Why did you confound their language so that they did not understand each other? Languages are a precious gift, and do not need to compete with each other. Whether it is racial difference, national difference, political or gender difference - whatever the difference I instinctively want to honour it. I have this deep desire to cherish difference. Differences provide the joy of choice. Differences can provide a wonderful sense of mutual respect and interdependency, and even extol what I would call a warm mellow glow of muted competitiveness. I see this being nurtured in the United Nations, the Olympic Games, World Soccer and World Cricket. Though some will see this perhaps primarily as an aspect of globalisation. Yet as I write I'm much aware that this inter-dependency can foster both co-operation as well as anxiety. Insularity can breed a kind of 'cocky confidence', but simultaneously it can sow seeds of fear, when the unknown is confronted. Humanity is afraid of the unknown. These feelings are complex and not easy to understand, and can resist rational exploration. Our age of unrestricted travel has accentuated the importance of cultural, religious, social, and economic differences. But it would seem that humanity has yet to acquire the emotional and intellectual maturity that will be required in order for us all to internalise them so that we all become rather more multi-dimensional in ourselves as persons, and in our community self awareness. Somehow or other fine principles feel flimsy and impractical when faced with poverty, hunger, unemployment, deprivation and the tyranny of dictatorships - either political or economic. Justice has to be the cornerstone when building a mutual inter-dependency, because preferential differences will shatter any dream of a 'beloved community'. Colour prejudice along with religious and political fanaticism breed on poverty and destructive discrimination, and put our long term future as a civilisation in peril.

The saddest realisation for me, as I write to you dear God, is to acknowledge that, none of my reasoning is new, This truth has been known for decades, even centuries. Humanity appears to be impotent to overcome the fear of having to give up comfort for some so that the rest, deprived and devalued, can, as it were, join the human race! This is the most serious issue for all of us who cherish our planet Earth and who desire to claim the future, without prejudice, for our entire one humanity, irrespective of differences. It is this vision that will not let me go. And I suppose the struggle within will go on for the rest of my life if I can be strong and determined enough.

Cultural mixing goes on all the time. For instance inter-marriage inevitably is increasing. When this is comfortable for both partners there is a tinge of wonder as boundaries are eroded, or at the least are of diminished importance. Some would claim that You, God, made the races quite distinctive. So will it matter if over the next century or so humanity achieves a racial fusion where distinctions diminish and a bland similarity takes over? For myself I prefer the Ghanaian to be black, and the Brazilian to be coffee coloured. Their distinctiveness has, for me, some inner satisfaction about it. And deep down I feel I would prefer the British to be white! So what does this say about me - am I being just conservative? Across the United States we find a remarkable cacophony of colour and race. For some this is highly prized but for others it is dispensable. We come up against the sharp edge between similarity on the one hand and difference on the other. So underneath it all the fundamental issue has to do with the nature of identity - outwardly and also inwardly. I'm wondering how you feel about the 'cross-fertilisation' that is taking place? I know there can be a beauty about distinctiveness. But there is also another kind of beauty that comes from crossing colours, with subtle shades that are scintillating and even exciting. Nonetheless we require a sense of wonderful objectivity to allow citizens of each colour to stand for themselves. However this complexity may be understood, but the differences of religion and politics may not be held with the same kind of objectivity. These differences appear to have firmer boundaries, where a muted cross fertilisation could be seen as a clear denial of the value of each religion and each political persuasion. A monochrome culture racially will lose much that has the wealth of diversity. A political and religious monochrome image will discourage the fertility of ideas and ideals, leading to a barrenness that will be suicidal emotionally and intellectually. So for me any tinge of absolutism points up a signal danger. Openness has wide open arms, and if the arms are a symbol of love and of belonging, then any sense of fear may at least be diminished. There is a good deal of evidence to suggest that individual identity as far as race and colour are concerned may not always determine one's own future happiness, though it will have its own importance.

However as I write this I'm also aware that I'm a product of an inheritance that has been rooted by living here in the U.K. but within the history of the British Empire. I'm reflecting with a very mixed sentiment. My own impulses about Empire fill me with uncomfortable regrets. For me this 'cupboard' is full of skeletons! The British Empire was a mood and feature of its time, but now such empires have no future because they were built on ideals shaped by arrogance, greed and exploitation. Our National Anthem is not without some sentiments which would be better omitted. It has that element of pride which from time to time whispers that the British Empire was not all bad. Of course, this is true but I prefer to banish these thoughts from my struggling mind. My ambivalence is too uncomfortable!

One of the other aspects of similarity and difference but which currently offer enjoyment is the shared delights of food and drink from a multiplicity of peoples and cultures. It seems as if in a quiet way many of us are being introduced to some of the more intimate aspects of other cultures as we allow our taste buds to grow and include culinary delights which are very different from our own. The 'roast beef of olde England' and the 'enigmatic' Haggis of Scotland both appear to be as intriguing to people of other cultures, as their curries, stir-frys and rich sauces are to us. There is a wonderful diversity of food and cooking world-wide. I'm wondering if this could have sprung from your imagination, God? Another gift to the whole human race? The versatility of food and cuisine remains a treat for us all. Perhaps the best route to better racial harmony might be via our stomachs and our taste buds, rather than by the violent elitism of rampant competitiveness? Food, music, costume, agriculture, sport and architecture all have the potential to give harmony to difference in a culturally evolving society.

How are we going to solve the dilemma of our search for diversity and difference on the one hand, and on the other our deep need for similarity and uniformity? Attempts at resolution bring us to the basic crux of today's conflicts, which emanate from violent uncontrolled anger, akin to a crippling sense of frustration, impotence, and having no sense of control. When, for instance, a woman and man fall in love and decide to share their lives, they enter into a fused journey where both difference and similarity fertilise each other and offer something known and unknown, which is mutually explored and accepted. But on a different level I think I have been forming with my Nigerian neighbours what I see as a parallel relationship. Our boundaries of difference and similarity are being worked out as our relationship grows, but of course, not the same intimacy of a marriage. There will be between us, as neighbours, benefits from the occasions when we will explore new realms and discover boundaries whereby we may find that at a certain point our exploration begins to feel too invasive. The time may come for an element of some sensitive withdrawal and reappraisal. From experience I am aware that unthinking acceptance of similarities and differences can invade our assumptions and abruptly show us that we have assumed too much of each other. So that the uncomfortable hesitations indicate that our mutual journey onwards requires a break, some reflection, and perhaps a new mutual assessment before we can proceed further. There will be benefits when as neighbours we recognise the boundaries which have evoked mutual disquiet. For instance my Nigerian friends and I may enjoy a game of tennis, or a film, or a shared meal. This is pleasurable. But it may overlook a deeper difference, such as for example our individual customs about the place which children have within our separate families. I think similar sensitivities to difference are required when we explore political and religious differences. We need to be alert to each other's inner world, with an awareness to history, language and assumptions. Deep listening and sensitivity to silences will provide an experience out of which understanding may slowly grow. Patience is required. This special sense of journeying is far from straightforward, and unexpected reservations or hesitations will never be far away. Agreeable guidelines on this journey will need careful flexibility. Along the way when other economic and social factors arise, then mutually agreed objectives will require more time and patience.

However, as well as these complex personal explorations there will also be what I would call the public journey as well. I consider myself fortunate that when it comes to the public arena of relationships, my history teacher at school provided me with ready insights which have influenced me to contemplate the importance of reconciliation, dialogue, as well as an introduction to the belief that the pursuit of peace by peaceful means was preferable to violent and autocratic strategies. He taught me about the strengths and weaknesses of the League of Nations of which he was a fervent advocate. I know I caught his enthusiasms, so that I began to consider myself a potential internationalist, and by implication a pacifist, though at times a reluctant one!

From your eternal perspective, how does all this seem to You? How I wish You had a mobile phone! It would never stop ringing, would it? In this complex scenario, which I have tried to describe it seems that elements of competition, proselytising and rigid evangelism will be counter productive. If in our day and age there is a priority for us all to understand the complementariness of difference and similarity, then the Christian Church faces a dilemma.

Jesus, prior to what is known as 'the ascension', is reputed to have said, "Go into all the world and preach the Gospel to every creature". In my view this has caused much bloodshed, bitterness, and pain. A fanatical belief that only Christianity can be supreme in our world displays unpardonable arrogance. It also devalues the sacred beliefs of others, who though they are different, remain an important part of the human race. I'm one of those who thinks that if for instance, the Church was true to itself, evangelism would be unnecessary. If the Church were 'the beloved community' then many people would be impatient to join in. But clearly this is not the case. So I think that this is a powerful message in itself, isn't it?

I'm wondering if it is possible for those who have a fervent belief in anything to be able to learn the skills of dialoguing? It's true, if I have something that I believe is good, then I want to share it. But if the person I wish to share it with, declines my offer, then I'm left with finding the grace to accept their response. This can be tricky. Proselytism, the making of converts stirs up all kinds of anxiety. This is true whether it is religious or political, and the undeviating enthusiasm of converts is well known! So the skills required to enable converts to dialogue with others of cooler perceptions are not easy to learn, and even more difficult to practise. I'm left wondering whether it is possible to extract politics and religion out of the 'competitive frame', and find a way of transferring this into a 'co-operative frame?' I can't help wondering God, if you are a competitor, or a co-operator? Is it possible to be both? For myself if people lived co-operatively then I'd be ready to be very tolerant of their religious or political beliefs. But those who are strident, and certain and ready to push others into their own frame of religious or political belief, I want to avoid like the plague! But again, I can recognise that enthusiasm and conviction, in some, has its own power. I feel split, and unable to resolve this dilemma. Is it a dilemma to you? Or is it that, in the realm of 'the eternal', this dilemma is resolved by perhaps the practice of extravagant love? Whatever this may mean, I remain unsure!

Perhaps it is that in this complexity I have so much to learn. But who is going to teach me? Can reconciliation respect deep difference, and yet enable those of strongly differing views to find a common ground? I have had the experience of creative reconciliation in minor confrontations. But in this raw realm of colour and culture the spikes of deep prejudice are not easily blunted. Widespread across the world the so called ultimate force of macho-strength and invincible violence is practised, threatening us all to the power of the nth degree. The appearance of weakness is not to be tolerated. This is visible, in the fraught anger of personal relationships; in the bids for power in the Company Board Room; as well as across community and national boundaries, and in global politics. Compromise is out of the question, and saving face becomes too costly. You see, dear God, reconciliation in spite of its excellent pedigree is not trusted when both or either side are unable to guarantee effectiveness.

My recently arrived black neighbours, I have discovered, are as puzzled as I am, just from their experience here as neighbours. There is a paradox somewhere in this tussle between the inter relating of difference and similarity on the one hand, with the frustration that comes with a sense of impotence and weariness on the other. My hunch is that you will be hoping that humanity will discover the vision of 'inner longing' which will allow our desire to grow at its own pace, so that eventually we 'see' the hidden message contained in the new perception that shows how reconciliation is a new sense of powerlessness - the notion of a muted force that reaches beyond aggro-power. But I'm still left wondering if this might still turn out to be a quagmire of hopes and disappointment. So you see, from this complex evaluation, I'm dependent on You blowing away the dross of confusion which in itself will give a new clarity of the mind and the heart. If clarity remains possible? But sadly I have to admit, I'm doubtful I can trust it, even though I want to believe it! It's hard when you want to, but can't.

Letter 17: Facing up to being human

Dear God,

Today I hardly know where to begin. This letter has been rumbling around in my mind for a couple of weeks or so. I'm aware that I'm feeling in a bit of a muddle. It's hard to think straight. I need to sort out some earlier experiences which, in a way, continue to distract me. I've always thought that I was an objective person, but recently I've found it hard not to be trapped by persistent subjective judgements which prevent me from 'thinking straight'. So I'm feeling unsure. This is all about being human - being focused - and in particular facing the complexity of personal sexuality. Gone are the days when I thought sex was simple and straightforward. I'm baffled and feeling in something of a turmoil.

I can remember the time when the common view was that sex was to be 'kept in the closet'. It was regarded as something done in privacy. It was customary not to talk much about it, and still less to openly flaunt it. Nonetheless in retrospect I know now that sex has hardly ever been 'kept in the closet'. Of course sex has been part of human life since the beginning of time. It's had its place in every culture, religion, tribe and class. None of us would be here but for the sexual activity of our parents. Sometimes, when I remember my parents, I hope I'll be forgiven for wondering how on Earth they managed it! My recollection from childhood is that we did not talk about it at all at home. It was a 'dark' subject. But I remember that when a baby was born along the road, or in our own family, there was always great rejoicing. But sex itself had an air of anxiety, and I never heard anyone talk about it. At the Nursery I attended I remember noticing that little girls wore knickers, while little boys wore trousers. And I never knew why! One day years later at Senior School I can remember when a classmate brought a copy of *Razzle* into school for his pals to look at in the playground. It was full of nudes, sexy stories and jokes. He loaned it out to his mates for two pence a day! I remember finding out about masturbation. It was popular with many of my classmates. We did it in small groups, and I joined in. I felt I had to - usually after our weekly trip to the Sports' Field, for football and cricket. So in spite of the outward impression that sex was a no-go area, at school it was a frequent talking point within the closed clique of my friends even though we did not have the now proverbial bike shed!

Pardon the big sigh! But why am I telling you all this? Well, because since those days two things have changed for me. Firstly, the sexual landscape of my own personal life has changed, and secondly the sexual landscape of society has changed too, almost out of recognition. I'm feeling gratified with my own personal sexual growth and development. Marriage and the companionship of my loving 'wife' - (how I hate that word!) - has played a major and loving role in my own sexual maturing. The wonderful discoveries we have made together has been for both of us truly liberating, and such pleasurable fun. Sexual intimacy has brought us joy, and given added meaning to our relationship. However, the other change in our society has been very different and quite far reaching. We now have what is called 'the Sex Industry'. Sex is no longer regarded just as an intimate pleasure. The tabloid newspapers compete with 'page three nudes', TV programmes of 'disclosure and invective', cert 18 films, and a plethora of pornographic magazines, along with the Internet and its chat rooms, make me feel now that sex is 'pushed in our faces' - a far cry from yesteryear. Sex has become a major pre-occupation in advertising, the clothes industry, and is featured as an attraction in selected holiday resorts. And there are the increasing number of Show Bars along our High Streets. I don't think I have overstated the situation. For some sex has become an obsession. Whatever the boundaries were, now they are disappearing fast because sex has become a highly valued money spinner.

Sadly, some experience sexual desire as an obsession. They can't help pulsing it out subconsciously, 'I want, what I want, and I'm not waiting!' Others fear that they may be in a sexual minority, because they find satisfaction with a partner of the same gender. Then there are those who have a relationship with a partner where sharing and exchanging a mutual love in intimacy and living together with fidelity is regarded as inhibited and "odd". And with all of this my own inner reflection has led me to feel there is a creative link between my sexuality and my spirituality. Words can hardly define it in its intangibility. But I know that for some their sexual behaviour and their inner perception are bound with an integrity that acknowledges fidelity. Sexual love is an engagement between body and spirit, and this sharing bequeaths a sense of unique joy which can only be understood by those who have actually experienced it. Erotic love itself has an energy of its own, and outstrips all of our other desires in the search for true fulfilment. All of this You will see is quite personal, and I can't help but wonder what You make of it yourself! What I have tried to describe is all part of being human, so can I simply say that I hope You will agree that our human experience of the wonder and even mystery of sex is of the very best of your provision. Will You affirm it with a big "YES!"?

Nonetheless with some apprehension I feel that I now have to turn to the misuse of sex within society today. As I have intimated sex itself can be a powerful force and influence. Sexual chaos threatens the speciality of the notion of 'sexuality as gift'. Today to all intents and purposes sex has become a 'free-for-all'. It can appear as a selfishly motivated extravaganza in which unbridled desire is paramount. I'm not wishing to 'over-paint' the scene, nor do I want to be part of any polarisation, and the competitive stance of 'them' and 'us'. It is so easy to be negative and judgemental. I'm all too aware of the 'them and us' syndrome, and the temptation for some to be 'holier than thou' in sexual matters. I'm also aware that there are worse sins than sexual sins. But the gluttony of our society for sex for some has almost reached the point of despair. I think we need to gently encourage and acknowledge the social implications of present sexual trends with their commercial exploitation, if only to remain compassionate, sensitive and quietly understanding. Both our thinking and our feeling need to be rigorous. In this complex arena I'll need your support, particularly when I'm aware of those occasions when I feel discomfort and anxiety because 'I do not know' when I think I should. 'Not knowing' means it feels hard to discern 'the truth' which sometimes seems to be made up of insoluble contradictions. You see, it's when I come up against others who think differently and who seem so adamant that I fall back to being over defensive. But it's when I remind myself that someone in a reflective yet perky frame of mind havered that if You, God, had something better than sex, 'up your sleeve', then you must have decided to keep it for yourself! I acknowledge of course, this is hardly in keeping with the traditional image of You. Even so, it is clear that all the boundaries of our corporate life economic, social, religious, in the shopping mall, the cinema, and even in the Radio Times - in and through and over them all, sex exercises its drastic influence. But we are told that this is how it has to be because 'the market' will decide.

On a visit to Brussels, outside the main railway station I saw a huge public poster. It showed three beautiful women, scantily clad, with a speech balloon from the mouth of one of them saying – "We're not looking for the right man, we're looking for the right-now man". This poster played on the insatiable desire which needs instant sexual satisfaction. It promoted an appetite that has no boundaries. I don't think I am a spoilsport. I can identify with the sense of excitement suggested by the poster, but I'm also keenly aware that it was an unashamed advertisement for 'the sex trade'. The poster diminished the three women. This kind of exploitation will not be contained solely by legislation, more rules and controls. Rather we need a conscious programme of promoting the intentional virtues of fidelity, respect, corporate regard, trust and mutually shared fun. This will stand a greater chance of winning the confidence of singles and couples, presenting personal discipline in a positive mode. This would do more than anything else to diminish the cult of 'raw sex'. For instance it could also become an effective force to reduce the number of Clubs where condoms are issued with admission tickets.

Currently society is caught up in a 'cult of the body'. I agree there is nothing more beautiful than a beautiful body. The urge to keep fit is positive, as it is to pay attention to what your body is telling you, in response to the way you behave to it. But the insidious competitive incentive is never far away. It wears the guise of the caption 'Size Matters'. Of course this is meant to relate directly to the male penis. Men can be embarrassed with a small penis, even though it is well known that it is not always the size that does count if it is going to enable its owner to be an effective lover. Modes of different contraceptives are marketed with a competitive edge. It can be difficult to ignore 'great offers', when it comes with a variety of choice of sexual aids. We are assured 'you must have'....The promotion of sexual appetite assuring instant satisfaction is hard to resist, especially if you are anxious to gain your partner. However, the experience of loving and being loved can more likely be assured if the couple together look forward to a longer term of satisfaction and mutual learning from each other. I hope it is still true that the majority of us grow towards sexual maturity naturally - it's inherent in the very genes of our unique creation.

Having the right size of penis, if there is a 'right size', as well as having all the other multiplicity of sexual aids, along with a 'good figure', the right clothes, car, with lots of money in your pocket, to be spent easily on 'entertainment' - yes, I suppose it sounds well and fine. I might sigh, yes this is just what I feel I need. But then my anxiety is centred round having a sense of appreciation for the wonder of the body, and what it is capable of, with an instilled sense of reverence and even humility. The first sexual triumph of a mutual orgasm in the adventure of love making, must go down as one of the real experiences of utter joy. This is what 'making love' really means. How I wish that our society had such a perception. Sadly the alternative competitive raw sexual attitude, even when laced with humour as it has been portrayed in the BBC2 offering 'Coupling', does devalue the 'sacredness of intimacy', turning it into just a free-for-all.

When it comes to looking for some guidelines with regard to sexual behaviour where do you think we should look? 'The Song of Songs' in the Old Testament, in my view would be a good start. On a cool reflection there is no shortage of wisdom and mature experience going back to Freud and before, and others who have amplified and developed his thinking, such as John Bowlby, Melanie Klien and Karen Horny with lots of others. There is the popular handbook 'The Joy of Sex' and preceding this centuries earlier the mature text of the Kama Sutra. So I find it re-assuring that positive concerns and teaching about the mystery of sexuality do go back into history, and that in recent decades thoughtful and sensitive guidance has been and still is available. Yet when overwhelmed by what at times can feel like 'the hysteria of sex today', it feels like a hard struggle to get back to a more mature and objective frame of mind and attitude. Within the world of counselling I know of the many opportunities for learning about the intimacies of life. Couples and singles can avail themselves of therapeutic learning, with practical insights, and I'm sure this is beginning to stem the tide a little against the generously funded Sex Industry which is pernicious in its competitive obsession.

It needs to be said that those who are content to keep themselves from the popular sexual scene, and who have no desire to indulge in what might appear to be the sexual 'melee' do deserve to be left quietly to live their own lives with relaxed satisfaction. Not everyone is crazy for a florid fun fare of sexual extravagance! If sex is your gift then humanity can appreciate it in a wonderful variety of ways without feeling that everyone has to be put through the 'sexual hoops' as a preliminary to fulfilled adult living.

In today's society the parental task of guiding children as they grow into adolescence is not an easy one. It used to be assumed that one of the tasks of parenting was to guide our children through the initiation of sexuality. To be available when a daughter is having her first menstruation, and a son having his first wet dream, and placing these experiences within the safety of 'normality' is assuring at a time of rapid growth. However, my reflection would lead me to guess that this aspect of parenting is not, in fact, widely practised. The majority of young people 'stumble' on their sexual initiation. Sadly this kind of quiet support is needed in a world where sexual activity 'pokes its nose' into the lives of the young - and frequently the very young. Currently there is a growing awareness of the increase in the incidence of sexually transmitted diseases. This is, in itself, a threat to sexual health. But the current culture might be called 'hedonistic' – perhaps this seems extreme when it is contrasted with the suggested behaviour at the other end of the spectrum which is absolute abstinence of sexual activity, until a faithful partner is found. Some may feel this kind of comparison is unhelpful, whilst to others their 'sexual horizon' is given a touch of greater hope along with perceived reality. Young people struggle to discover their own sense of responsibility, and as adulthood dawns many have a keen sense of wanting to be 'the best'.

The felt gap between what might be called the gauche sexual scene on the one hand and on the other the instinctual deep desire of young lovers who are committed to each other, who are discovering the joy of shared and faithful sexuality, puts the meaning of 'making love' as a wonderful experience inducing a deep sense of satisfaction. It is the responsibility now of all the aspects of our social scene to affirm this ideal which perhaps could begin to erode the hedonism and exploitation which the sex industry has bequeathed on us all in these 'modern times'.

You know, I have my own anxieties about the future of marriage in our society so I'd like to share with you a little of my thinking about the practice of co-habitation. Traditionally the Christian guideline has maintained that sexual intercourse is primarily for those who are married and in a stable relationship. After the wedding, the party and the celebration, the couple go off on their honeymoon. It has been customary that on the night of the marriage the couple will share their first sexual experience together, on the 'honeymoon bed'. For many this is a wonderful fulfilment, though it has to be said that for some it is a dismal disappointment. From this point onwards the married couple learn to 'make love'. For some it is a rich reward. For others it feels like an anti-climax.

Today the scene is changing fast. The majority of couples now cohabit - that is, they live together as partners maybe for a year or two before they marry. The response of society has been mixed. Some think it should not be encouraged because they say sex is for marriage. Others fear that during this period of cohabiting the relationship could break down, and the couple would be 'living in sin'. However, for those couples who use their cohabitation as a period of preparation for their marriage, this has a clear logic and wisdom of its own. If marriage is to remain the desired state of living, on which the wellbeing of the family is to be based, then the 'trial run' of cohabiting has to be seen as a wise step. On the other hand if cohabiting has revealed that the couple are not going to be able to make a secure marriage bond, then how much better to learn it before entering into a marriage that will be untenable for both parties. From this perspective marriage will be seen not so much as a legal arrangement (which of course it will still be), but rather as a mutual style of complementary sharing and caring based on the desire for fidelity.

However facing up to being human has more to it than 'fixing the sexuality' of humanity in such a way that it brings the benefits of all those high values for which every human being yearns. Laws, moral principles, ethical integrity, and basic attitudes to justice and compassion all together mould the changing face of being human. The parity of women and men, the sacredness of childhood, the right to health, mental, physical, and spiritual, are all precious if life is lived to the full. Being a homogenous society is always in the state of becoming - the vision that goes before us, which surprisingly can etch itself on to the conscious and unconscious sense of self, encourages a positive perception of humanity's future. Sadly it is the fact of broken and fragmented relationships which can sabotage the vision, which makes me all the more committed to offering that aspect of committed ministry which is singularly about promoting insight and enlightened understanding into opportunities for reconciliation, renewal, and fertile forgiveness. So if marriage is to remain an important corner stone of tomorrow's society then the therapeutic tools, with spiritual insight will have an important role and function.

I think it can now be argued that the widespread sense of instability in personal relationships encourages those feelings of uncertainty which in themselves upset the citadel of the individual from within, by which we each formulate our own choices and desires. So it would be wise, I think, to now openly acknowledge that a 'trial run' which uses the practice of cohabitation has the potential to strengthen relationship bonds, rather than weaken them. This 'trial run' for the couple living intimately together will provide the opportunity to manage financially from a joint purse, to learn to share choices of furnishings, pastimes, and also to exchange insights about their work, their own families, as well as testing out whether they can begin to share and experience the unison of hope for a marriage based on long term fidelity.

Should this become unstuck in this experimental period, then the couple would be wise not to proceed with marriage. But if cohabitation confirms their inner desires tested by the actual stringency of living together, then it could be that many marriages based on this experience will hold the hope that long term living together will be mutually blessed and enjoyed. I believe there could not be a better foundation then for their ensuing family life. So the notion of 'living in sin' whilst not altogether without meaning and relevance, might be tested rather more pragmatically, because cohabitation will become the route to a life lived together without 'sin'.

It's hard, but I think I am learning not to be so judgemental of the behaviour of other human beings. But as soon as I have written this I am aware that there are behaviours that are not acceptable in a civilised society, and perhaps even more so in a Christian culture, or even a post-Christian culture. The experience of personal violence, betrayal, abuse, exploitation, are examples that need a sharp and clear denunciation. However the personal idiosyncrasies which are part of the exciting journey to loving and being loved need to be addressed with pastoral tenderness. I'd want to exclaim, let's have a passion for the possible - let's have a passion for individuality - let's have a passion for the mysterious secrets of love in its many splendoured being. But also we have to engage with the evil, which is ever present in our society. So we can then point to the better way, and focus on the values and the virtue which cradle each of us in the comfort and adventure of loving, which I guess mysteriously has its source in You. The cultural blight which kills the healthy desire for wholesome sexual satisfaction within a mutual loving relationship needs to be eradicated.

I hope you will rejoice at this sculpted vision which is emerging from this letter. Again I'm reminded of the scripture which recorded that 'Jacob wrestled with God in his vision of the ladder that led to heaven'. This letter has been for me a tough exercise of wrestling with the complexity of being human. The emerging insights and the sexual vision unites tactile satisfaction with a spiritual notion bonded within the warm embrace of sexual delight.

However I'm aware that the prophets of doom are advocating an alternative message - that the clock of society points at 'five minutes to midnight' and all too soon the factors and philosophers of sexual chaos could have their way.

But I am not being moved. I am ready to invest all I have in my vision which I believe will push back the boundaries of stubborn custom and flabby thinking. I believe that 'the market' in sexuality can be moulded to the new vision. But tenacity will be required. Beauty will flourish. This is the beauty that is known in lives touched by an intimacy of love that is generous, accompanied by vibrant hope, and with that deep sense of contentment which will be both our haven, and our reward.

Letter 18: The purpose of money

Dear God,

The other day I was out doing bits and pieces of shopping. I put my hand into my wallet, so as to pay a bill, only to find that there were no bank notes there! I was stumped, and the shopping trip had to be abandoned. My immediate feelings put me in touch with the disquietening experience of being, albeit only for a moment, penniless. Being without money in today's world leaves me with a sense of desperation and impotence. This has caused me to go through a period of pondering as well as questioning some of the issues about money and its importance in our society. It's a matter which has complexities, and a language of its own. I feel I need a steadying hand, as well as an imaginative heart, to help me through what feels like a jungle of jargon.

I'm mindful that in the first flash of wonderful and extravagant creativity which brought this world of ours into being, the fruit of your generosity has left me feeling lost in wonder and with some incredulity. I'm feeling overwhelmed with both searching questions and exhilarating joy. In my best moments I'm ready to accept that you made this Earth, the sky, the air, seas, rivers, trees, animals, fire, and humanity in its exciting diversity, and all with a purpose. Of course, I'm at a loss to know how you did it, and I suppose I might never know. I'm ambivalent about whether or not it makes a difference whether I know or not if you did in fact, make this world, Mother Earth. Nonetheless it feels like a shattering insight to recognise now that even my own beginning has its roots back then. It's all told in picturesque language in the beginning of Genesis. This is a story I love to read! Again and again! At the same time I'm aware from scientific research that the actual process expanded over millions of what we call years. But this makes it no less remarkable. I still feel lost inside myself with this fresh wonder of it all. The continuing act of creation, no matter how it all came into being still 'blows my mind'. You have provided the basics of a foundation out of nothing, which gives some resemblance of order and purpose. But again, this is not, without its doubts and questions. Why? How? What for? The questions perhaps will be endless. And the final question? What do you expect of us, in return?

Over this course of the long history of creation, humanity has grown, and in due time it discovered its own creativity. Following in your path, as it were, humans have been busy making and constructing ever since. For instance the wheel, primitive weapons for hunting and survival, shelters, boats, clothing, roads. Gradually bit by bit women and men have not been slow in supplementing your original act of creation. Looking at the world today there is a whole gamut of humanity's creativity - frozen food, penicillin, videos, split atoms, D.N.A., dish-washers, electric blankets, credit cards, radio FM, electric shavers, music, paintings, languages, and we have even put men on the moon! And so much else besides! Really the spurt of communication technology has brought about a worldwide revolution in both communication itself and travel. We continue to probe space, the stars and the planets, as well as the seas and the depths of our planet Earth. Our present fascination is with our neighbour Mars - its mysterious red glow, so tantalising as it appears in our telescopes. It seems as if today there are no boundaries to the explosion of inquisitive exploration. The drive of human curiosity knows no limits, and at one and the same time feels exhilarating, but also forbidding, because the known, as well as the unknown has its own sense of mystery and even seduction. Strangely so much of what I know, or think I know, has its inset of wonder with apprehension, a mysterious ambivalence. So I'm left wondering about the deeper questions as to whether there are to be limits to the penetrating curiosity of humanity? I'm wondering how it feels to you, as you observe the onward march of human discovery, following on from your own creative genius? Perhaps you have mixed feelings?

In my own inner questioning, with the welling up of doubts and mixed uncertainties, I'm aware that one of humanities primary quests, has been the creation of money. Of all the 'trinkets of discovery', perhaps money itself is ambivalent. It has potential for good. On the other hand money takes control not only of itself, but also those who use it, trade in it, and those who make it their 'god'. You did not make money, dear God, for as I see it there was no need for it in those, what, we call now, primitive times Mind you, having regard to the complexities of the money culture of today, those primitive times must have had their own 'innocent' attraction. I'm aware that from the earliest beginnings there was mutual trading, bargaining, and a growing process of exchange, But as the story has unfolded, the creativity of men in their drive to live and grow has brought about decisive changes in the day-to-day life of our world. You planted this instinct in us, didn't you? The desire to improve our daily routine of living, from simple basics of contentment to our increasing desire for more comfort and more control. I sometimes wonder whether you have ever regretted endowing us with such powers? As it has turned out, cultures in different parts of the world have developed their own experimental communities and co-operatives. We have learned to trade with each other. Neighbours loan tools and resources to neighbours, as well as skills and energy. This was a simple and natural phase of growth with a blend of dependence, interdependence and independence. But with age and growth and the advent of the consumer society today, at least in the West, everyone wants their own tools, their own necessities, and this in its wake has led us to the situation now where a lust and greed for power and strong independence has created the division between those who have wealth and plenty of possessions, whereas the larger sector of the population across the world are able to enjoy only the very bare basic necessities. And beyond them there are the dispossessed who, literally, have nothing.

Today we are all immersed in the money culture, and there is constant speculation about money, its price and its value. Over the centuries we have become alert to the misuse of money, the danger of usury, and the ever increasing charges for interest rates on loans, and mortgages. For the uninitiated money means worry and anxiety. There never seems to be enough of it! It has not taken long for the 'wise guys' to discover that there is a whole new world for profiteering and getting rich quickly, and at others expense. We have currently a popular TV programme 'Who wants to be a millionaire?' Down the centuries the Jewish people became notorious in the money profession. For some, the portrayal of Shylock in Shakespeare's 'The Merchant of Venice', may be distorted and unfair, as he exercises his determination to secure at all costs his 'pound of flesh', to seal a financial transaction to his advantage. This example has tended, some say, to encourage racial suspicion of the Jews. It became a slur that sticks hard. However, it is the Stock Exchange located in the capital cities across the world, in the offices of banks, investment companies and commercial companies where 'the pound of flesh' is secured, without question, and where the safeguarding of the interests of shareholders becomes the overwhelming guideline of practice. We live in a broken world, between the very rich and the far larger number of the absolute poor. Some friends, with me feel guilty as we find ourselves caught up in the grip of an uncaring and selfish society, which allows too little compassion, for instance by requiring the full repayment of debts. Defaulters lose their homes, and join the queue for 'benefit' with its local search for self respect. We are told by those who are secure in their financial 'palaces' that it is 'the market' that decides. It is not difficult to see how this process can readily increase the number of homeless families, with dire consequences. The unfairness of it all is placed in a stronger light when it becomes known that we now have more millionaires than ever before - the largest number for all time. But the rub is that the people who live in poverty may also be at an all time high. This inevitably leads to corruption and communal disintegration.

I don't think I am mistaken, believing as I do that you, dear God, have a heart of compassion. I want to think this anyway, even though 'proof' may be circumstantial, to say the least. I'm all too much aware of what I don't know about you, in spite of the scriptures and the story of the saints, but, for me, there is a recurring theme of your concern for 'the underdog'. Scripture refers to the various forms of exploitation, including usury. In the book of Leviticus we have the radical and fertile notion of the Year of Jubilee, though this is entirely discounted now. Today's economists dismiss the policy of a fallow year every seven years; resting on the 7th day of the week; and the radical Year of Jubilee, i.e. 49 years, that is seven Sabbaths of years for resting the soil and acknowledging that the resting process has within it a therapeutic benefit potentially for all the various aspects of farming. As I am writing this I'm conscious of those who laugh at this programme in their believed self superiority of modern agricultural practice. A society where money is the supreme guideline is blind to the benefits inherent in the Year of Jubilee. For today's economist a Year of Jubilee does not feature anywhere in their strategies. So the land continues to be exploited.

However, there are those who would argue that money itself has brought higher standards of living. It cannot be denied that many families do have a better lifestyle and quality of life, because they have exercised a responsible stewardship. Making the most of what you have by planning, and carefully exercising a personal strategy that looks responsibly to the future, will bring its own dividends. All of this can be done without being unduly self-centred. Indeed I would argue that it is tantamount to responsible living, i.e. safeguarding your own life and the lives of your dependants. Nonetheless, the bigger and complex question remains. Do you think the notion of The Year of Jubilee could be reintroduced into the world economy? Could it be under the jurisdiction of the United Nations?' Could there be what I might call a Commonwealth of Agriculture? Would it not stand the same chance of success as the weak International Monetary Fund, and the blemished World Bank? I 'm tending to think that this could be understood as a requirement for compassionate living, which might create a better prospect for the wellbeing of our planet Earth. I acknowledge all of this needs to be carefully explored, but the dilemma is, how? Is this practicable in our modem world? Is it more than an unrealisable dream? If not, then the current prospect is dire, the more so if we just go on in the present mode, which to be crude seems like 'dog eats dog!' A fundamental change in the way money is used, and the way it exercises its power in our society is urgently required. And the prospect of introducing the practice of regular fallow years in agriculture might be more far reaching and ultimately productive than is currently believed.

I'm wondering what you think about this dear God? I'm assuming that somewhere within your Being there is an insight, of which humanity today stands in need? Could this be made accessible, to us? Recently I came across what might be reckoned to be 'a straw in the wind'. I read that in the run-up to Christmas, our major spending spree, for one day, agreed worldwide, shops without exception should remain closed, and that St. Nicholas' day would be an appropriate day. Yes, of course if it actually happened it would be nothing short of a miracle! It would be a recognition that even in contemporary society one 'fallow shopping day' could be a symbol of recognition that 'giving up' had a restorative and remedial benefit, potentially for all. I imagine that such a suggestion would send shock waves, through the financial community. Would it 'buck the trend of the Market'? Being a realist I think there is no chance of this 'flash of insight' being taken seriously. Yet the idea, for me, remains potent, and might be taken up in smaller communities which may escape the long arm of financial institutions. It could be a metaphor that would provide a starting point for a strategy that might begin to modify the relentless drive for more and more wealth.

There is one other example of exploration motivated by the greed for money, and it is the growing practice of putting the poor under pressure to 'donate' an organ for financial reward.

This benefits wealthier persons in need of an organ transplant. Bodily organs are collected, usually from ignorant and unassuming donors, living on the breadline. They are led to believe that, for instance, if they sell one of their kidneys they will solve their own financial problems. However the transactions are carried out by unscrupulous racketeers. They take the money from the recipient and the donor is left without an organ and without the financial price. It is an extreme example of callous money making, within a society that has not been able to construct adequate safeguards for the exploited. Achieving a compassionate society seems to be an unrealistic objective. I'm left wondering if you share something of the depth of frustration which is beyond tolerance. The pain of knowing that such practices are widespread, with the accompanying sense of impotence that results.

Today the advertising industry has a big hand in the promotion of the money market. We are fed up with notions such as 'Size Matters'. We are told we deserve a bigger car, a bigger house, a bigger drink, a bigger diamond - indeed a bigger 'anything!' You don't need to be reticent about your wants - just indulge yourself - be conscience free - the bigger it is the better it is! Society today has a multiplicity of Temples. The majority of these Temples go by well known names - Asda, Tesco, Sainsbury, Somerfield etc. They are dedicated to giving all of us a choice, from what we are told the Market says is good for us. These Temples are dedicated to the worship of shopping, pleasure spending (even if you can't afford it) for food, drink, clothes, the latest 'toy', aids to beauty, health, and the trendy 'mobile', fast-track music maker and the increasing superfluity of communication technology. It's not that any of these objects are bad in themselves, but they have become the dominant necessity that 'the Market' says are essential for a happy life.

There are other Temples, to the god of money, and we call these Banks! They are to be found in every High Street, as well as in the remotest locations. These Temples have their own 'priesthood' - customer advisers, managers, under managers, financial advisers, actuaries, estimators, and debt collectors. They each have their own space and place in the priesthood hierarchy. The transactions within these Temples have a semblance of liturgy - paying in and drawing out, checking the overdraft. Everyone sings from the same hymn sheet, and no one can deviate from the agreed norm, called 'the conditions of banking' .Shareholders and directors have an annual festival called the AGM, when the few at the top do all the talking, and the congregation is 'swept up' in singing from the hymn sheet, which is called 'The Annual Report!' Your money is safe in our hands'. However as in all human institutions things do breakdown, and on occasion catastrophically. Dividends, pensions, may not 'perform' well so some less fortunate customers face severe overdraft charges, loan interests which fluctuate wildly: and dividends do not always realise their promised targets. Worship and membership in the Temple of Money is a risky business. A few do win, but many lose!

Money is powerful, It is seductive. If I am to worship you, living God, then I'm not going to be able to worship money or wealth, am I? Living in a society of financial arrogance, puts pressure on even the most warm hearted worshippers of yours, good God. It's difficult to keep face when there are the uncomfortable customs and attitudes which the influence of money has acquired within today's society. Money has its tentacles everywhere, even in the heart of your Church. Society has not been able to devise a taxation system which ensures that the wealthiest pay most tax, so that the impoverished pay much less. The unscrupulous power of money devalues a painting so that it is not admired for its artistic excellence, but for the price tag given it 'by the Market'. I'm remembering that when Van Gogh was approached by a wealthy industrialist for one of his paintings so it would hang in his Board Room, Van Gogh's question was "How many people will see it?" "Oh" said the industrialist, "It's just for my Board members". But Van Gogh responded that he wanted his paintings to be seen by lots and lots of people. "I don't want my paintings to be seen only by the privileged few". Today's society has put a financial tag on everything, and thereby devaluing it, whatever it is. Even our highest aspirations which hitherto have been sacrosanct are in danger by being dominated by the Market!

In this reflection I 'm recalling the encouragement felt because of the vision of others - for me 'the saints' of radical Christian socialism, established on the teachings and lives of Amos, Micah, Isaiah and some of the writings of Deuteronomy. Jesus himself was not slow in his fiery words for the poor, the prostitute, and the manual working fishermen. And in our recent times George Macleod, Donald Soper, Dorothy Day, and a whole company of others who have lived out the belief that you God are primarily concerned for the poor, the moneyless, and the bankrupt. So all is not lost, and the vision of a society based on the relationships of love and justice still has its own energy. Jesus drove out the money-changers from the Temple in Jerusalem. So here I am, wondering deep inside myself. How would you deal with the money merchants in today secular 'Temples?' No, this is not a rhetorical question! But as I ask it, I'm left wondering whether you have an answer?

Finally before I draw this letter to a close, there is one more factor which is important in any serious dialogue about money, and it is this. Over the last fifty years the value of money itself has, in hard terms, declined. When I was a child I could buy sweets for an old half penny. Today in the sweet shop you need at least about thirty new pence to buy the most run-of-the-mill sweets. Everything today costs much more. Incomes have increased too, and this has brought an acceleration in comparative prices. The cost of living index has 'shot-up' and this has been occasioned to some degree because of the decline in the value of money itself. I can remember when 000,000 was the maximum for the biggest figures. Then it went up to hundreds of millions, quickly followed by the billion indices. So it's not unrealistic to expect the trillion indices soon. The sums go up, but in so doing the actual value declines. There are those who maintain that the actual figures should not be taken too seriously. It is easy to say this when you are well off! The higher quality of life for some should not be decried. But it is now clearer that the gap between the rich and the poor is bigger. It is older people who are more likely to have experienced the decline in the value of money - they have the longer memories. The poor feel impotent with the contraction of money and its declining value, and impotent to do anything about it. The pound note has almost had its day, and the coin is just another coin. The one pound note in

Scotland will soon disappear, and will be replaced by a coin. And it is not a wild guess to anticipate that the £10 note will replace the £5 note. Where, I wonder, will it all end? Billions will replace millions, and billions will be replaced by trillions. It is not out of the question that our notes and coinage will be unrecognisable by the end of this century.

Is there anything spiritual about money? Could there be? Is there a secret here waiting to be discovered? This may be an increasingly important question for all those who value the secular life but who also seek to 'embalm it' as it were with a spirituality which allows a sense of sacredness for all that undergirds the wellbeing of our planet and our own daily living. The route to monetary spirituality has yet to be revealed, but perhaps this holds the secret of cleansing all the monetary arena, so that at last it will have its own integrity. Recently there was the story; that a wealthy business man offered Britney Spears $1,000,000 for her virginity. She is a young pop star, contemporary 'icon' for the young club-going public. Well, Britney refused him! I bet he was surprised, and maybe with hindsight she was too! But I can't help wondering if her action, unknown to her, was a spiritually motivated response to a man who clearly did not have a spiritual 'bone' in his heart - or his soul? Currently the worship and untoward elevation of money is turning our world into a materialistic wilderness. If love and truth, integrity and beauty are to survive, then the wilderness of monetary greed and power has to be rolled back, and my guess is that for this to be achieved your insight is needed. Is there a blueprint? The vision of sharing, of promoting co-operation rather than competition which might enable us all to live without the untoward influence and control in our lives of the Stock Exchange? The spirituality of money is a path to be explored, and for myself once we gain the key it will, amongst other things, create the right conditions to achieve political and economic justice across the face of the whole earth.

Money may have become a convention, and a powerful one at that. Money creates money! But my vision is that humanity will learn to see the importance of values which in themselves have no oppressive economic power – no stronghold on the imagination, and the freedom of the spirit.

Hidden too within this web of potential discovery will be the recognition of the enigma of 'the power of the powerless'. Like others I need the flash of your continuing and incisive creativity. My work in this matter is far from done. And if I might offer a further evolving conviction, it is that your work is not done either. We look for a fresh picture - an image that will enable us to be creative where creativeness laced with love will help us to see the fresh and what will be the cherished sacrament of spirituality that equips us for the future here, the spirituality that transforms the task and value of money. Be generous as you digest this letter, with all its inadequacies. And I am hoping that my hopefulness will not be in vain. Yes, actually writing this letter to you has made me feel better – but I know this is not enough. But you see, don't you, why I write?

Letter 19: Going up? Or coming in?

Dear God,

Today has been a good day. I'm enjoying this holiday on a small island off the west coast of Scotland. A small Highland community live on this island, about eight hundred people. The pace of life is relaxed, and time is not the most important consideration. This is a refreshing change from the tense and unremitting hurry of city life. It's late evening now, and I'm looking out westward over the sea, lulled in a quiet calm with just a ripple here and there on the shore. I'm feeling a deep sense of calm. Cows are chewing the cud nonchalantly. There are a few hens pecking around, and across the grassy scrub sheep, some of them still lambs, are feeding on the brown tinged tufts. I'm just sitting here relishing the relaxed and seductive joy of being alone. It's all unplanned, and I sense it is good to be here just for its own sake. The sun, a red orange ball is sinking lower and lower, as I watch, and its size gradually grows as it eventually hits the horizon of sea and sky. What a picture! There is little to hear, but so much to see. I feel cocooned in this lay-by of solitude and reflection. It feels unforgettable. I'm unable to put into words precisely what I'm feeling. But I do have an accentuated sense of nourishment penetrating the fibres of my body. I just want to look, and nothing else. Yet I know that all around me insects and tiny creatures, for which I have no names, are busy scurrying here and there about their immediate business. No solace for them! There's life on the sea shore. It's not come to a halt. Unawares perhaps the hardly hidden activity of the sea and the sky, with fish and fowl, tells me how fortunate I am, that unlike them, I can rest and reflect. I do not need to be caught up with my own pre-occupations, not to miss perhaps the sights that stir the human heart. They have their own lives, and I have mine. But, of course, it is one world - theirs and mine - and not to put too fine a point on it, I'm left wondering whether they have a sense of your presence in this scene which for me is vibrating with, shall I call it, your energy?

Sitting here, all on my own, I'm drinking in the ecstasy. I'm watching a silent cloud move across the sky, so gently it's as if it knows where it is going. In a sense I'm jealous because it's just beginning to dawn on me that I am unsure of where I am going. What and where is my own personal destination? Am I going anywhere at all? Yet, in this reverie I can't help feeling that the cloud could know something I do not know.

The rhythm of the sea lapping on the shore, the noisy flight of the gulls, swooping and swerving against the strong light of the sun, clearly have a purpose. I'm sensing too that the earth is strong and secure as it awaits the moment of imminent darkness. Yet I feel uncertain even if this seems incongruous. Nonetheless the vivid colours around me, and the silence together seem like symbolic probings of my imagination, I'm strangely in touch with images that caress my deeper feelings and remind me of the nourished goodness and warmth which I can readily overlook. Foolishly perhaps even, there is a void pressing in on me with unremitting questions, why am I not able to rest my soul, to let go of my inner turbulence and share the peace that is all around me here? I wonder why?

In the midst of these ruminations I'm suddenly aware that today many are celebrating Ascension Day. I wonder if this may have been stimulated in my unconscious, moving me to a reflective mood, encouraged by that elusive image of Jesus rising skywards. Somehow or other I feel this has an escapist quality. What I wonder am I wishing to escape? I'm aware of a magnetic-like pull inside myself, and I wish I could pull myself up and right out of this world. To where, I wonder? Well, to be honest I don't quite know. I wish I did. It's as if nature in its multiple glories tugs at my immature sense of 'the other' which is transcendent and beyond my immediate grasp.

Last night I left the shore feeling as if I was well on into my inward journey. I slept well, and now this morning sitting in a quiet room with a window open to fields and hedgerow, I'm ready to return and pursue the exploration. It may have been Ascension Day yesterday, but for me it is still Ascension Day today. I've tried before, if you remember, to converse with you about some of the aspects and stories told of Jesus. I can readily accept that the record of his life in the four Gospels is not an accurate word for word account. It does paint a picture of him that has its own particular attractiveness. Being pragmatic I have no argument with the writers of the Gospels. How could I? Whoever they were, I enjoy reading the stories, taking in the insightful parables, and relishing the skilled rapport with those who questioned him, and who envied him. But the record of the final stage of his life, I think, is quite another matter. I'm not a scholar of ecclesiastical history. But for me the record of the end of the life of Jesus reads differently from the actual story of his teaching ministry. Scripture tells its readers that at the end of his earthly life Jesus gives his disciples a clear directive. They are to do nothing less than tell the story of him, his ministry, from beginning to end, to the whole world. The emphasis clearly is to everyone. It was an imperative command. I can't but wonder what those disciples thought had hit them when, as the words pierced their ears and their minds. 'The world is a big place, and we are a tiny group!' Then immediately the records tells that at Bethany, in the full view of them all, that he was levitated - he rose upwards by a strange invisible power. Upwards and upwards, until he disappeared it seems into the sky, the clouds, euphemistically 'to heaven'. Yes, just like that! I simply have to say this is incredible and rather frightening. I have nothing else in my experience with which I can compare it. So yes, in a way I'm speechless. Just like the disciples. I'm thinking that this is an act that no one else can better. It out-classes any other earth bound spectacle. It would stop anyone in their tracks. Jesus concluded his own earthly life. He came here in a strange manner, and leaves us in what can only be regarded as a stranger manner. Someone has described this event - the Ascension - as the crossing from earth to heaven. However, for myself, I can't imagine heaven, whatever it is, being up there beyond the sky. It's laughable. So I'm driven to ask, did this whole supposed episode really happen? And if it did was it a visual allegory, or an enacted metaphor? What was it that actually happened? This event to me is inexplicable. It's beyond my own mundane human understanding and experience. But then I suppose for someone who has 'triumphed' over the human experience of death, and who yet could not stay around for ever, what other way was left by which he could be translated from 'here' to 'there'? This world is not the scenario for eternity, is it? I do not know where the boundaries are, even in the light of this, that there are boundaries. To wherever it is that Jesus has gone it is not in our known human and transient location on Earth. Unlike any of us, he appears to have been released from all human conditions and restrictions.

To say I'm puzzled, is to put it mildly. His mysterious exit - his upwards journey, whatever his destination was, leaves me with anxiety crowding in. But again, part of me takes a little comfort from the insight which suggests that the image of the Ascension was the best that this small group of disciples could do, in their attempt to describe the indescribable. I'm ready to acknowledge it was a brave effort, and I'm not intending to be patronising in any way. I don't know anyone who could have done any better! In today's science fiction culture I can readily imagine that there are those who would readily take it for granted that this levitation could have been real - an act or an event before its time. But as far as I know it is the only happening of this kind in history. The location of 'heaven' is a dimension about which I can only be agnostic. It's beyond my experience. The sun sets and disappears each day. It disappears from our sight. We have all witnessed this. But could there be, I wonder a 'link' between the setting sun and the disappearing Jesus? Yes? No? Human ascensions are unknown to me. But with a modicum of hesitation might I guess that you, God, were powerfully present in him with your unique dynamic creativity, translating a human act into a singularly bizarre moment which could not be captured in human experience in any other way. Could it be, I wonder, akin to that moment when the sky itself was first shaped? I feel I'm in a realm where there is no ground under my feet! I don't have a language to cope with these 'reported happenings'. I like to think that I do know a little about the sky. I frequently observe it in its very different moods and its wonder never leaves me. But the Ascension takes more faith than the faith I have. It leaves me without conviction. The best I can do is to wonder whether this symbolic masterpiece was a brave attempt to try to put into human experience for a very few, something that was happening at a 'non-human' level? I cannot judge how successful it has been, because I do not know what criteria I'd use. Of course there are those who will be content to believe it. But though the boundary between the finite and the infinite must exist somewhere, as far as I can tell it seems to be beyond any human location. This Ascension experience, for those who were there, may be one of the few, or even the only occasion when this significant boundary was visible. Was this evidence that the finite could be transformed in to the infinite? I want to make sense of it. And I'm wondering if this is possible?

Today we know that it is no longer viable to think that heaven as being 'up there'. I'm just wondering if it is a place, or not a place?

Likewise I'm left wondering whether I can have any experience of Jesus - ascended - 'being with me?' In a way it's like my feelings about you. I've never seen him, touched him, or heard him. When I listen to the experience of some other friends, I'm left wondering, why I do not, for instance, hear him? I'm ready to acknowledge that beyond sensory experiences there are occasions when I have had a sense of a non-physical presence. It defies description. All I can say is that my person is, or has been invaded by an intimate sensation that harnesses my feelings of self - my thinking self. This can be both quietening and disturbing. Because it defies articulation as I struggle to live fully in my desire and my hope. It is also an experience which is not readily shared with others - because of embarrassment, as well as frustration. Is this what the Church has pigeon-holed as 'the Holy Spirit?' First recognised at the Feast of Pentecost, as it feels like a non-physical intrusion. To those who experience it, it is real. But the experience is not universal. When I take seriously the challenge to live as if I had only one day left to live then I may feel a non physical 'intrusion'? I might hasten to add that this does not, in any way, feel an honour. Why should it? But the vibration of tenderness is conserved within me, strangely without language. Impatient with myself I can only say, rather lamely 'it's a mystery' – it's beyond human description, and human language, and all I can do is to confirm that 'it' lodges in my inner self, and is contained by my dumbness!

In this reflection I found myself going back again to the recorded words of Jesus on that last meeting with the disciples. I suppose that being one who has been moved on many occasions by his 'servanthood ministry' I was rather taken aback with those words in the clear imperative, 'Go into all the world and teach all nations 'about me!' He promised them power, with the clear implication being that Jesus is supreme. I find this all rather indigestible. It contrasts with Jesus' own model of ministry, that of the Suffering Servant from Isaiah, on the one hand, and the crystal clear picture given by Paul in his own letter to the Church at Philippi, where Jesus is described as the one who took 'the form of a servant'. His lowly birth, and his frequent refusal to be honoured as a king, his Servanthood demeanour, which I think at least calls into question whether those selected words from the scene of the Ascension can be authentic? The truly humble life style has been epitomised by countless Christians, and this shines even today from the witness of those who have no interest in power seeking, and money making. The supreme act of humility by Jesus was that stark example in the Upper Room, actually washing the feet of all the disciples. For myself I find this example something that vibrates within me every day. This style is a far cry from the imperative command. Conversions and stacking up numbers seem a perversion of the fundamental servanthood ministry. In spite of what some right wing Christians think, talking at people, whether catholic, protestant or pentecostal, usually is non-productive. And it might be worth pondering on the life style of those communities, retreat houses and hospices, where service is the quiet priority. This resonates with the other paradox of the Gospel, expressed as a challenge, living by the 'power of the powerless'. You'll be aware of the long list of saints who have been ready to submit themselves to service rather than the seduction of authority. I can't help but say that were the Church and religious communities just to live out this dynamic, evangelisation itself would be superfluous. That's a thought which I hope enfolds a revolution! And now as inter-faith dialogue progresses, evangelisation can only been seen as another dimension with the obsession of being competitive rather than co-operative.

Becoming poor for Christ's sake will make its mark on a paternal and patriarchal society where authoritarian gender bias sadly is experienced in too many religious settings. Gender equality will enrich all those who seek religious integrity. Yes, the roots of paternalism run deep. It is only the ethos of mutual servanthood that provides an adequate setting for all valued relationships which interweave across today's society.

To finish with just one last reflection arising from my own contemplation of the Ascension, it is, to be ever aware of the sad fact of history of how religion has too frequently embraced violence, war, oppression and tyranny. Religion has its roots in many violent situations. Today 'the West' is experienced as a threat to other parts of the world. And other parts of the world are experienced as threatening to 'the West'. Terrorism is the new warfare, and Christianity and Islam between them now hold the key to a future of possible co-operation, or alternatively to competition both as far as trade is concerned, as well as in the race for more oil, more armaments, more money and economic superiority. One of the frightening indications is the belief held by many who are on the Christian right in their 'doctrine' of 'Armageddon' - the supposed final battle between the Christian mould, against all others, and the believed imminent victory which will come to 'the soldiers of Jesus!'

It seems a long while since I embarked upon this line of thought. Contemplation is rich when experienced within the goodness of this natural scenario, even though it defies verbal description. Last night the stars were bright and there was a narrow slither of the moon climbing quietly on its appointed route across 'the heavens'. I imagined my own resting place, like Jacob, finding the stones for my pillow. And as I glided into sleep I hoped I might have my own ladder that would stretch from Now to eternity. His journey seems to have come near to that Ascension journey of Jesus, but I know in the depths that Jacob's 'ladder', and the upwards sweep of Jesus are but fertile pictures of a truth which I have as yet to understand, with a reasoned judgement. It feels as if this will be a task for the rest of my life.

I know I stand in need of a revival of my own religious imagination, so that I escape my own spiritual rut. I hope the Ascension will be a lively metaphor for a forward looking promise, the essence of which, for the moment, appears to be clouded with uncertainty. Does it matter that I am having difficulty to validate it all intellectually? If I am to grow in giving, healing, listening, with my sense of wonder, perhaps I'll sense it all in the very tips of my fingers!

Living God - by invocation, I would feel you.

Living God - by approach, I would hear you.

Living God - by vision I would see you.

I seek to embrace your mysterious power even with my flawed faith. Lubricate my imagination. Project me from my clouded reality, to a clear and uncluttered vista of a renewed humanity.

Join me to a life unencumbered by time and space - unscarred by the worn out hindrances of history and everlasting regret.

Refresh me! With the clean water of ascended purity -

Provide me! With the comfortable clothing of the Spirit -

Translate me! From the tiredness of stale and sullied love -

And then, on the wings of hope and gifted desire, let me see the perfection of that new love in revelation, which is unspoilt and so delicious, that it will blot out for ever the power of human evil.

Amen and Amen!

Letter 20: Does time have a meaning?

Dear God,

The clock has just struck midnight. It's the beginning of a New Year. Time flies! It's a special time - a holiday - and I wish to explore with you some thoughts and feelings that recur at this season of the year. Behind all the jollity there is an insistent question. Time flies, but where does it go to? Another year has gone. But to where has it gone? Another year has arrived, but from where has it come? This brings a strange sense of mystery - something intangible - and it has struck me that in a way, for me, time seems to resemble something of you, God - something more than just an association of ideas. I can't see time itself - I can't touch it - and it's silent. But in a way, I feel as if time is 'wrapped around me'. This is the only visualisation that gives me any satisfaction. And this has some similarities to my feelings and thinking about you. Clearly there is something immediate about time. It is here and now. The seconds tick away and the minutes are soon gone. When each tick has had its own time, then it is no more. This has a strange feeling to me. It is as if there lies here something significant, but deeply hidden. Each moment is complete in itself, and yet it has passed before it is fully able to be. Time could be said to be the measurement between the ebb and the flow of the sea's relentless tide. It does not stay still and there is no end to it. Could it be that this goes on for ever? As well as the fleeting present, time also conveys a sense of history, and simultaneously has the sense of stretching into the future, and on in to what is called infinity. So I'm intrigued to understand, if I can, what time has to do with eternity, that supposed existence which is 'out there', in front of us all. It is said, God, that you are in eternity. Could this mean that presumably You are beyond the territory of time and its boundaries?

When I think about time and wrestle with its meaning, it helps, of course, to have clocks, which tell us the time in seconds, minutes, and hours. However, I am also aware that sometimes my mood allows me to feel that hours may seems like seconds, and at other times a minute may seem like hours, if I feel in a threatening or frustrating situation. Chronology attempts to place all events at correctly proportionate intervals on a fixed scale in the order in which they occur. We have also the calendar which records the days and nights, the weeks and months, the years, decades and centuries, all in their fixed order. But having said this, the insatiable question remains - what is this elongated and stretched out manifestation of time? It cannot be pigeon holed in any way. So I am left feeling that this has a striking resemblance to my perceptions about you, God. For me, my letters are a serious attempt to discover you, because I feel I hardly know you. To me there seems to be a link between Time and you. What is it, I wonder? Time is unstoppable - will it go on for ever? And you? Are you for ever too? My hope for understanding and meaning feels quite slender, and the sense of unknowable mystery remains. But at the same time this process is searching me. I feel enfolded by and in something that for now remains indescribable. The words that bubble into my mind - 'Unresting, unhasting, and silent as light' - and 'We blossom and flourish - and wither and perish, but naught changeth thee'. These words written by Walter Chalmers Smith a hundred or so years ago are still sung in our churches today. There is an enigma, called T I M E - just four letters for one of the biggest mysteries of our human experience!

Every human being is contained in time, by time, from the moment of conception to the moment of birth. We are born into time, and in due course at the end of life's journey we will arrive at the time of our dying. What is there that is left at the end of this personal experience of living? We know for sure that our time will run out. Some talk of 'killing time', and some spend a lot of time, killing it! But then again I'm wondering, can time be 'killed'? And if it can, does this in some way injure or harm the being and even the prospect of what is called eternity? I think of eternity as that existence which is outwith the time span of this mortal world of humans and animals, and insects - a 'place' beyond the allotted space of our world. We don't appear to have any choice about 'our own time'. I did not have any choice when I was born and came into time. It was out with my control. And I wonder if I might have some figment of control, or at least awareness, or influence, in my own death? I like to think I can live my life to the full. But parallel in my reflection is my realisation that the actual measurement of my life which is called time, does not, finally belong to me. It belongs elsewhere, but I'm not sure where, and to whom, if anyone. If I have been given time, which feels like a gift, and a precious one at that, my sense of control over this time, my time, appears limited, to say the least. Though I cannot stop the clock of time, there may be occasions when I might consider stopping my personal clock. This decision is loaded with personal responsibility. Sadly I know for others the choice is too predictable. Those whose own time is a heavy burden, and too heavy to bear, face an end of agony. For them killing time, sadly, is a release. Yes, time does not stop, it rolls on and on. In the mirror of Time I can reflect on my sense of fragile control, or on occasion the lack of control altogether. This is salutary, to say the least - the intangibility of Time - from the past, to the present, and then into the future. My sense of lack of control, seems to be augmented by the control of Time itself. But for all that I hold securely to the immediate task and face the challenge to be present in the present. Marshal McLuhan has pointed out that for tribal humanity it was space that was the uncontrollable mystery, whilst today he says in our technological age it is Time that now occupies the same challenge. It feels unfathomable.

Looking back, on past epochs, I am aware that women and men had a shorter life span. Scripture records this as three score years and ten. Large numbers however did not reach this 'target'. They had less time in their lives. Today longevity provides a longer life cycle. In a sense life seemed cheaper then. Today we have more time, but it is unclear to what extent this means it is more highly valued. Within modern technology there is the temptation to assume that we do have more control over time. Nonetheless we cannot speed it up or slow it down, can we? There are those who appear to be more adept at saving time - remembering the hare and the tortoise! Whether our life span is short or long, does this in any way affect us in our perception of the probable value of time? For me life - all life is sacred, but does this imply that time is sacred too? And could this depend on the amount of time I think I have? Perceiving that only a little time is left, could engender a sense of time. But to see the whole of your allotted span of time as sacred, that is, to say the least, far reaching, and in a way inspiring.

Longevity of life is experienced far less in what is still called the Third World. Life is shorter and tougher, and expectations tend to be modest. In the West our go-getting society is driven by a time table of obsession, whether of our own making, or imposed by the competitive culture that has an insatiable urge to acquire more and more. Whereas elsewhere, life is experienced as a labour grinding existence, where achievements are attained only by long hours, and primitive processes which in themselves can be responsible for shortening life expectancy. However, there are other cultures – Aborigine, Native American and Maori, to name a few who appear to be freer of Western constraints because time is not manipulated by utilitarian categories of production and worth.

The demands of work and or love, have a distinct effect on how we regard the time we have in any one day, or on any one night. The more time we have, the more we want. The less time we have, the less we expect. Those who feel they have no time are tempted to 'let go' and descend into a spiral of unsatisfied and diminished self esteem. It seems to me that having a sense of time within your control, then the more likely we are to have the satisfaction of achievement. However, this may also widen possibilities of error, pain, and frustration. The use of time can foment evil desires, as well as facilitate goodness and hope. On the other hand our own contemporary obsession with pleasure, can make a fetish of enjoyment, and in so doing will devalue it. The subtle influences of time, whether in plenty or in short supply, will make the difference as to whether or not we give time to build a compassionate society or whether we complacently pass our time to satisfy our own personal needs with a diminished social conscience for others. But it is not that I want You to think that the enjoyment of pleasure itself is a bad use of time. Perish the thought! But I'm still wondering whether time itself can, as it were, be impregnated with a sense of integrity which will create some thing for the common good? Or is time neutral? These reflections gush up, from 'time to time', especially when I feel I am burrowing deeper into my inner self, so as to be more aware of time's influence, without being captured by it.

Why, I wonder, does time travel at the speed it does travel? I'm aware of shorter days and longer nights, or shorter nights and longer days. But 24 hours is still 24 hours. The orbit of the sun stipulates the regularity of days and nights. This tunes in with the moon as it traces the ebb and flow of tides on every shore. What a remarkable system, so meticulous in its every day detail, its regularity, providing us with a sense of security and wellbeing. But there are those who respond with a sense of fatalistic frustration and who desire only that for them time would stop. We know without doubt that each day will have 24 hours and each year twelve months. I wish there were a greater recognition of this every day gift, rather than taking it all for granted. Recently I have been endeavouring to focus on this as I wake each morning, and then again each night, as I gaze at the splendour of the night sky. This does help me in an age of unpredictable social and political flux to access for myself regularly the order and quiet certainty of each day and each night.

However the mystery of time is here to stay - I hope! For me if I focus on small bits of time, it becomes that bit easier to comprehend. For instance I can take an hour and settle down on the settee to read a book, or to watch TV. This piece of time - an hour - assumes a more focussed relevance for me, and I become aware of being quietly changed. In a way, I feel I can hold this particular piece of time, as it were, 'in the palm of my hand'. In a real sense, it is mine, and I use it for a personal purpose. And I'm aware of my satisfaction. I know it will last for as long as I read the book, or view the programme. When then I have finished reading, and the time has moved on, I can reflect on it with a sense of pleasure - the pleasure this hour has given. Time has been used and something achieved. Maybe God you will be thinking this is beyond question. Well, not in the world where I live my life. To have a sense of achieved happiness, and to experience how time pays dividends is a fertile insight for me. The longer the span of my life, then the deeper the sense of value and appreciation. But it still remains true, that the more time I have, the more I want! For me it is still the case that there is something insatiable and yet absolute about time. It's like, "now I have it - now I don't". When it's gone, it's gone for ever. This sometimes leaves me feeling that my grasp on my own time is weaker than I'd prefer. On occasion, I feel that Time itself has a grasp on me. It surrounds me, driving me into activity, and I have this sense, of making up for lost time.

Today the spring sunshine beams through my window, reminding me that Spring comes after Christmas, and after Easter Summer will arrive. After Summer there will be Autumn the harbinger of Winter

- full circle, a circle entire in itself. This cycle of time has its own reliable rhythm, with a deeply embedded sense of ongoing purpose However there are indications that environmentally the seasons themselves, these days, are not as tightly bound to the framework of time as they were in earlier decades. The reliability of the seasons has been as a gift of creation, so that when for example snow falls in summer and expected rains do not come, does this cause you pain? Scientists and environmentalists observing and recording the phases and changes across the globe, of our menu of weather, with its increasing unreliability, are now asking questions which strike at the heart of the supposed inter-linking between time itself, and the hitherto assumed inter-relatedness of weather patterns within the overall framework of the seasons of the year. If, for instance, you imagine that Spring is shortened and Summer is lengthened does this not suggest that the timing of the seasons has, to some degree, cut adrift from the hitherto assumption that time would ensure the regularity of the seasons, each in its allotted order?

For me the bigger question in the back of my mind, which I don't explore too frequently is, what would happen if Time itself slowed down; or speeded up, of even stopped? No, I do not think this is an idle question! If there are creeping signs that we are moving into a period of uncertainty and irregularity of the seasons, then could it be that Time itself could stop? What would this feel like, I wonder? If there would be no time, could the world function? Is this a matter that is in your hands God? Or is there yet to be discovered truth which for now lies beyond our own human comprehension? Time speeded up or slowed down seems a scary notion. I have days that speed by, and nights that seem slow. I'm unable to sleep! But I know this possibility is not real - at least not yet. Even though the thought of it quickens my pulse. For now I'm ready to accept we cannot manipulate time. This confirms a certainty, in a world where some certainties feel fragile, I am thinking of that well known image, the Rock of Ages which helps me to picture the link between you and Time. This is profound and strangely comforting. One of the blessings of everyday life is the gift of memory. Memory is entwined in my sense of time. It safeguards for me the earlier experiences of my life, or at least some of them. The older I grow the more precious memories become. But within this is the growing sense that memory itself is fragile. Memory can find itself less able to cope with the totality of one's own time span. The more time I have, or have had, the more remembering there is to do, even though it is less effective. But memory can sharpen the highlights of one's own past time, which in a way ensures that one's past does not become full of emptiness. Comparisons can be disturbing. For instance even only momentarily comparing my slender slice of life, and then contemplating the age of our universe. Scientists estimate the age of the galaxies of our universe is something like 45,000,000 years old. How can anything be so old? So Time has been ticking away endlessly, 'for ever' and it feels both wonderful and yet full of mystery. So my own years on Earth by comparison fade into utter insignificance. My life feels like the millionth of a second! But whether all of this is 'old' to you God, is a question whose meaning I might not be able fully to understand. So I'm left with a strong sense of wanting to cross the time barrier, and yet not wanting to, for fear of finding myself beyond the reality I have come to accept as my one own fragile life. I can't peel time back from its original start, and I'm not able to project myself forward into a future of which I will experience very little. So being present in the present feels the most comfortable place to be.

Isaac Watts had some of the same revealing insights which he transposed into a hymn. 'A thousand ages in thy sight are like an evening gone'.....'Time like an ever-rolling stream bears all its sons' away. They fly forgotten as a dream dies at the opening day! However, some dreams remain. They do not die. Dreams frequently are timeless. They stimulate insight, even though the detail may remain vague and not understood. But whatever else, dreams are not time bound. Watts' sense of poetry turns this mystery of time into a fertile and nourishing reflection. At the same time, he opens up a hopeful dimension to my thinking, and to some degree takes away or at least diminishes the sense of hopelessness about, for instance, the meaning of history. By this I mean the history of each one of us, and, of course, all of us.

His second verse, 'Under the shadow of thy throne thy saints have dwelt secure...sufficient is thine arm alone and our defence is sure' - presents a view of history which today some would question. Time in itself has not defended us at any period in the course of history. His verse is too sweeping a statement. But then again, there may have been some particular events when time has provided safety from enemies – for instance at the evacuation of British troops at Dunkirk in W.W.2, when it seems that time and tide provided a unique space to permit an unlikely evacuation, and so saving the lives of hundreds of soldiers. Recent memory still holds on to the miracle where time and tide, and circumstance conspired together. As they say, 'The rest is now history!' The words of Watts may have lost some of the meaning felt by the writer. But we cannot evade the experience of impotence which on occasion humanity had to experience when Earth's future seemed so uncertain. Now looking back, the passing of Time, with reflection can breathe hopefulness. But, similarly history is capable of provoking memories of despair.

There is the further notion of time as Kairos - the imperative sense that <u>now</u> is the appointed time. It is here, in the here and now. This moment has come and will not come again. Some theologians have marked this as 'the Eternal Now'. It provides the experience of 'venturing into now', because in the fullness of time, now is here, and can be delayed no longer. The advent of Christ, it is said was a 'Kairos moment' - likewise the death and the new life provided at that first Easter. This was the once and for all moment that could not be delayed. I suppose in a sense it might be said that at this happening Time itself stood still. Time standing still fertilises the imagination, and has a profound power of its own. The Kairos moment can never be repeated – it is once and for all. Procrastination is the enemy of 'the Eternal Now'. Perhaps Dunkirk had that sense of 'the eternal now'?

But again reminiscent of paradox, the 'March of Time' cannot be hindered, and it will also pass into the mystery of the future. In all this I have the present sense of being controlled, and finding myself in a process of passing time, over which I feel I have no control. Then there follows a sense of freedom when I can deliberately give myself up to the March of Time, and to have that new sense of being able to swim in the Tide of Time. This might enable me to 'peel back' the memory, the time which I might have missed or foolishly misspent. I know that it is not for nothing that three small words, when taken seriously, transform a hopeless situation. The words – 'do it now'. Like nothing else they address my languid and tepid state, accelerating me into the mood that will grasp the opportunity which has the potential to change and to transform.

The sense of 'the eternal now' with its immediacy allows me to venture into a time line that may straddle that gap between now and eternity. It's here that I sense that the 'veil will be, or could be, lifted'. Then hopefully there will be greater clarity. But the risk of unintentionally assuming the eternal now continues to lurk in my heart.

Before this letter is concluded I have one nagging irritation. In the context of now and eternity, wrestling with the sense of the inevitability of time, for some their eternal now is the wretched daily life of severe mental illness. Incurable it destroys all the sensitivity of love and belonging - I guess you know this. Likewise there are others who are unable to forgive themselves, or who remain unforgiven by others - their souls are deeply scarred - and their lives are the epitome of eternal misery. 'Now' for them defies any sense of healing. Can 'the eternal now' vouchsafe a gift that dilutes the pain of eternal punishment? I suppose I'm hoping to discover that you can intervene. But can you? It all feels so difficult - either you can, or you can't. If you are powerless, then the mystery has to be beyond me. Is there any means by which you too can fully identify with those who suffer the pain of knowing there is no release. This I suppose could be the power of powerlessness?

This letter explores something which has been difficult to put into words. I need more insights, knowledge, humility - but in addition a well meant insistence that can question, only because this may be the only possible route to a clarity of cloudless understanding of that 'Now' which will be realised! However if this is not so, and realisation turns out to be 'mission impossible' at least I have pursued my course with all the integrity that I know.

It is the notion of 'loyal dissent' that supports my enquiry. In the scene of humanity's pain and disarray, I trust that your compassion will 'gather up' the dregs of bitter mistakes, so that in the closing stages of my life here, the grounds for hope will expand.

Dear God, read - listen - and despite troublesome religious jargon, use this letter for your Presence to be searched, so that I will be understood. Each minute ticks by, and could bring further revelation. Hopefully my writing will link us into a new sense of intimacy - the joining of love and truth.

Letter 21: Is sex about being different and being the same?

Dear God,

These letters are proving to be important for me, because they are helping me to give expression to concerns which are difficult. They expose my vulnerability and anxiety, but they also push me to explore and to wonder. They are reflections on everyday life, but they also help me to go out on a limb and look at matters which over the years I may not have given the attention they deserve. Like others, I'm not too ready to face the things where I feel uncertain. So at the moment I'm taking my courage in both hands to look at some aspects of everyday life which for me bring confusion and doubt. You see, I can't always see the wood for the trees! When I'm at my best I can be penetrating and creative in my thinking and questioning. However, there are also occasions when my 'wells of compassion' dry up, and I'm unable to get to grips with problems because they threaten me. On the one hand I don't want to be seen as 'one of the herd', but at the same time I'm anxious not to be regarded as 'too far out'. To put it simply I don't want to be too different from my fellow human beings, but at the same time I want to be myself.

I'm going on a bit about this because when it comes to behaviour, I feel I can become judgemental, and perhaps superior. I can on occasion recognise that I'm not always able to be as open as I would wish. This can inhibit my lifelong search for integrity, at any cost.

These concerns are never far away in my practice as counsellor and psychotherapist. This is my vocation, and it has given a great deal of meaning to my own life. I have provided therapy for women and men – singly, in couples within both short term and long term partnerships. Some couples appear to enjoy short term relationships, but others have long term love affairs that seem to be for life. In the last five or so years I've been called on to explore same gender partnerships – with women who are lesbian, and men who 'are gay'. Contrasting my therapy with heterosexual couples and with homosexual couples has directed me into refreshing dialogue – refreshing yes, but nonetheless complex and open ended. I want to be open and non-judgemental with couples in either group. This is important if I am to offer myself as a credible guide and counsellor. But I am aware of my prejudices, just as I am aware of the prejudices of the women and men who make up the couples. Part of therapy is the offer of the ministry of listening – deep listening. From experience I know that this can bring about change, the change that can turn anger into reflection and neutralise violent attitudes. So I submit myself to the same process as I do those who come to see me.

I know that for too long, gays and lesbians had to go about their daily lives furtively and secretively. Family, neighbours, work colleagues and members of clubs and churches had to be kept ignorant of the nature of their own sexual orientation. Some have feared being ostracized by those of rigid and intemperate views. But now the practice of 'coming out' has gained some credibility, and gays and lesbians have been brave enough to be more open about their gender partnerships and their sexuality. In fact now the custom of 'coming out' is for most almost superfluous. Being open is preferable to being secretive. It has taken courage to be open about same sex relationships, and then to live together with your partner. It seems to me that courage may still be required to say 'this is how it is for me / us'.

In spite of hard-line homophobic behaviour and attitudes, gays and lesbians are making a place for themselves in society. Their lifestyle is normal for them, and they make their own authentic contribution to community life. However, the struggle for acceptance goes on. Bigotry and prejudice remain, and at times Gays and Lesbians face 'closed doors'. This is as likely to be experienced in the Church as out with it. The Anglican Church is split over whether or not it should have gay priests or gay bishops. I'm very much aware of the acrimony and fanatical behaviour which mark both sides of this controversy. For myself I really am glad that gays and lesbians have not adopted a secretive culture, like for instance, the freemasons. Openness is always preferable to secrecy.

In this matter scripture is not really very helpful. 'Text bashing' is non-productive and only enforces prejudice. Rigid thinking has never been of much help when exploring the scriptures. When I reflect on the haphazard way in which the scriptures have been written and come down to us over the centuries, with the added uncertainty of authorship, 'text waving' in itself is not helpful. The variations of meaning of texts, resulting from the complex issues regarding translation, require of all readers some magnanimity of meaning which will in itself fertilise avenues of truth for exploration and for ultimate understanding. Texts waved around indiscriminately can become traps, rather than new insights into truth. We have to continue to link creatively similarity and difference. When it comes to different styles of human behaviour our prime need is for intellectual rigour along with deep sensitivity and empathy to a wide spectrum of feelings. The rise of rabid discrimination with unhealthy judgemental attitudes is bound to set up barriers which then establish no-go zones, socially and intellectually. The objective has to be an open society which aims to be inclusive rather than exclusive. Isolationism is dangerous. You are the one who promotes compassion and respect, irrespective of behaviour and beliefs. But we – or at least I, need to know how to do it, that is, not to let the behaviour of others deter us from building a society that tolerates or even encourages difference.

However underneath all the debate and controversy there remains one basic question, and though I hesitate, I want to put it to you. Even my asking of the question makes me aware of my own anxiety. However, I believe that my question is also the unspoken question of others. The question is something like this. As the Creator of humanity – women and men – did you intend that male / female relationships should be entirely complementary? Did you intend that women and men, within a stable relationship should procreate and have children so as to ensure the future of the human race? And did you intend that the gift of sexuality would be designed as a female / male shared experience? Was sexual intercourse, as far as you are concerned designed to ensure the bonding of couples? If, for you, the male / female bonding is a primary feature of human life, can it then be assumed that it has a special significance? These are the sub questions arising out of one question! I feel they are all 'heavy' questions. For some, they are charged with considerable emotion. But within the complexity of human relationships and morality, there has to be a base upon which the viability of human behaviour is understood. In spite of the anxieties and confusion I'm looking for 'firm ground' on which my exploration can proceed. I feel quite relaxed about the sexuality of my own life. However, I'm also aware of a sense of sexual chaos in society. I'm not obsessed with sexual sin, nor are my feelings in any way legalistic. I'm clear that the heterosexual partnership whether long lived or short lived is partly designed for mutual sexual pleasure, for fun, enjoyment and fulfilment. I also think it has its own sense of spirituality which multiplies the pleasure and enjoyment of sexuality, when it is shared with a partner, with the intent of giving pleasure. And though, of course, the enjoyment of mutual sex is the entry into parenthood nevertheless I'm sure that the choice of parenthood needs to be more than just a sexual flourish!

My question(s) is about having to face up to the different perspectives of a homosexual approach, rather than a heterosexual one. Homosexuality describes a spectrum of relationships between persons of the same gender. It has its own complexities. Within the term homosexual there are men who may not seek female sexual relations, just as there are women who do not desire sexual relations with men. Sexuality itself may feature very little, if at all, in the lives of some women and men, There are women and men who seek a same sex partner, for their own sexual satisfaction, as well as for all the other reasons one chooses a partner. Some same sex relationships will be long term, but for others they will be short term, just as it is with heterosexual couples. There will be promiscuity both in heterosexual and homosexual couplings. Multi partnered women and men whether heterosexual or homosexual will contribute to what I have called sexual chaos. But couples in long term relationships, both homosexual and heterosexual are contributing to stability within society, based on a sense of responsibility and their own sexual integrity.

Do you think all sexual behaviour is natural, or are there some deviations which you consider unnatural? I know there are different feelings about oral sex. Some think it is exciting and pleasurable, while others feel it is disgusting and dirty. Is it just a matter of choice, as far as you are concerned? For myself I think there is something of mystery about sexuality, and there is much we don't know and have not yet discovered. What is it that leads some to consider themselves homosexual, whilst others are content to be heterosexual? But then there are others who are bisexual, or transvestite. There is a sexual mystery that has potential for both pleasure and pain. The pain of not feeling comfortable with one's own sexuality can send sufferers to breaking point. A deep empathy is required to be able to enter into the depths of suffering, for instance when a person is unable to use with comfort their own genitals. Some resort to genital surgery, in response to deeply perceived need to change one's gender and sexuality. We know that human beings have female and masculine traits, and this influences one's personal appearance, dress habits, and emotional wellbeing. But in this arena of human complexity it is preferable to desire to understand rather than to indulge in rigid prescriptions. Your response to these ruminations would be more than satisfying, but perhaps this is asking too much of you?

In these delicate concerns privacy needs to be safeguarded. The more so, when each of us explores our own sexuality, within the context of intimate personal relationships. Sexual intercourse between lovers who are women and men, normally takes the form of the male penis entering the female vagina. Sexual manuals spell this out with clarity, but perhaps without much imagination. Sexual intercourse is an imaginative diet of fondling, caressing, kissing as well as touching and fingering erogenous zones of both partners. We call it 'Making Love'! A telling affirmation!

However, when it comes to sexual play for men with male partners, and women with female partners, the act of sexual penetration becomes something of a conundrum. It's something that has to be differently understood. Because this is such a sensitive matter across society it needs to be spelt out, quietly, and with your blessing God, because with you there are no forbidden zones. Men with male partners enjoy mutual masturbation, and discover satisfaction from a manually induced ejaculation. Women with female partners have their own modes of intimacy and sexual pleasure and comfort. However, I believe I would be evading the discipline of integrity if I did not refer to a sexual practice about which there is, I think, some understandable disagreement. I'm referring to the sexual act where one male partner penetrates the anus of his partner, for sexual satisfaction. There are also women with male partners who practice anal intercourse. This is both controversial, and for some repugnant. I have to say that for myself I find it unpalatable. But it needs to be explored sensitively, for in spite of what I feel, there are those who find it enjoyable. If I may, I'd like to pursue this exploration by recalling that in heterosexual intercourse, for the man, his delight is in the sexual pleasure afforded by and to the vagina and the clitoris of his partner. For the woman this sexual technique provides her with pleasure and satisfaction. However, when a man enters the anus of a male or female partner, I think it might be likened to intercourse within a vagina without a clitoris. So in a sense the anus is expected to give both pleasures of vagina and clitoris. This explicit expectation cannot be achieved. Fundamentally, the purpose of the anus is to be a channel for the evacuation of human waste (faeces). So using the anus for sexual pleasure will require previous careful cleaning, after evacuation has taken place. Of course the importance of cleanliness of the sexual organs prior to intercourse is widely recognised. But with the anus it needs a particular thoroughness. Anal intercourse can also cause membrane fragmentation, which in itself is painful, and slow to heal.

I hope you will understand why I have gone into this detail. I feel I have to be modestly factual. There are those who maintain that in homosexual anal intercourse that the prostate gland can add a sensation of mutual pleasure. But for myself, more research will be necessary before clarity about this can be established. Important considerations are at stake, and openness is essential. The present acceleration of the spread of sexually transmitted diseases has created world-wide problems. Today HIV / AIDS is a pandemic crisis. Those who are experts are warning that infection through anal intercourse cannot be ruled out. Nonetheless I would not be responding by endorsing fundamentalist views that HIV / AIDS is your judgement God on a 'wicked society'. Such a stance is flimsy both intellectually and emotionally. It's quite against my own belief, because I believe your nature God is compassionate and forgiving. I'm ready, on this matter to put my trust in you, in your mercy and tenderness for all who stray, who need your forgiveness and the forgiveness of humanity. But now I come to a question I can't avoid. Does my writing to You about these issues of sexuality evoke in You some hope, or do they leave You with sadness and disappointment? I'm searching for clarity, so if You can open up avenues of insight which might then create a new direction for sexual wholeness and integrity, then that would be a breakthrough.

Even though gays and lesbians have different sexual orientations they remain an important sector of the human race. They are common in every country and we need to value them for who they are, and what they do. Promoting tolerance would be easier if agreeable boundaries of sexual behaviour and practice were clearer. We have to discover an equitable way of sharing all the delights of being human, but how? I'm not wishing to diminish the quality of the love and affection shared between women, or between men. I cling to the persuasion that where love is – the genuine desire for the wellbeing of the other, then ipsofacto your Spirit is present. This is of great comfort to me. Respect and a deep sense of positive regard is valid and integral to all inter-personal relationships. They are all 'special'. Sexual love and pleasure when highly valued are then elevated above meanness and the obsessive intention of those who would misuse and exploit the natural joys of sex.

One of the delights of long term heterosexual partners is the desire and gift of having children. Parenthood brings a new dimension to the loving relationship between spouses and partners. There is something natural and authentic happening when partners share the joyful act of bringing a child to birth. The process of conception and birth is at the very heart of creation itself. In this women and men are participants with you! Of course, family life can be strewn with hard, uncomfortable and chastening experiences. None of us have been trained in parenthood, but the experiential learning – learning by the actual doing of it, flourishes where it is rooted in loving fidelity and mutual assurance.

However, I'm also aware of a sense of sadness, because those who are gay and lesbian, and who share a loving fidelity face stress and disappointment because their sexual loving will not enable procreation towards the birth of a wanted child. I think those of us who are not gay or lesbian need to acknowledge the pain and frustration this brings to faithful homosexual partners. But I'm remembering too that sometimes heterosexual partners discover they too are impotent and infertile and unable to conceive. This realisation floods the soul with agony. And to talk about the 'rights of parenthood' is singularly unhelpful. These two different experiences of infertility have similarities as well as differences. My 'gut feeling' leads me to guess that you, God, will also share in this desolation. I've written elsewhere of my perception of your own impotence – your inability to act – of not being able to do what is desirable, but is also practically impossible. Whatever else boundaries cannot be ignored, nor can they readily be changed. This is, how it is! Nonetheless the hypothetical question emerges, is there any sense in which omnipotence – the authority that is all powerful – of finding its way to diminish the incidence of infertility, of those who are heterosexual, as well as venturing into the condition of homosexual women and men, so that they too could create their own embryos, and so to permit them to experience their own parenting. I can see that the ethical issues are complex. But would you, God encourage or discourage these paths of research and enquiry? Pushing back boundaries is always controversial. But the wisdom to perceive which of these choices is in the best interest of your entire creation is necessary. Can humanity discover and find this?

But there is also a further factor, and your insight into this is necessary, if 'rightness' is to be ensured. For most of us the hard question is whether or not gays and lesbians living in long term relationships should parent children? In the heterosexual family children have the benefit of mothering and fathering. The traditional family has a mother and a father. However, for different reasons this has become a little less common because spouses are not always able to maintain their partnership, and hence the mother or the father may have to move out, leaving an inevitable gap in the parenting task. When homosexual partners desire children, the implication may be that children will find themselves with either two mothers or two fathers. Ad hoc arrangements may be possible in individual situations, but this in itself may not be entirely satisfactory. This is volatile ground. Sadly we know that humanly designed outcomes can go disastrously wrong. Growing up in today's world might be difficult enough without anxieties that arise from deep personal doubts and uncertainties. But again, if love is present in the adults in any family, then perhaps this is all that is required? Magnanimity is required in these explorations. But simultaneously gentle research in a climate of openness, without competition, may offer potential new insights which hitherto have remained hidden and unexplored. It may seem idealistic, but the hope that adults who are heterosexual and homosexual, mutually supporting each other so as to provide a compassionate society might be a big adventure which could yield wonderful new outcomes within family life.

The increase in the incidence of child abuse and cruelty will require of us all a stringency in parenting. Children need to be defended from painful exploitation, whether it is from heterosexual or homosexual adults. Some might say that consideration of this issue without prejudice is unlikely. Ultimately the wellbeing of the child has to be paramount, and sexual mores and behaviour will be of only secondary consideration.

I can't conclude this letter without reference to women and men who have opted for life-long celibacy. They tend to be overlooked. Women and men, though celibate, and even perhaps because they are celibate who in particular offer 'the casualties' of our society the tender caring that so many need. These are the adults who are 'misfits', for whom no one else will care, who frequently find themselves supported and loved by dedicated celibate women and men – both priests and nuns, and other single men and women. For myself, I'm of a mind to give credibility to those who have decided to live within a life style of sexual abstinence, and who offer gifts to us all. Free from the need of sexual and other satisfactions, they make a unique contribution to the greater good. They have their own value, and like the rest of us confront their own weaknesses with varying success.

I'm aware that this letter contains the hard grind of questions which may as yet still provide no reliable answers. But being fully human requires us to explore modes of behaviour which are not readily understood, and to keep an openness of attitude so that we may discover truth in unexpected places. There will be situations within which palpable answers are not possible. And in our differences we need to preserve integrity of motivation. So perhaps, again, the discipline of waiting may have its place together with forbearance. Those of an adventurous spirit will want to go forward, whilst the more reticent will wish to hold back. Wherever we find ourselves, my hope is that fundamental to the future of us all there will be discoveries that will enhance the wellbeing of sexuality itself so as to ensure a new ecstasy of fulfilment which will threaten no one. Whatever our individual sexual orientation, I hope God, with some spiritual input from you we can formulate a complementary society where difference and similarity provide the caring fabric for us all. For me, I feel that this letter has, in a way, 'spread a fleece' before you. Come in your gentleness so that I may 'hear' afresh and 'see' anew the uncharted path forward leading to a humanity bathed in the light of your face and invigorated by your distinctive voice.

Letter 22: Wrestling with uncertainty

Dear God,

Putting pen to paper today is going to be a struggle. I think you'll see why. I've just wakened up, and the morning is black! It's as black as night. There is no sign of life, or light, other than my own erratic breathing. Inside I feel utterly empty - hollow - cold as ice, and yet at the same time, stupid as it may seem, there is a burning ball, as it were, in my head, and it feels as if it could explode at any moment. It's hard to know where I am. I listened and there is nothing but silence. A strange uncanny silence out there, in the cold. A desolate silence, and I feel utterly alone. My body is prone. I'm scared to move. My eyes flicker and I can move my toes, so somewhere there is life within me, but it feels precarious, fragile, and uncertain. I'd like to move, but I can't. I feel exhausted, as if I had spent the night not in sleep, but in combat, with who or what I do not know. It all feels so evil. All I know is that I'm on my bottom, and I'm afraid this is where I'll remain.

From where has this all come, I do not understand. I hoped my sleep was renewing me cleansing me, giving me new strength, and leaving me refreshed for a new day. But at this moment all that the new day has brought has been darkness - black, black darkness. It's as if the sum total of thirty November dawns had been telescoped into one big black hole. It's extraordinary, and I am facing it quite alone, and it's not nice. I wonder whether my senses are almost disintegrating? Am I dreaming a wretched dream? Or has it been a nightmare? Am I losing my body, I wonder? Or my mind? The dark threatening void out there is real enough to me and the other dark void inside me is real enough too. I am left with nothing but nothingness and emptiness. Momentarily I wonder which is worse, and then I realise this is a stupid question. They both generate a tortuous fear. One fear after another. It is so wretched. I feel bad about me and I feel bad about the world too. I'm grasping at the present, and the future too - if there is one. Perhaps, I wonder, is this the end - my end? Has my life been about coming to this end? Not that I feel it is a good end, but perhaps an ending that might hopefully just pass quickly, so that this suffering is as brief as possible. At other times I don't want my life to end at all. Today is my dark night of the soul. This is a chunk of the wilderness of my life.

When I'm able to think about it, and try to calm myself just a little, it feels as if I'm in the grip of something that feels evil. It seems as if there is no way out. There are barriers, invisible ones, and they hem me in and this allows evil to assault me, threaten me, and I feel so vulnerable in my mind, my body, my soul. The essence that is me is exposed and encompassed by a glass shell through which others peer and intrude. I have an enemy that I do not know, which actually not only sees through me, but gets right inside me, and I'm exposed for what I am. So it's not a matter of being off guard. Rather it is having to be on guard all the time. This tortuous evil penetrates my inner citadel, afflicting me with wild thoughts, fantasies, moods, and horror scenarios that turn everything to bitterness and to utter helplessness. Whatever has been beautiful and enabling from all those times of remembered wonder and exhilaration, now appear squashed and trodden into the ground. All the attributes of goodness are damned and demolished. As I lie here it seems as if nothing good exists anymore. I can't help but recall when I lay in a hospital bed in pain after some unpleasant surgery, and quite unable to do anything at all for myself. It was so embarrassing. I found myself dependant on a young gentle nurse who quietly relieved me. I was moved to the deepest experience of dependence and thankfulness. And now, at this moment following this morning's nightmare, I can again sense the same all black, slimy, cold stinks everywhere with no solace. But today there is no gentle nurse. It's as if the light at the end of the tunnel has been switched off. It is true isn't it – there is a real presence of evil in the world? I feel it!

I hope dear God that you can recognise these feelings. For me they are so real. Now, when I have had a little space and air, and can think and reflect a passing mood of contemplation suggests to me that this nightmare has encapsulated those shadow experiences traversing many years. This is more than a mood. Squashed together in one solid lump, like a never ending struggle with regular blows of setback, dereliction, and the blunt end of sheer undeserved defeat. I'm being sucked into reflecting on the sad and disappointing experience of what being so human feels like today. I feel my own poverty of desire. Passion is spent. I feel as flat as that proverbial pancake. It's as if my desire, the guardian of my vision has been tarnished and distorted so that now everything, in the end, turns into rubbish and ridicule. Sneering cynicism scorns whatever might have been good. If only the good had been allowed to survive. At this moment I'm feeling as if the reservoir of goodness, which I have cherished and guarded over the years has all been flushed away, but not before it has all been terribly polluted and abused. No sun, no stars, no hopes, no love, no people, no music, no imagination. No! No! No! No! Nothing! Just emptiness. But dear God, why? It's been hard to find the words that penetrate and sensitively describe how I was earlier today.

But it's important for me to tell you and to try to describe it. Though it started earlier this morning, the sense of it lingers on. It's as if the tentacles of evil stifle the goodness of life out of me, and I'm unable to stop it, or even to slow it down. I tell myself, when I can, that this travail of the soul has afflicted many of the saints. But it also afflicts those who have no sense of being a saint either. I hesitate to say it, but for me this nightmare has felt like a crucifixion of my identity, that precious bit that is 'me'.

As I write, creeping into my mind is that reminder of Alcoholics Anonymous, 'that it's not until you have been to the very bottom of the pit, that you can then, and only then, take the first faltering steps for the climb up, and eventually out, to start again'. But this is hard because no one can do it for me. I don't feel me, this 'me', climbing up and wanting so much to be a new 'me'. A 'me' that in the future will not be demolished as I come up against the 'brick walls' that in all the sectors of life seem set to frustrate and diminish all that is best in me. Rejection, unfaithfulness, betrayal, feed one's sense of disillusionment, and ears are deaf and confidence is waning. I know this cripples my sense of judgement, and perhaps my insight is blurred. The power of evil, I have found is not to be trifled with. Even though my hopes have been scattered, I can say, it hoarsely, I have survived - though by the skin of my teeth! But the rest of the day now lies before me, and I approach it with some timidity. I'll need your companionship as I step out one pace at a time. I know now as never before that there is no hiding place. This feeling of gradually being alive again is as near to death as I have ever been. This essence of death has shaken me to my very core. I have a flashback to Psalm 22, where the psalmist writes, "My God, my God, why hast thou forsaken me?" "Why art thou so far from helping me?" How is it that You remain aloof from my suffering? This is how it seems. In this agony confidence evaporates. But it is, in a way, a relief to be able to identify with others who have also the agony of unknowing. However perhaps the Psalmist had something I do not have, because within a few verses he exclaims a stanza of praise and affirmation. He aspires to the life of the meek and he feels affirmed by you. But the mood swing remains threatening. Reflecting on the agony of Jesus' death on that timber Cross, is a mystery far deeper than mine earlier this morning. Calm can be inter mingled with pain and hesitation. Out of that stark dark Calvary scene I can feel my own crumbling identity. Ignominy devours pride, but even at my lowest point I had an instinctive need to search for a renewed vision for my life. Where did this come from? There is a tissue of sensitivity so tentative, which might point to my failure being nothing other perhaps than an evolving gracious stillness within which I can now taste something that is akin to surrender. Is there a paradox here? Failure and defeat of the magnitude I've been trying to describe have uncovered a perspective which shows that in the end, my scenario of meaninglessness has within it the secret that eventually concedes a gracious culmination. I do hope so. To be clear, I'm not feeling like any hero. Rather spurts of positive regard have now begun to well up, so that the struggle to describe this epic of the soul surprisingly offers up an unexpected solace, followed by what I dare to think may be even a sense of sacred achievement.

I feel that now may be the time to try to explore with you perspectives of hope on the one hand and defeat on the other. Gracious perceptions have appeared out of tensions, and even frustrations, but I have struggled to remain a realist, committed to being present in the present. I've tried hard to remain coherent to myself. Through the storm I clung to the hope that a greater flexibility of spirit would enable me to tolerate violent swings of mood, only then to discover, surprisingly, my tenuous readiness to wait and even in the midst of my chaos to wonder. The feelings of malevolence gave way to the recognition that if, in spite of feeling impotent, I stayed with the experience, eventually it would reveal some hopefulness. My terror diminished and I was relieved to feel that this was not to be for ever. I was able to grasp the possibility of a renewed future, and this strangely rewarded me with further glimpses of virgin hope - a hope that was fresh and unsullied at that very moment. I had this picture of a ray of warm sunshine falling on a mellow ice-bound flower.

Until this morning I had felt that I was not easily pushed over. I've been used to trusting my own sense of committed tenacity, whatever the struggle. Hanging on to my vision, and feeding my delight in life itself has been part of a vivacious spirit. But now it seems that since this morning all my vivaciousness has been vindicated. From that momentarily overwhelming sense of defeat and terror has come a lively awakening that goodness and right can prevail, but at a price! So perhaps for the moment this is enough for me, but I remain unsure that the world itself will come eventually to share in any sense of ultimate triumph over evil. For the moment I know I have to give myself space to savour my own discovery, and perhaps for the time being to leave the world in its struggle to find its own space and a new sense of priorities which will disclose new discoveries and new radical directions.

However, I do not want to let myself too easily off the hook, and evade the true meaning of this morning's experience. I have to continue my search for the understanding that will confirm my new sense of fulfilment. This will be interwoven with my own reflections on the present stage of my life's journey. It is not always easy to be able to let go of past experiences. Memories can hold me back and seduce me with confusion which readily disarms me with further indecision. But the prospect of the joy of new achievement can counter negative notions of losing the race. In the present competitive culture of our society with its distorted wisdom, on occasion this can, as it were, push me back into a box from which I stupidly think I can just be a spectator rather than a participant. On the other hand I can honestly say that I do not have any fantasies to be an Alexander the Great in waiting, nor a Mozart, nor a Michaelangelo, a Martin Luther King, nor a Julian of Norwich. No! I am clear beyond doubt that I am 'me', and no one else. I have no desire to be anyone else. I'm now comfortable within my own skin and I deeply desire that freedom which will allow me to continue to be me - yes, and with warts an' all. To explore creatively this wonderful possibility is all I ask - and with the risks that will be involved. After this morning's trauma, this is not too much to expect, is it?

Perhaps now I need to face the other hesitation that dogs me from time to time. It is the fear of future failure. I can put past failures behind me. They hold no further terror. But it is the possibility of future failure that saps away wasted energy. Success may be evasive but it confirms rather than negates my ageing ego. A friend challenged me, saying, why should I be afraid of failure? And my reason is that humanly speaking, for me, there is a limit to the overbearing nature of failure which saps energy. My deep desire is to bear a more successful reputation. And more bitter than all else is the trauma of believing that my own failures too frequently are not of my own making. But I readily now have to concede that I have learned so much from the experience of failure. Even though this in itself does not guarantee future success. I recall occasions when failure was born out of my own inner self. On other occasions failure was inevitable because of circumstances over which I had no control. Failure is a 'slippery' business. It erodes confidence in the future and the extent to which I do lose control over my own future. This 'shadow' is never far away. So in my contemplation of you and me, peering through the mystery of your eternity, I'm beginning to get the sense that with you it is always NOW. For my failures there can be no past and no future. Out of the NOW there is a spirited birth of hope, with its imminent horizon enfolding my failures and removing them beyond the sight of this frail world of mine. If NOW is ever present this assures me that opportunities will remain for new beginnings and new endings. Seasons come and go. Things wear out. Opportunities are to be taken whenever they appear. Being in the NOW at all times sheds a new perspective for me on the realisation that my life will have meaning, enriching a creative dialogue between failure and success with a liberating touch.

This morning's trauma has not been without its hard earned enlightenment. I'm beginning to recognise my inadequacy within the experience of uncertainty. Uncertainty is ever present, about the meaning of the past, my past. It faces me too as I contemplate tomorrow. But in this present moment I'm searching for a greater security, intangible but laced with a sober expectation. From this morning until this moment I've been through some sense of transformation. My transformation does depend on being in touch with you. This is what these Letters of mine are about. There feels to me as if there is warmth within the transformation experience. It's a sense of warmth for which I have yearned. To desire transformation, is to know that within the new sense of being I find myself within a sense of equilibrium which refreshes my whole and entire person.

But, I can't help it. I'm wondering how long this will last? Will it last? I've struggled through this experience and grappled with the deep desire to describe it to you God. I'm left now feeling the satisfaction of the physical and spiritual effort. Indeed whatever else this sense of journeying provokes and yet satisfies, and I have learnt that I can't have one without the other. I am aware that my ageing ego feels a greater sense of readiness for the on-going journey, but I hope my spirit will flower to grow closer to you. From my waking time this morning, to now - hours on - in spite of the pain, I've grown that bit - not quantifiable, but etched deep into my being. Though near to exhaustion, I'm ready to rest, and as you'll notice, with a smile on my face. This smile itself a new beatitude. I'm open and ready to grow some more, with you around and within.

Letter 23: The story of Gladys

Dear God,

I've been thinking a lot about Gladys. To look at her you'd think she was past her prime - perhaps even a long way past it! She lives on her own in her sparsely furnished flat. She's plainly dressed. She's quiet - no airs and graces about her. She'll always stop and talk if you meet her along the street or in the local shops. Each Sunday morning she's sitting in the front pew in the local Cathedral, at the Eucharist. She walks there and back most Sundays. She's had a full life - in business - helping families -and she has been content to do her bit in the Church, over the years.

For the last few years she has had one overriding priority. This has been at the local Children's Hospital. Like all hospitals it is a busy place. In the Wards there are children who have undergone serious surgery, usually to be followed by long months of treatment and nursing. Many of them have suffered the long term trauma of serious illness. Some of the children look quite frail. Some look burdened by their illness. Others though, have a mischievous look in the eye, and though immobile, you can see that they are mentally alert and are looking for attention. Some are quite restless, just itching to get up and play and get back to normal. But they can't do this, just yet. Many of the children are a long way from home, so that the visits from parents and friends may not be frequent. The staff at the Hospital became aware of how alone some of the long-stay children felt. Some may not have a visitor for many days, and even weeks. Some of course, know that "Mummy and Daddy live a hundred miles away" - and some even live further away than that! So visiting is difficult. It's easy for children to feel very much on their own, in a busy Ward, when Mummy and Daddy can't visit very often, even though they may understand the reason. Children come to this Hospital because it provides the special treatment and expertise, with longer term care which they require. Though it was not easy to put it into words, Gladys felt there was something 'special' about this Hospital. In fact there is something special about any place where there are lots of children, and more so when they are suffering from illness and trauma. The Wards are very busy. The children need a lot of individual attention. So when Gladys became aware of how things were she offered to set aside three periods each week to be with the children in one small Ward. She made time on Mondays, Wednesdays and Fridays in the late afternoon and early evenings, when the long Ward day was beginning to wind down. The children were being prepared for feeding, bathing, and hopefully sleep time. It's a time in the day when children feel the need to talk - for closeness - for intimate cuddles - a story - a conversation - some 'nice talk' - jokes, questions, and inner hope - a sigh - a glance - a whisper - and maybe a quiet tear. They are waiting for the time when Mummy and Daddy will be there. Their Mummy, and their Daddy - yes, just there in the Ward beside their bed. But they weren't! They may be a hundred or so miles away, and no doubt many of them feeling what their children were feeling. The aching - the longing - the wanting - the void and the uncomfortable emptiness.

The Wards were fairly small. Gladys offered what perhaps she would be able to do. To look in on one Ward three evenings in the week. She would be there when the bathing, the straightening of the bedclothes, and the cot covers was needed. She's there with her story book, picture book, and perhaps a few sweets, if this was allowed. With her warm hands - her open face - her smile her quiet touch and her free spirit. There she is with a small group of two or three - one on her knee, another at her side, and one holding her hand, all looking expectantly at her, fiddling with her jewellery, but listening intently to her words, with the occasional guffaws that could make the stitches twinge! But always eager to get on to the next page of the story book. In this way she came to have a special relationship with a small number of the children. They came to expect her. The children wanted their parents to meet her when they came to visit. Many of the parents were not slow in expressing their own appreciation for her quiet kindness

Dear God, you will know, I suppose, how that sometimes even a Hospital can feel like a wilderness. It has its own smell, its own atmosphere, its own particular furniture, and there's an etiquette though it is not easily described. For patients, and probably more so for child patients, and the staff too, it's not surprising that the medical atmosphere can inhibit and create tissues of anxiety. But on the Monday, Wednesday and Friday, each week, from 6 to 7pm regular as clockwork Gladys was there offering what some might call 'good enough mothering', or 'good enough sistering'. She wasn't replacing Mum and Dad, but she was standing in for them, as well as she could. She's never had children of her own, but she has known many children, and how to be with children. In a sense she was 'a natural' - and you could say she was still a child in herself. She wouldn't argue with that'! Unlike some adults, she was still in touch with 'the child within'. She knew what children knew, and over the weeks and perhaps the months there were children who in spite of their medical treatment, and the artificial situation, were able to look forward to the special times when she would be there just for them. Her closeness confirmed their own growing hope to live and 'get back to normal' - to face their own future, being sure that in it there was going to be Mummy and Daddy, and in her face they glimpsed it all.

Over time Gladys earned the trust and thankfulness of the busy nurses and the auxiliaries. She had a special place in what came to be known as 'The Gladys Ward'. Over the years there were other ladies in other Wards, and on occasion a male Gladys or two! It had become established, quietly, that this was a Hospital where long stay children, a long way from home, had a special service provided. It was a voluntary service, with no publicity, no advertising, no ceremony, just a quiet and discreet personal service. A quiet offering of something special. The kind of service that enables institutions to remain humane. I recall how years later, by which time Gladys herself required daily care, in talking with her, of how she felt so privileged to have been able to be so close to the children. She had a good memory for names - Jackie, Don, Blaine, Samantha, Mary, Fraser, Bert, and Judy - and I guess many others.

These days in cities and towns across the countryside, there are women and men who do invest something of themselves by giving free, voluntary and caring service to others. There are many who need this, and for some it can be for them literally a lifeline. But alas it is becoming harder and more difficult to find enough people ready and willing to give this service. It feels as if now the need is greater, and the response for volunteers can't keep pace with the growing need. These days it is not uncommon for organisations to experience a shortage of volunteers. In a way this may not be surprising. Some people face hard personal economic difficulty.

Others find themselves having to do two or maybe three part-time poorly paid jobs 'to make ends meet'. Others are stressed because they are expected to work long hours, and in stressful conditions. They carry big responsibilities with little support. Parents with their own family demands, along side their working lives just do not have much free time, and if they did they would need it for themselves. Now the fast developing 'Leisure Industry' - Health & Fitness Clubs, Night Clubs, the new fashion of Clubbing makes its own inroads on the leisure time of society, spawning more short term poorly paid auxiliary jobs, whilst at the same time providing attractions for those able to pay. The media and advertising industry is hard at work to persuade us all that we need 'to enjoy ourselves' and find the cash so we can patronise the surfeit of entertainment in bars and clubs. It is said you deserve a break and if you spend scarce cash on yourself it's okay and its good for you. If you work hard, then, it is said, you need to play hard, enjoy yourself, even if it leaves you with a hangover! This will leave little time, if in fact any time at all, for helping here or there, or giving time to someone or a group who need your help.

Society is experiencing a decline in the valuing of public service. The economic ethos of the country has created an acceptable 'habit' which gives priority to making money. This overrides the validity of prudence. The value of money has become an obsession. Your bank, your shares, your insurance policies and the number of credit cards you possess, will, it is said, give you confidence for your future. And though there may be something here not altogether invalid, it all too easily creates the assumption that 'looking after number one' becomes the priority, and for some an obsession.

Nonetheless there are those who, for instance, decide to retire early, so as to give up 'the rat race' and enhance their own quality of life, which may find its expression in a creative hobby, the garden, developing a skill or craft, travelling, or passing on to others a learned skill or interest.

Voluntary Service Overseas, and Community Service Volunteers, along with similar groups recruit a steady stream of ready volunteers who undertake a form of service either here or overseas. For some there is still an attraction in giving service on a rota of a charity shop. Until recently many served Meals on Wheels which was boon to the elderly and the disabled and those with learning difficulties. For myself I admire the volunteers who on a regular basis help disabled children to become adept at horse riding, valuing the exhilaration of those who hitherto have been chair bound.

On the 'volunteer front' all is not lost. There remain those who are good neighbours, even though from time to time the newspapers remind us that there are those isolated souls who die alone and whose deaths are not discovered until weeks afterwards. Yes, it's true, there are ghettos where care is scarce.

So God, you see my perception of the wilderness scene has a stark reality about it. Although altruism is not dead, thank goodness, there are clear signs that it may be in decline. And when I think about Gladys and those who mirror her commitment, there is a question that persists in buzzing round in my head. What is it, I wonder that occasioned Gladys's altruism? Where did it come from? Was it just 'inside her?' Did she learn it from someone else? Did you, perhaps, influence her? Was it that she just happened to be 'person centred' rather than money centred? She lived modestly, she had no car, none of the popular electronic communication and music gear. No holidays abroad. Not that there is anything wrong' with any of these 'goodies'. But she didn't need them. She was bright and lively, with no airs or graces. Maybe her family upbringing had been an important factor. I'm sure she must have imbibed from somewhere her persuasion about charity and service. She's been an inspiration to me.

On the other hand 'Red Nose Day', promoted primarily by the BBC, has made giving to charity popular, and the thing to do. This enables personalities, sportsmen, and the 'might from the media' to seduce from viewers the extra cash which when added up results in a tidy sum for charity. But whether this is enough of an effort when faced with the world wide need to combat hunger, poverty and disease because of contaminated water supplies, and the shocking daily deaths of countless children - well, I doubt it is enough. The personal sacrifice that clearly will be required does not look at the moment as if it is even recognised. This is the wilderness of millions of sisters and brothers across the globe. And our own wellbeing seems to be, in its way, a barrier preventing us from really identifying 'with the poor'. It might be advocated that there is a state of 'compassion exhaustion'. Because I know of some who are just that - 'exhausted'. Our entrepreneurial culture has not yet penetrated the 'mire of poverty'. There are those who will be awarded with an M.B.E. for service, whilst the higher honours are reserved for those who gain status and who are integrated into the money culture. If you read the honours list, published twice a year (I'm wondering if you do?) the segregation between the levels of awards is clearly distinguishable. Others will be 'seduced' by a prize of some kind - a holiday for two in the Seychelles! We are encouraged with short term goals, and consistency and continuity tend to be somewhat devalued, and this in itself diminishes confidence in the future of society, or even of ourselves. The long term future is eclipsed at the present. But with an increasing number who are over 70 years, this brings with it a further demand on the public and private purse. So the need for lots of Gladys's it could be argued will increase in the next few decades. But the current decline has a serious hard edge to it. They will be missed! They are being missed!

Gladys, though unwittingly, has opened up 'a niche'. But it could be argued that it is a very different story helping the homeless, drug addicts, violent and drunk adolescents, as well as the anonymous who starve on the streets of wealthy cities. But I'm not forgetting those who bring hope in our Prisons, in our Social Work Departments, at the Children's Hearings. There are those who purposefully venture into blighted tenements. Today's world seems to have an 'under belly'. There are the bad, the sad, and the mad! And I'm aware that I'm quick to do the labelling, but too slow to realise that the actual labels do not solve the problems. And I can only cry with some exasperation 'Oh dear how feeble I am'. It feels such a mess and I feel impotent to bring even at least a modicum of enlightenment, and relief.

Are the beggars, the poor, the disadvantaged, 'the wretched of the earth' to be left for ever on the scrapheap of time? The way I'm feeling at the moment this appears inevitable. Is this how it looks to you? I'm desperate to know whether you think I'm being unrealistic - too idealistic - and whether there is a bottomless pit of injustice that has a depth which is unfathomable? I'm remembering that over the years the Church has taught that 'God loves everyone' - do you? Of course this idea has to be welcomed, but the implications are not clear. It only feeds my sense that I'm not coping with the dilemmas - in a sense I'm at the end of my tether. This one saint of a woman has stirred up in me the realisation of how deep lies the frustration in my heart to struggle and to achieve an antidote to the repetitive sense of impotence. Clearly society is unable to build a fairer world. Do you think that inevitably there will be beggars and demented people just 'left over' on the scrapheap of time? Your response on this dire question would be enlightening, to put it at its simplest. Would your view be such that *You* might have the authority to transform this wilderness with its penetrating agony of failure? You see, I'm left feeling that humanity 'off its own bat' is not and will not be able to solve the problem. And I'm hating the thought that the untold unborn of future generations will be doomed to a life of pain and failure. You'll know better than me, I assume the story of the Good Samaritan and of the rich land owner whose barns were bulging with wealth. Their message after two thousand or so years has failed to improve the life and existence of the untold poor of every century since. Would you be aggrieved if in response I could only mouth those words of agony – 'My God why have you forsaken me?' 'Forsaken us?' I can't help but feel there is anything worse than being forsaken.

Thinking back twenty five years ago in what became known as the Velvet Revolution in Czechoslovakia the slogan that galvanised thousands was 'Socialism with the human face'. It was the human face that was able to challenge the sterile doctrinaire notion of the politics of Eastern Europe all those years ago. I think it's unlikely that Gladys was 'au fait' with politics. But it was her human face that had that special impact and charm which rescued those children from being afraid, and losing hope in themselves. Her humanity was genuine and it became a special kind of presence to the children, their parents and the nursing staff. Gladys was, what she believed. She did not have to explain what she was doing. Her life had a poetry about it. As the children sat and listened, touching her, feeling close, in a strange way they knew intuitively that each of them was to her 'closer than breathing, and nearer than hands and feet'.

In the midst of reflecting on Gladys, this morning I was hit by a newspaper headline which bluntly stated that 35,000 children under five years, die every day of preventable diseases. Of course it's just a statistic! But what a statistic! It still has power to shock, but not shock enough. Kids born next year, in the next decade, and in the next century are fated to die prematurely even before they are born! A pre-meditated death! This is shocking and I hope you are shocked too. This now forces me to recall the occasions when I have heard it asserted that to seek and find understanding for this insoluble dilemma, there is a facet of truth that has the key. This says that you God are a suffering God. You enter humanity's pain with its sense of meaninglessness. You are the God of the poor. You are the source of compassion, giving rest to the weary. And then most tellingly of all, when Jesus hung on his Cross, it in fact was you who hung there at Calvary. This is hard to believe. This paradox of powerlessness being the new power is seductive - one might deeply wish it is true. But is it? When love searches and seeks, and is then rejected, can the rejection and the ensuing suffering be experienced as a victory?

I may not be putting it very well, but is this the 'secret' of your own involvement in the world? There's a difference in thinking about this, from actually believing it. I'd like to believe it – yet it does not seem to change the here and now. I can't get out of this sense of defeat from all the stacked up obscenities of our present situation. The implication is that undeserved suffering is redemptive. But I do not know how to demonstrate this, or even acknowledge it.

All of this has been pertinent to the 'Make Poverty History' campaign and the simultaneous G8 summit in Scotland. The words of John Drinkwater "knowledge we ask not, knowledge thou hast lent, but Lord the deed, give us to build above the deep intent the deed, the deed!".

What I do know is that Gladys was a powerless individual. She did not count for much. But in fact she did count in the lives of actual children. We need an army of male and female Gladys's. But we need more in addition to them. If you are what has been asserted, then we need to see it, hear it, feel it, that's what would count. I've read the scriptures. I've taken account of the lives of the saints. I know too that there has been and still is a multitude of those who have put their hands to the plough, and have not looked back. And thank goodness for them, and for the treasures of the scriptures. But today, this very day the power of evil will go on assaulting humanity. There will be incidences when evil is personified in women and men, some willingly and others unwillingly. This is the 24 hour a day dilemma. No matter how we struggle, the truth is that there is a huge shortage of 'Gladys's'. Yes, I have a vision, but alas I'm unsure whether it is achievable, even though I wish it were so. My soul feels stuck and defeated. It might seem at one level to be unrealistic, but it would help me and others who falter, to have some clarity from you. Could there be a new incarnation? When and how, I don't know. But I'm feeling that the 'ball is in your court'. And I'm deeply hoping that my waiting, and the waiting of 'those children' will not be in vain.

Letter 24: The dilemma of loving

Dear God,

Though in my better moments I love humanity - at least I try - there are times when I have serious doubts about loving 'everyone'. Sadly, and surprisingly I have to admit that on occasion I actually hate people - especially when I'm on holiday! Yes, I'm kidding - a little! Holidays for me are occasions when I can evade contact with people, though of course with a few notable exceptions. There are the occasions when I prefer not to be disturbed by 'people'. They seem to 'get under my skin'! I find myself wanting to evade people, and I'm more reluctant to get into conversation. I'm not the most gregarious person, and sometimes keeping myself to myself feels like bliss.

This morning in a quiet reflective moment I found myself surprised when I was struck by the idea that perhaps, after all, I'm not expected to 'love' everyone. To even think so, just for a minute, seems quite presumptuous. It felt a little arrogant. Of course, I do not wish anyone any particular harm – that is most of the time! But there are those who, on occasion, get a wide berth from me. However there is a lurking question which will not go away – it is persistent and it pushes itself into my thinking, and feeling, catching me off guard. At one moment I tell myself I'm not expected to love everyone. But at other times I'm quite unsure about it. The notion of 'blanket love' for the millions who I will never see, and never know, but who with me inhabit this planet Earth, leaves me with the vague feeling which may approximate to goodwill. But I'm not at all sure that this will achieve anything. Some of the saints in their contemplation allowed their love to expand with no inhibition. In my own contemplation, when my focus may be on a painting, a scene of nature or a beloved face, then my insight gains a greater depth. And then when I take time to contemplate what love itself is, in a strange way, I find it discloses itself, and I feel freed up to actually erase the boundary between them and me. It's hard to describe. It's not that I feel I have to do anything, but rather there is within me a new awareness exerting itself. And I feel renewed.

Maybe you will remember that in an earlier letter I shared with you the notion of 'paying attention'. I attempted to explain how for me this was quite central to the discipline of prayer. Practising positive regard to others helps love itself to become palpable – really real! However, a life-long discipline of contemplative silent loving of everyone, I feel, is not for me. But should it be? How can I know? For those with whom I have no outward relationship, am I meant to be aware of them and to have some inner regard for them, which will make any difference to their lives? There is so much pain in the world, so could my contemplative love for them – my silent vigil – really affect them in any positive way? If I thought it did then I would make time for it. But at the moment I'm not convinced – should I be? Can I live my life without any boundaries on my loving? It remains a haunting question.

As I attempt to stand aside from the busy world, I feel I'm being overtaken by a crippling sense of un-ease. There are 'choppy waters' within me. They represent the ways which on occasion I have been badly treated. When I come off the worst in an argument, or someone lets me down, or I'm pushed around, or even purposely ignored, the hard question really penetrates me. Can I be a loving person in return? I know I do not readily have this desire, but I feel I should. But I can't. Are these then the moments when most of all love is needed? I have a sense that perhaps the actual word 'love' is losing something of its intrinsic value. It's as if its deeper currency has been devalued, or even corrupted. So what can I mean by using the word? Love? Help me!

The experience of the wilderness of my earthly existence has not been condusive to fertile acts of love or genuine positive regard. You know I'm not a great philosopher, but in 'my gut' I have this restless desire to empty out everything that feels like 'the rubbish of argument and controversy' from out of my head, and out of my heart. Will you companion me so that I discover the creative love I sense the world disregards, but which I see, inwardly could be the inner secret of fulfilment? I want to take seriously the sense of freedom you embody which enables you to love without restriction. Your loving of our creation – this planet Earth – implies for me that you have hope for it. But when I face this prospect, it leaves me feeling inadequate, even forlorn, because I know in the depth of me that to try to follow you feels beyond my most creative potential. In my impotence it is so hard for me to get tuned in to the love that I know is so desperately required 'out there' – in the hard stressed lives of women, children, as well as men. I struggle to love, as deeply as I am able, but I know it is never enough. The world's need of love is insatiable, and then I wonder if even your love is enough, in this heartless wilderness? The world I live in is more likely to give priority to quantity rather than to quality. In its fragmentation the insatiable desire for more and more only disregards the tragedy of those who find themselves with less and less. Those who are at the 'bottom of the pile'.

All of this leaves me feeling rather like Paul of old. You'll remember his yearning, 'The good that I want to do, I don't do; and the bad I don't want to do, I do'. For me this sums up my feelings about myself, in a nutshell. I'm feeling so small because the quandary of loving the world seems so huge. My faith, if that's what it's called, seems a mixture of a little strength with lots of weakness. Of course I know there is no arithmetic to loving. My superego which feeds my need for success and my desire for reward, has become an obstacle which hinders the selflessness of what I think I want to call my potential for my loving, pallid though it is. Your love, it is said, radiates outwards because it can do nothing else. At least I'd like to think this is so. My loving on the other hand is a struggle. Putting this all in a letter is, in itself, a struggle. But I hope it will prove to be worthwhile. This kind of examination is tough, but I hope it has within it the potential which will enable me to grow.

All this seems to be, in a way, a struggle between awareness and a lack of awareness. One can't help these days of being aware of living within the ethos of the consumer society. The fact is that society is based on the process of supply and demand. Living successfully depends a great deal on whether I find myself among the managers of supply, or whether I'm caught up grappling with the competitive demands of need. This style is about the survival of the fittest. There is no space for the balm of mutuality and co-operation. For many families living is about the struggle to make a profit – a reasonable return or a sum which indicates there is stark exploitation. Wanting more! Or 'needing more'? More possessions, more money, more adulation, all with insatiable satisfaction. Ultimately this has led to a society that has an uncompromising 'banner' which promotes 'the self' first, as the beneficiary whenever and wherever it's possible. In this promotion there can be no compromise nor deviation. For instance this is reflected in the current craze for what are called 'Award Ceremonies'. Prima Donna 'personalities' push their egos so as to claim the status of 'a star' – famous for being famous and promoting cult 'goodies' designed for desperate fans who seek to bathe in the reflection of fickle popularity. This craving for more and more notice edges 'the star' up the ladder of fame, but dependent on a fickle market and fickle fans. This generates money and waves of advertisements and media kudos. Top places cannot be shared, so this existence eventually proves to be a decline into a loneliness of what was, but which passes quickly. This struggle to survive goes on at every level of our society. But it is not in any way conducive to any notion of loving – 'love is for the birds'! So each of us has to contrive our own survival, if we are lucky. It's not hard to delude myself with exaggerated persuasion that 'I' need to come first. There is a subtle dividing line between the co-operation that leads to openness which will promote love and positive regard. But any of my preferential self, designed primarily for my own wellbeing, will rest upon the hard competition which has no regard for others.

Building a society on the basis of loving and positive regard will conflict with the social theory concept of a consumer model of society. To daub women and men as consumers rather than citizens and persons, devalues the whole of humanity. Nonetheless I'm aware that I have, on occasion, had to play the consumer game for my own personal survival as well as the survival of my family. I am doomed to live with this constant choice between these two life styles, each exclusive to the other. On occasion I've considered withdrawing into a disciplined community, adopting a John the Baptist persona, living on the contemporary equivalent to locusts and wild honey! And the blunt alternative is to remain a pragmatist. But to value integrity in this quandary leads me to speculate whether I can live within the consumerist ethos but simultaneously cultivate the mode of selfless love, which I think I would want to call a 'one-for-others' life style. This will be fraught with hard choices, but it might be a style that would have at least some similarity to the teaching of the Sermon on the Mount. But I'm wondering if I am strong enough to wean myself from consumerism? Being responsible for my own life is one thing, but to set out on the path of liberalising society away from rabid consumerism which kills the love inherent in the notion of the good neighbour, is something else. I guess it would take a great deal of tenacity, to the nth degree. And clearly a mammoth campaign would be required. To face the discipline and stringency of inclusive loving within a consumerist society has to be a hard choice. The tide of consumerism turns students in school and patients in hospital into consumers, diluting the spirit of education for a living, and caring being a fundamental ingredient in the healing of illness. Even small children are regarded simply as customers as parents struggle to find the cash to clothe them with the up-to-the-minute styles. But then everything feels compounded when I recall those incisive words of Jesus, spoken following one of his terse stories – "unto him that hath shall be given, but unto him (or her) who hath not, shall be taken away all that he (or she) has". Would I be forgiven if I thought that this seems more extreme that the most rabid capitalist! His words are perplexing, though I have witnessed them come true both with the poor being stripped of meagre belongings, and in other circumstances profits being heaped upon profits. There is a harsh clash here, for to have and not to have, penetrates the daily life of millions. Confusion and uncertainty is spawned, and I'm faced with the inevitable task of shifting my love from that which is conditional and preferential over to a selfless love committed never to give up on openness, fidelity, generosity, and truth. It's not enough to shore up our crumbling society, is it? Rather the individual – the unique person intrinsically, is valued solely because of just who and what he and she are. Without judgement each of us is to be valued, beyond any price, and this comes very near to the genuine expression of magnanimity. Thinking about this reminds me again of what was coined 'the velvet revolution' in Eastern Europe in the late 60's – 'socialism with a human face'! But I guess what is needed is the human face to be transformed into the divine face. Hopefully, could it be that we might be in for a big surprise?

There is one other aspect of this theme of the dilemma of loving, hidden somewhere in our human need to understand better the struggle of children and families as they face, what can seem like a baffling world. Within families children struggle against their own doubts about their own need to be loved, and to love in return. I'd put it this way. Children love Mummy and Daddy, partly because it gives them a good feeling and some sense of assurance. And they enjoy their love being reciprocated. This bonds children and Parents together. In the family love is given and love is received. However, as childhood proceeds children become aware that on occasion they need or want to do something, or say something which Mum and Dad will not like. The child faces the experience of possible disapproval. "If I displease Mum and Dad will they go on loving me"? It's an important question, and it's very real. However the child discovers that the love of parents for them, does not depend on the child being obedient or good. Part of your story good God is that you still go on loving a disobedient world – that's our hope! So hopefully children grow in insight, and parents grow in understanding. Children discover that the love of Mummy and Daddy is not conditional, even though sometimes they would like it to be. Love, being love, is safe. It is a gift. It does not have a price attached to it, does it? When children grow into adulthood, it's a precarious journey, just as it is for parents too. They too have to learn how a love matured, will grow and accept their children, as they grow into adulthood, forging an adult to adult relationship. It is then so rewarding to discover that the love between young adults and parents is not based primarily on what is agreeable, but rather on what is mutually discerned, enjoyed and willingly reciprocated.

This exploration of the dilemma of loving would not be complete for me without a more penetrating look at the hard and nasty things that have caused me pain, through my life. I have to ask myself can I begin to love those who have caused me personal hurt? I know that 'turning the other cheek' makes adult loving perhaps the most costliest demand of all on an individual, a couple, or a group. When I'm in the role of recipient of betrayal and intrigue, then a loving response does not come naturally. I rush to defend myself, and pour verbal hell-fire on those who, in my eyes, do me deep wrongs. This segment of my experience at various times in my life has been seeped in hesitant and even erratic regret, feeling I'm unable to extricate my own self esteem without it being blemished. On occasion I've felt a failure, though I lodge the blame for this on others. I think I'm not easily bruised. But at the same time I acknowledge that the pain of a lost friendship or a flawed confidence, usually perpetrated behind my back, cuts a deep wound in my own self esteem, and plunges me into despair. However, it is my hope that I will grow into a greater maturity, based on a new perspective of the meaning of integrity. I know that I'm required to forgive and to love, but this remains an insoluble dilemma when 'the other' does not recognise the need for forgiveness and reconciliation. How can love – yes, love – how can it heal the breach? I'm not sure that I have the resources of the love to forgive the proverbial 70x70 times! I can feel stingy about my loving when I already know I should feel magnanimous. But this particular loving, more than any other needs an impetus beyond my own. I'm reminded of 'The Everlasting Mercy' in the profound poem of John Masefield. I know I need the 'ploughing in my heart, the ploughing through the rottenness and the decay that will revive the frail flower of shared love'. How often have I wish it were to happen, just like that. There is the sense once again of mystery. But I'll tell you once again, if I may, the mystery of itself is not enough – that is, unless it is shot through with an effective and mutual pragmatic change – and I know that this is not readily achievable. The bottom line has to be that there is no room for revenge. The deepest sense of being wronged has to be swallowed up by the all pervasive in-coming tide of reconciliation. But still, I know I have a lot of learning to do – yes, even at my age, but I hope that this learning curve of mine will bring me face to face with the price of undeserved love. Love suffers pain – the pain of pain itself. And the suffering needs a deep well of patience – sadly, I know, not my strong point.

This whole expanse of thinking, probing, feeling, wishing, leaves me sensing that in these issues, age itself is hardly an important factor. Nor is it a helpful criteria in assessing my skills of judgement and assessment. In a strange way there is something of simplicity in the midst of this profound complexity. What I mean is that the challenge of loving, at one level, appears simple, but on the other hand there are real complexities that disturb and frustrate. I know this life is not 'a Garden of Eden'. And though, for all I know you may yourself walk through it in the cool of the evening, for humanity it provides the mystery of pain, suffering and evil itself and it remains quite hard to believe that love will prevail. My own learning curve, when it comes to loving, will have to be very steep, but I hope it will also provide a newly revealed panorama of a prospect where loving will increasingly be the preferential choice and encompass everything in the here and now, and beyond into tomorrow. Being unalterably human I'm still searching for the divinity of yours that will bring us all the deepest love and comfort. I know it might be said that I'm fortunate enough to have had the experience of some happy endings. But the 'therapy of loving' has the potential to provide the essential ingredient, so this makes my search imperative – yes, even compulsive. Coming to the end of this letter leaves my mind sharpened, and my spirit provoked and hopeful. I hope I'm on track, and that you'll touch that bit of me that still needs to be loved and forgiven. It's not easy to rest with the assertion that you God are unknowable, because to love requires us all to know!

Letter 25: Meeting the painter
extraordinaire

Dear God,

Not long ago I was on holiday in Cornwall. I visited the small coastline town of St. Ives. For me, as well as being a small holiday resort, it is associated in my mind with art – painting – and sculpture, and the group of artists who lived there within a sense of community. One of the artists was Patrick Heron, and some years ago I tried to negotiate with him the loan of some of his larger canvasses to hang in the Wester Hailes Education Centre, situated in the urban housing estate in south west Edinburgh. But because of insurance requirements and an assurance of safety for the canvasses which could not be guaranteed, the project fell through. So an imaginative vision of art at the heart of an urban community was lost, to the sadness of many. As I have said he was a member of the St. Ives group, so it was particularly of interest to visit the place and see it for myself. This group of artists explored the essence of art with a renewed and refreshed imagination, using the inter-play of light, colour, and texture within an ambience of a tangible setting, but which also had a creativity interwoven which seemed intangible, and which seeped into the hearts and minds of the artists themselves, and eventually of the viewer too. Intrinsic to the shared life of that group of artists was not so much what they painted, but rather why, and how their creativity was implicitly of the mystery within the hand and the eye of the painter, rather than just the factual paint itself on the canvasses. I was unclear as to what much of their search was about, so I wanted to see something of it for myself first hand. I guessed it was about something that lies between the human and that other realm that is just out with the human grasp.

Sitting high up on the cliffs, eating lunch, I was transported into a world that was about the evocative out-of-doors, garnished with peace and silence, interspersed with the intruding cries of the gulls, and hemmed in by a kaleidoscope of endless colours and shapes, with the sea and sky nourishing the inner world of my own imagination. If I have a soul, it was on this day, and at this time that I felt an inner core of my being, richly refreshed. It is hard to describe. I'm unsure what the inner core was or is, but I felt it inside me, not my physical self, but that other part of me beyond the flesh. My mind was dancing. And in spite of sounding a little dualistic there was and still is an inter-weaving of the intangible with the rough and everyday ordinary things struggling for attention. After lunch I went down in to the town, along the narrow winding streets near to the beach. At the far end stood the New Tate Gallery, an imaginative modern building – a beautiful and exciting venue, with its profile clear and inviting against the line of sea and sand, an attractive horizon where the air and water meet.

When I went inside I found myself in a state of mild surprise. It felt as if a powerful magnet was enticing my feet, even a little against my will, I suspect. I was drawn up the stairs, and almost unaware of other visitors, I came face to face, for me, with the symbolic canvasses – some large – others smaller – and all I could do was to stand quite still, and stare, and gaze, and drink in the visions that stroked my eyes with quiet ecstasy. It was an effort of will to move from one to the other. My eyes were, it seemed, harnessed to the canvasses, and I could not let them go. As they hung there they had a power which I am unable to describe. They stood 'off the wall', and every element of them seemed to travel through and inside my head. And my heart too. These paintings were the work and the joy of a Jewish Russian émigré who, in the days before World War 1, had settled in Portland Oregon in the U.S.A., along with his two sisters. The family was poor. As a child he had been torn from his familiar world of political uncertainty. Life for him had had a particular unpredictability about it. Russia was on the verge of revolution. He found himself in a new culture with the social strengths of a diverse people emerging into a nation which was adopting a cross cultural identity even though it was still restless within itself. This restlessness at times helped the painter to shape his own view of his intimate world, which eventually became vividly represented on his canvasses. In the seesaw of unharnessed change he sought the line of stability and certainty, as it straightened out across the vivid colours of canvasses born out of his inner search for a fresh and richer identity.

Years later in 1959 Mark Rothko during his European travels visited the St. Ives painters' colony. This proved to be a mid-life adventure for him. He stayed but three short days, yet inspite of the brevity this provided a new rush of power to paint, and to paint, and to paint! But though he had long since left, it was to me as though he was still present. The enigma of presence and absence in a way reminded me of how it feels with you God – strangely present and yet strangely absent. As I moved around the exhibits it was as if I almost expected to see him look out at me from behind the canvasses – or unexpectedly stride across the Gallery.

In those canvasses, the large and not so large, there were vibrations that told me life was here, and within the painting this sense of life evidenced his presence, but without the actual person. Much of his art would be labelled abstract and representational. But this categorisation, for me, was and is without meaning. I can't help but wonder, and keep wondering whether what Rothko was to his fellow painters was something akin to what Jesus was and is to you God? This transparency of his work with colour, line and shape revealed a beauty which entered into my inner self. I thought and felt in a fresh and revealing way that this experience of the present moment with him might be illustrative of how Jesus may have enabled in his own life and his own death – his living canvas – to be in a special way a key opening a door to you God and maybe to secure your closeness to us? Rothko's painting spoke to me as if there had been a complete elimination of every obstacle between himself, the painter, and himself through his ideas. One critic has suggested that his abstract paintings allow the viewer to travel without having to endure the tedium of the journey. For me, however, this was strange because I'm not one to actually evade the 'tedium', because I find myself caught up more in the experience of arriving at the destination. After the tedium of the journey, the destination is wonderful! For him, I think, in a sense, the travelling was intensely bound up with his anticipated destination, perhaps more than the actual destination. Each pictorial floor of colour reflected the journey of his life and I am still left wondering what this has to tell me, and humanity itself, about my own journey, the stops on the way, and what I expect at the final destination. Can my journey be separated from my own eventual destination? I'd like to know! My own dilemma remains acute as long as I am unsure of my own destination – as I am! But this wrestling of the spirit between the journey and the destination gently pushes me in my own inner quest to know better whether you, God, are a part of this dialectic? I'm hoping you are with me on this journey, but will you also be with me at the destination? It is a struggle to find the words which will match this incandescent desire for the deepest illumination, yet for it not to be diminished by flippant articulation.

The one canvas that pushed me beyond myself was his 'Blue & Grey'. I remember it as a rectangle moving beyond the creamy yellow and grey, hovering above a horizontal rectangle of purpled blue. There was the dark grey base, and as I looked, it was as if the night was being relieved by the lightness, from a sense of dramatic movement, but perhaps declining somewhat into a suggestive darkening, ominous and yet with a tentative sense of threat. This sensitive vibration still lodges in my inner self, and hopefully one day there will be a flurry of deeper understanding which I feel still remains to be born and known. I recall that twelve years earlier Rothko had said "I think of my pictures as drama: the shapes in the pictures are performers. They have been created from the need for a group of actors who are able to move dramatically without embarrassment and execute gestures without shame". He had, I think, a naked sense of the sublime. Something which I find alluring in a spiritual sense, taking me into a world which is fading from the material into something which as yet I cannot name, nor even describe. I now think he may have held the conflicting boundaries of severe geometric measurement, as over against his intense awareness of sensual pathos and even despair – and all tinged with a melancholic embrace. Though faced with anticipation referred to earlier, of whether to be classified as abstract or as representational, his canvases reveal a creativity which makes this issue meaningless. Maybe, with hindsight, and in response to his own searching he, in fact, found himself somewhere which felt a little less than comfortable, but also knowing that for him his work might be judged as both. For him there was a significance in the symbol of the rectangle. It held together the colour he poured into it, suggesting something at ease with itself, unlike the other conflictual images of the triangle with its sense of division between two and one, rather than two and two. For him large canvasses had intimacy, and as I walked close to them I entered them in a sense of being mentally stimulated, physically provoked and even refreshed. I think of him sometimes, as a poet – a poet of paintings – of line and perspective – his paintings, which all have colour, both daring and beautiful. Some of his canvasses almost appeared with the inner eye, to be gothic cathedral windows, austere and withdrawn, and yet as if behind their colour there lies a cataclysm – perhaps an endless abyss. There is nothing to suggest, as far as I know, that Rothko was in any conspicuous way a religious man. This somehow allows me courage, for he had, and still retains the gift of showing what are essentially sacred thoughts - sacred things - sacred in the sense that one finds oneself 'caught up' in them, sometimes even I suspect against one's own will. Yet I know that in the presence of his painting, deep inside myself, I am in 'a presence' that remains yet for me defying description, and beyond understanding of the mind, and then only near definition within the heart.

Rothko the painter, the traveller, the secular mystic, the one who moves on from one pregnant canvas to another, leaving a boon of anticipated discovery, also seems like an enigma, albeit a rewarding one! I find myself puzzled and uneasy when I recall that in 1970 he committed suicide. In a sense this affronts me. Surprises me. It makes me feel afraid. And in my imagination I can't help wondering if his suicide, for him, in his death was his 'stretching out of his uplifted arms and acknowledging that his cross of agony was too much to bear? For him, his own inner invitation to let go of the searching, and make one final plunge into the mystery of the future – his and ours! I'm left wondering if he had an analogue to the act of crucifixion, which might suggest his transparency to reality showed he had fewer protective skins, than most of us. This may go some way towards validating his sense of his own inner suffering and his turbulent discomfort which he transcribed in not a few of his paintings with his vitality and clarity of sight, and thereby transporting us all further on our way to the ultimate mystery of life and death, yet to be hopefully, eventually understood.

You see dear God, for me in a poetic sense, this man has left me with a number of oases in this terrestrial wilderness. As I make my way today through the mire and ugliness of our civilisation, marked by a new millennium solely as a date devoid of hope, he enables me to turn from this meaningless life to something other – implicit yet not explicit – something half hidden, and something that can possess me, but not own me. But which eventually I might even possess. It is, for me, as if I get caught up in a sublime moment of relief from the tremors and vulgarities of this life, into a language of knowing, finding a spirit that assures me that there is yet more to be discovered which affirms and does not reject. I have struggled in my search for meaning and hope, passing the contradictions, the seductiveness of narcissistic power, so that now I am more aware and able to ponder the inexplicable, and to be overseen by a sense of wonder, yet without certainty – yes, the inexplicable! I admit to a sense of envy for Rothko's uninhibited ability to let go of tradition, and custom, and with a mixture of quietness and flamboyance to declare who he was, as far as he knew himself, and to then reveal what he was about, living his life and in a sense offering it up to any who would identify with him, and accompany him in his insatiable search.

If I may say so, this reminds me so much of you, God. Yes, it does! With some sense of bewilderment, I honour your canvasses – your use of both delicate and extravagant colour. However, when I try to talk with you, I'm left with words that seem to have no immediate meaning. Your silence in this wilderness leaves me with frustration, emotionally and intellectually. But since my Gallery visit, it is as if I have discovered that the strength of my ankles comes from the energy of his wonderful canvasses. Could it be that perhaps even the texture of an intruding solitary hair has within it the self same glories that are intrinsic in the very hairs of his creative brush? Or again that even the tender intimacy perhaps of the human face, be it of the new born, or the aged and wrinkled, could be revealed perhaps from within the inner mysteries of some of his structured canvasses? His daring creations may in some mysterious manner mirror something of the vulnerable fertility of your own creation? I am aware that this is tantamount to acknowledging an enigma. Your creation flourishes and withers and then flourishes again, yet it is not without its flaws. Rothko's inspirations was wedded to despair which had within it a sense of defeat. Here was the conflict between the positive and the negative. We need both, and on occasion freedom from both would be more than a blessing. This then reflects the truth hidden in our humanity, which underlines the gap between our lives and the hoped for prospect of eternity. We are, again, left with the embedded good and the pain of the embedded evil, another dimension of the immeasurable gap, keeping me from you, and you from me. This reflects our shared unsolved mystery, the struggle between life and death. Rothko chose death inspite of his creative and imaginative genius. I'm left feeling doubly sad, though also paradoxically enriched from his strong fertile craft by which shape and colour contained a mystical meaning within the wilderness of my earthly existence.

Rothko as a mediator has stopped me in my tracks, and has pushed me back to the ultimate things. His canvases belong to him. Their bits and pieces of colour and strokes and form disclose an accessible excitement, like nothing else. But you God, 'painter extraordinaire', you seem to be less accessible, and the threat of your remoteness is a burden without logic and crushed with ambivalence. The signposts appear to have been tampered with, pointing to ambiguity rather than clarity. Even so I discover kernels of love in the desert, and in the midst of disaster there are hidden moments of ecstasy, which fuel the wells of hope. The words of Charles Wesley, "lost in wonder, love and praise" on occasion have a genuine ring, but they intermingle with memories of sterile contradiction, on the rough edge of existence. Can it be, do you think that the sacred and the secular are after all complementary? Is the boundary between so fluid that the space allows a coming and going that in itself facilitates a dialogue? Your world can feel quite religionless, but also I have discovered that this neutralises those vestiges of religion that foster bigotry, violence and oppression. In the moments of glory I don't need the furniture of religion, all I need is your embrace, and when I feel it then I know that I am possessed by the Spirit. But sadly, for me it is a rare experience, and if it is to be highly valued then maybe its rarity is an important dimension of this almost indescribable experience. I think I am ready for my own next step into the unknown, the unknown that Rothko was intent to explore back in the 70's. The 'sting' of our existence may remain, but the sense of wilderness and isolation hopefully might be diminished if you offer me a new sense of intimacy that acknowledges my desire. For me this is a sacred anticipatory moment. So, come to me – I'm waiting!

An Epilogue: Into the future — keep travelling to God?

GOD

is a circle whose centre is
everywhere, and whose
circumference
is nowhere.

This book is a serious attempt to describe my search for God. This search will continue till my dying day - and perhaps thereafter? It has become a pilgrimage, which when shared will I hope, be an encouragement to other seekers. We share the same wilderness, the mystery of God, and the dilemma of language and communication. But I expect too that somehow we will also share the hope for exhilaration, as discoveries are made, and new understanding emerges from these explorations.

Seeing, hearing, and touching are the means whereby I know I am in relationship with another person. Within this threefold experiential context my relationships grow. From within this fullness of relationship, each dimension has its own significance. Most of us are practised in the fusion of all three, and particularly so in primary loving relationships within our own personal and intimate lives. It is as if touch, sound, and sight each become conductors of knowing, growing, and discovering the comfort and satisfaction of human contact. In this way I come to know someone, and I find satisfaction in the richness and gladness of mutual and multiple relationships. I am glad to know that I am known for who I am. Intimacy itself grows as I move on from casual seeing, to more purposeful seeing; from casual hearing to a more intent hearing. The more intimate practice of touching may enable me to feel in the profoundest sense that I am loved, and that I am not alone. This threefold process enables me to enter into a relationship which has the potential to be deeply personal, bringing with it riches of loving mutual regard. Nonetheless, this threefold process also enables me to enter into patterns of communication which I will practise at varying levels according to the intimacy, or in some situations the inappropriateness or lack of it, with the persons who surround my daily life, in all its variety. But from a personal stance the closer and the more intimate the relationship, then the more I invest in the actual experience of seeing the beloved, looking at the beloved, hearing the beloved, and most sublime of all, touching the beloved. Human experience is blessed by the mystery of this journey of intimate personal knowing, providing me with the rare and relished blessing of a partnership which in some sense, I believe, comes near to a recognition and indeed an experience of the sacred. So, for me, my own brief exposition of the human experience of knowing, and of using the 'three tools' available to me, enables me to establish a pattern and a process that has its own validity. Much of the understanding and the practice of these 'tools' will be helped or diminished according to the tender loving care that has been given, or not given, parentally to the person in early childhood. For myself, as well as others, the chance then to go through this relational learning experience will determine how I will, myself, fully become a person in my own right. But the wonder of it will be the magnanimity which will enhance the seeing, the hearing, and the touching.

In my own life, relationships have been something of a bedrock by which I have been nourished and fulfilled. Included have been my own 'successes' and my 'failures'. These inter-mingle and the resulting life patterns may take unexpected directions. Clarity is not guaranteed. Failure and success can change places, but between them a sense of personal identity has been fashioned, and this is what I have to offer companions on our corporate journey.

When it comes to my own religious experience, broadly speaking, I have found it has not been easy to discover exactly who I am, nor how to use effectively the 'tools of knowing'. I feel I have been something of a failure when it comes to having a relationship with God. My human experience has taught me that failures in making relationships are contributed to by both parties - him and her. But in this realm of relating between me and God, would it be fair, I wonder, if I suggested that part of the responsibility might rest with God, so that I do not have to feel that it is 'all my fault?' I'm not meaning to be arrogant, the more so because apportioning blame hardly ever helps. I'm aware that I have not seen God. I have not heard God. So sadly I'm left wondering what is the hope for my experience of knowing God? My 'three tools' have not functioned at all in this particular search. But these tools are all I have - humanly speaking. So the only question that can follow is, 'Who is responsible?', 'Me or God?' But then again, the question is perhaps without meaning. What a struggle!

Is God inaccessible? Is God unable to take initiatives in our world? Is God tuned into an 'eternal' constellation, which in itself is different in every way from the constellation of our human world? As I try to trace out something of this complexity, I'm not overlooking that there may be the experience of those who do believe that they do have a relationship with God. There are those who believe they actually talk to God, and some believe that God speaks with them. The conversation, it is said, is not a one-way conversation. As I contemplate this experience of others, I'd find it helpful if I had a glimpse of the 'picture' that is in the mind of the persons engaged in this conversation. By this I mean the person's interior picture of the God with whom they are speaking. Does it help to have some kind of identification? Much of our time we are visual beings and much of our understanding comes from seeing. So when there is an exchange between God and the person, what does the person 'see'? Perhaps for some these are inappropriate questions, but I cannot help asking them. As I have said, I have not seen God. As far as I know I have not touched God, nor has God touched me. If, for a moment, my searching is valid, then how can I have a 'relationship' with God? And God with me? I can speak only from within the limitation of the finite world within which I live. So when it is said, for instance, 'God inhabits eternity' then my question is, can a creature of this finite world have a relationship with God dwelling in eternity? Scripture reports that 'Moses was afraid to look upon God'. However, I'm not sure whether this is meant to be taken literally, or whether it is a picture trying to explain something about God, and if so what is it that is being explained? If God cannot be seen with the human eye, can God be seen with the inner eye, and if so what does this mean? Does this help humanity to come closer to God? These, I know, are deep and profound questions. They indicate something of the complexity of the dilemma. It's a dilemma that will require the insistent single mindedness of the searcher, in the hope of discovering the truth.

Liturgies from earliest times have declared that God is Spirit. Well, yes, from my notion of Spirit, I have a glimmer of that which is transcendental - beyond the material - experienced perhaps in the mind and the soul, but really beyond definition. But I also perceive that women and men have their spirituality - a sense beyond the here and now - in the depths - but again beyond definition. And sadly I'm not unaware of those few people who have an air of preferential spirituality, believing they are one notch up on their fellows. This in itself detracts from the pursuit of the spirituality that is open and non-judgemental. I'm wondering if there is a difference between 'the spirit of God' and the declaration that 'God is Spirit?' This searching can feel like cleaving the air, and having nothing to show for it. But the mystery of God remains. God is a small word. But the notion of God appears to have no bounds - is limitless - and yet remaining so difficult 'to know'. I'm left wondering if God perhaps has a priority with concerns outwith our world? This is perhaps what is called eternity? It's not easy to get one's mind round it because from my worldly and human perspective eternity seems to lack what I can only call substance and definition. The purpose of this slender volume of personal letters to God is primarily to enable me to explore this baffling puzzle, and to discover, I hope, some enlight-ening conclusions. On the other hand, I suppose, it feels like playing around with ideas that are too big for my own very small boots! But in my sober moments I feel that this enterprise is the biggest issue facing humanity, as well as facing me! There will be those, looking over their shoulder, doing their best to read these letters, who may conclude that I'm being far too pragmatic in my exploration. But for me, this is the only way I know. Pragmatism does not thwart the deepest sense of thinking and exploration. Pragmatism has its own discipline. This enquiry and exploration is the most important task of my whole life. To come equal with the notion that God is Spirit, and ineffable, poses the question as to whether or not human beings can have something approximating to a relationship with God? I can't help but hope that the description 'Spirit and ineffable' is incomplete. My judgement is that there has to be something else that can be added to the description. But what is it? This, for me, is the profoundest question yet to be posed. The dilemma of communication remains.

Religious language and experience are littered with metaphors for God. Metaphors attempt to give a quality or identity which in itself is not literally realistic, but which has within it a sense of relevant meaning. As an example, it is common place to talk about a person having 'nerves of steel'. This does not mean that he or she has actual 'steel' within them physically. It is however an attempt to describe the person's valour, endless energy, toughness, or fortitude. In this example I'm suggesting that the communication with the person who has nerves of steel is unimpeded by the use of the metaphor. This metaphor gives illumination. But with the subject and 'person' of God metaphors provide all too little illumination.

So in conversation with God, or hoped for conversation with God, how and where does one begin? I can mouth the words, use sacred images, and even adopt a special and sacred language. My imagination may be about to manufacture 'pictures' in my head which give me solace, or hope, or tenacity. But they inevitably turn out to be blurred pictures, ill defined, vague, and of little help. Over the years of contemplation I have become familiar with this process. My interior life is not a stranger to the silence, the sense of 'holiness', created by music, colour, poetic words, memories, and the speciality of intimate experience of oneness with a beloved. However with honesty and after rigorous scrutiny I find I am still left searching, because I am still aware that I have no actual relationship with God. I remain aware that the Very God of Very God is not in any way personally accessible with an experience of communication that touches me in my own inner self. Being finite I do not know how to operate within the context of infinity. I have not been able to discover any 'entry points' which offer even a chink of hopeful meaning. My search is for experiential enlightenment which has the touch of human reality about it, and which provides my personal accessibility to God, to which my heart and mind can be positively attuned. The much recited words of the Revelation of St. John the Divine - a religious metaphor, "I stand at the door and knock; if any man hear my voice, and open the door, I will come in to him, and will sup with him, and he with me", has a spiritual/religious seductiveness. The music of this metaphor has resonated down the decades. But for many, including myself, the knock is so quiet, that even when responded to, sadly, it would seem that the door is not opened. In fact the pain is that it remains firmly shut. But of course this will all depend on whether the handle is on the inside or outside of the door, and the Holman Hunt painting does not show whether the handle is on the inside or the outside. The hoped for relationship evaporates. In my mind I'm aware of others who seek desperately to 'enter the door', but who find it firmly shut. In spite of the hope, and the pain, and the inner knowledge of need, 'the door' remains tightly closed. The hoped for welcoming hand of God does not materialise. So my question remains, how can humanity have personal access to God? It seems as if the avenue of approach is littered with those all too familiar bollards of restriction in our city streets - 'no parking' - and in this case the limitations are being strictly implemented!

However, there will be those who will suggest that the truth of the Holman Hunt painting 'I stand at the door and knock', is that 'The Door' can only be opened from the inside. Well, yes, this is the common experience of everyday life. But, is it not also the case that if the person standing outside has their own key, then they too can open the door? So am I pushing this point too far to suggest that God too has a key to my door? And if, for any reason, I find I'm not able to unlock my door, then could God unlock it for me? To do so might be acting as a good neighbour. It's worth pondering.

But I must hasten on. Even though this could feel like a negative perception, it does not in any way diminish my sense of wonder for creation, and the mysteries and confusions of everyday life. I know full well that our human lives are touched by experiences which in themselves confound adequate rational description and understanding. These letters are my personal search, undertaken in a positive mind and hoping they will help other seekers. I can vouch that in my life I have been deeply moved by the experience of intimate love with its indescribable wonder. This has overtones of a spirituality which feels profound. The beauty of mountains and the sea, sunset and moon rise - music and poetry of vision, and paintings of unutterable beauty are genuine and real. The perplexity of science in its thoroughness, and the instinct of discovery, with a human tenderness that in spite of an unutterable consumerism can still brings hope in an over commercialised world, I'm at liberty to say – or hope – that this is something of God? And even if this is the case, I can only reflect with some deeply penetrating disappointment, that the sense of 'knowing' which is the birth pang of relationship still remains absent - God is elsewhere. And this is a profound sadness for me.

On occasion I can recall the distress of someone who is dying in abject pain from an inoperable cancer. As I sit there, holding the hand of the sufferer, I have no certainty that this person is being touched by the hand of God. The person dies without a sense of triumph and the ignominy of their end appears to be devoid of meaning. This leaves me with the deepest of dilemmas. Is there any measurable sense that God, the real God, is here - in the here and now? Because it is in the here and now that the presence of God, experientially and in relationship is so keenly awaited.

Searchers over the centuries, in an attempt to get nearer to the 'reality' of God have used the anthropomorphic language and imaging of God. This 'cartoon' effect may appear to solve the problem of understanding, with a prospect of coming nearer to 'the person' of God. The anthropomorphic process endeavours to cast God in a human guise, usually making God male, a Father with the best of human characteristics. However I'm left with the feeling that this provides me only with what I sense is a 'mini-god'. If you like, God brought down to my level. For me this is devoid of integrity, and is without intellectual rigour, which I believe is the least that I hope God desires. To attempt to clothe God in human form is, for me, an escape from the very purpose of the task of discovering God for God's own self. I'm clinging to the hope that God is God. But the anthropomorphic exercise leaves me with the deepest sense of un-knowing. In this debate I feel as inadequate as anyone, be they saint or sinner or both! All the time, inside myself I know I'm only at the beginning, and the path ahead remains quite unclear. There is a sense of confusion between what I would call the 'substance' - if you like, the 'nakedness of God', on the one hand, and then the blurred image - the muffled word - the presence that remains always at a distance. Hopefully there is a link, but I'm not able to feel it myself. The anthropomorphic images cause more problems for me than they solve. The desire 'to know God' is not audacity on my part. It is a genuine search for a relationship. Nothing else will bring satisfaction. Is there, I wonder, a bridge to God? Might it be heaven, whatever heaven is, or could be? These letters of mine are attempting to describe what some will maintain is the indescribable. But I will not give up, at least not yet. Why? Because an experiential 'knowing' of God is the revelation that would make all things worthwhile. Idealistic? Perhaps. But as 'someone' has said 'No man having put his hand to the plough, and looking back, is fit for the Kingdom of Heaven'!

The wilderness?

The wilderness in the context of these letters approximates to a metaphor. I hope it will open up an aspect of truth about the world which I inhabit. I confess that for me this is wrapped in a context of uncertainty and discomfort. This is not solely an intellectual adventure. It has come to address every aspect of my own life with the perceptions I have of our world. The exploration has an impatient imperative about it. It is my hope that these letters will assist and support others to pursue their own journey of discovery across what I view as a rocky terrain. On the one hand there are the shared doubts, and. on the other awakening hopes of new certainties, perhaps, just 'round the corner'! However, to be honest, at other times, on occasion, I feel as if this entire exercise is in danger of being too tender, too precious, for expression. Yet, I am anxious to safeguard the very tenderness of it all. I think this is a deep and unavoidable ambivalence.

Our world contains stretches of wild, uncultivated and uninhabited land and water and space. At times it seems limitless. It has its own sense of isolation and it is not dependant on any human concern, or human interaction. There is little sense of time in this wilderness, other than the movement of the sun, the moon and stars, and the unrelenting tides of the shore. The wilderness is what it is, and nothing more. Simultaneously however I have my own sense of sadness when I see modern transport intruding this virginal map in its natural isolation, and cradled in interminable silence. This invasion, growing year on year, is a symbol of humanity's insatiable desire to possess and dominate, without discipline or respect. It is as if the natural wilderness is invaded by the consumerism 'jungle'. There is the Research Base in Antarctica; The Gobi desert; the wastes of Central Australia; the unchartered Patagonia Desert; as well as the desert of Nevada USA exploited for research in nuclear and biological weaponry. These barren spaces have become magnets for humans. Meanwhile others are intent on converting 'the desert' into paradises of pleasure for tourism. And yet there are also women and men who have the deep and insatiable desire to retreat and withdraw within a simple lifestyle of meditation and utter simplicity. Their urge to retreat and withdraw takes the soul on an inward journey in search for emotional and intellectual integrity. They require no luxuries, little comfort, but the sobering sense of silence. This pilgrim life offers a new valid meaning of existence with a sense of liberating honesty, which sadly in these times is all too scary for the daily treadmill of what we call civilisation.

Some poets have captured something of this sense of yearning and struggle with the wilderness. Bunyan – "Walked through the wilderness of the world". William Cowper yearned, "Oh for a lodge in some vast wilderness, some boundless contiguity of space; where rumour of oppression and deceit of unsuccessful or successful war, might never reach me now". Gerald Manley Hopkins shocks us with his questions, "What would the world be, once bereft of wet and wildness? Let them be left, O let then be left, wildness and wet! Long live the weeds and the wilderness yet!" Then Edward Fitzgerald, provokingly sighed for, "A flask of wine, a Book of Verse - and Thou beside me singing in the Wilderness - and the Wilderness is paradise now!" These poets cum prophets ease me into the way of the wilderness. But my own cry is deeper and more urgent. It is borne out of the punishing years of struggle, against what felt like overwhelming odds and unpalatable compromise. I have suffered and felt surrounded by the sense of inevitable encroachment of my own integrity, seeking to defeat me and obliterate my own precious identity.

The cherished hopes for fulfilment are readily lost in a void of daily frustration and anxiety. Limitless frustration readily turns to anger, which burns up all my good intentions, leaving me anxiously empty and vacant. This world has become for me a jungle, a threatening wilderness where the virtues and rich values of co-operative living are swallowed up in endless aggressive competition. It all feels an alien territory. It has to be endured, the product of human greed, political, economic, moral, social, and even on occasion religious. The feeling of being repeatedly 'worn down' overwhelms, and it feels as if the only alternative is the other wilderness of nature that beckons with its sense of the remote and the unimagined calm of joyful isolation.

Sometimes my life feels as if I am sunbathing in the rain! There are demons in my daily wilderness. I feels a thousand miles away from the popular oft imagined Desert Island where endlessly I could play my eight discs, till they wear out! My wilderness is between the reality and the desired sense for an impatient absence of reality. Too much reality paralyses the soul. In the most private part of me I'm in the desert of meaningless routine with unfulfilled desires I can hardly express. It is as if I am rooted in my own personal smallness and apparent insignificance. Trapped in my own inner self I feel terrified with the desire to escape - but to where? Instead I'm left to tread the path of pain with too much introjection, a sense of injustice and then - well, all too soon perhaps oblivion. In my deeper inner self - my unconscious, where thought and articulation are of necessity primitive, and at times even impossible, the refreshing inner well of grace, seemingly from 'nowhere', occasionally, and mysteriously creeps over me, lulling me into a frame of gentle repose, so that then all my fragmented parts struggle to come together again, providing a new sense of wholeness.

So I am confronted with the Wilderness that has, it seems, a double state. The wretchedness of the world which resembles a 'jungle' where ideas and persons are seduced by what elsewhere would be called 'sin'. But the other wilderness, located geographically in the natural world, which in spite of its inherent 'tooth & claw', withdraws me from the fray as it were to where beauty and quiet harmony co-exist, nourishing me both within and without and cherishing my precious ideals even though they are seldom realised. Albeit, rationally I know that within this natural wilderness lurk the terrorising primitive forces struggling for survival. So all of this needs the energy of potent paradox, enabling a reconciliation of all that appears to be beyond any fusion of a creative union. Moving hesitantly between the wilderness and the jungle that I know all too well, to that other wilderness that beckons, when I'm moved to cry, from the depths, 'Where are you God?' Even if I knew where you are, I'd still be left with the enigma of how to communicate with you. Yes, perhaps your otherness encircles, but it seems only in a mystery that I find too deep for articulation. So this is where there is the possibility that these letters might, hopefully rescue me.

Letters?

I'm not a Man of Letters in any academic sense. I am someone who has come to be aware of an expanding ministry of letters. By this I mean that over the years letters I have written have been fertile modes of personal conversation and communication. This has required listening, sympathy, and the actual discipline of writing - a putting into personal words experiences which shape and support relationships at significant milestones of life - the good and the bad and the utterly inexplicable. Letters are about valuing the person, the cause, the predicament, and acknowledge the potential for good, and simultaneously stare evil, as it were, in the face. My letters have been vehicles of truth and integrity infused with compassion, within a process of searching and reflection, and pointing forward, journeying into discovery. This process, I think, is laced with regard and fearless goodwill. So whether it's a celebration or a mourning with dereliction, a hope or a despair, a victory or a defeat, the letters themselves transmit a sense of solidarity. Each letter stands only for itself. It may make a statement or ask a question, but it rests solely on its own motivation. Letters of support - of protest. Letters which will wing the seeming insolubility of a critical moment, and transform it into a hopeful perspective. Letters transmit a generosity of informed and temperate care. This is something of the endless ministry of letters, whether written 'off the cuff', or with agonising, wrestling investment of evaporating time. Letters, I know, have taken 'bits of me' to where I know I have been wanted and needed. Then, on occasion, in return on the personalised page, written in another hand I have received something of the person, the cause, linking with me in a bond of exchange and personal sharing, revealing a sense of vibrant unity. This giving and receiving though seldom in equal parts represents a mutual vivid totem of trust and identity. I learned these letter writing skills from an early age. Later in the Peace Movement a colleague demonstrated to me how invariably the letter 'would get through', when all else failed. So, when I slip a letter into the postbox, or when the postman calls, with letters dropping on to the hall mat, I have a thrill of anticipation, whether or not the news is good or bad. A personal bond - an understanding - a new perspective from this personal living link is alive, and this means there is hope.

In present times letters have gone out of fashion, in a world that has no time to write them, and still less time to read then. Modern communication technology thinks it knows best, and impatiently is moving on to the next insatiable discovery which it is believed will hold within it a financial bonanza! Messages swan across computer screens; the slimmed down language of the hasty text; the mobile phone that carries messages which invade the personal space of others, intruding with their oft irrelevant murmurings. In the light of all these pretentious communication tools, the heritage of letters deserves to be re-valued. Something has to be preserved of the highway of personal communication which bears the mark of a human(e) stamp. Letters transmit the personal stamp of the writer, and indelibly reveal her or his personality and grace, and on occasion 'warts 'and all'. The letter is a harbinger of personal interaction and becomes a medium by which others grow strong enough to cope with their future, whereas otherwise capitulation might appear to be the only other option. But the key question has to be addressed, as to whether or not, in this attempt of mine to learn something about communication with God is whether the letter is a possible model which in itself feeds the mind and heart of the writer. Will I feel differently, think differently? Will there be a resonance in my being that will provide some deeper understanding which illuminates the spirit? Does the ethos of the letter, its process, and its arrow-like access to the heart of deep and sensitive enquiry initiate a valid start to break the timeless sense of isolation that surrounds the epic search for God? Is there a sense in which God will read these letters? How can I know? We know of other narratives which have described 'the breakthrough' of God. So why not a breakthrough from a personalised letter - written exploration? But a letter which has a special, if not unique message, which traverses the space between my life and the transcendental realm of God is like an arrow, shot into the future and taking with it a message for the unique moment of its arrival, when ever that will be. Perhaps there is a parallel with the probes made to the planet Mars, travelling unlimited space for a period that outstretches months and years, but which we know will eventually arrive. If God is so inaccessible, then nothing can be ruled out in the search for a relationship, which will grow from fertile and imaginative communication. Somewhere there is a key, and for me these letters have provided a means of dialogue, knowing that from questions posed, new hope arises in the heart. If the revival of religion is dependant on a revival of the imagination, then an access to God will no less require the imaginative audacity that formulates an attempted route of communication, and for the time being is ready to rest just here.

As a letter writer with Amnesty International I know there are writers who possess resources of hope who never give up their mission in the face of unanswered letters. The letter sent to a prisoner of conscience that has no response, remains a letter of witness wherever it is eventually opened. Letter writers are faithful in their purpose and in completing the task. When you know you have done all you can do, then the issue is left to prospects of hope, silent or otherwise. I recall that some years ago I wrote a weekly card to an anti-apartheid activist who was in solitary confinement, within his isolated location. I never received any response. Some years later when the transformation of South Africa was assured, this activist visited Scotland, and at a memorable meeting he shook my hand and hugged me fervently. His being vibrated with limitless appreciation. Those apparently endless cards had enabled him the better to withstand the terror of absolute isolation. I know the same is true for the young Israeli conscientious objectors to military service in the Israeli Army, who though shackled and silenced in their cells receive letters that transmit warmth and solidarity. Letters have a special facility to provoke a mode of personal, and on occasion intimate communication. This, in itself, redresses the impersonal, the isolated and anonymous ethos of our society, particularly at the significant moments of crisis in our lives.

However, and of course, I do not know how God will regard my letters. There is a real sense of risk for me, the risk that there will be no response. For me, the writing feels sometimes like a struggle in the dark. But in the dark, to light only the tiniest candle when it is the only means of illumination, is to know that nothing else can be done. All other modes of power are inaccessible. So the candle has to be sufficient. These letters are my bid for communication, and I think that because they are directed to God, then implicit in my writing is the hope, no matter how unformulated, that they will 'get through'. But 'getting through' implies something of a mystery, because I recognise my hope that this actual communication is at a deeper level – 'in the spirit'. These reverberations, I believe, will not be limited only to that which is accessible to the questioning mind and heart. But again, whatever the responses expected, pragmatically they cannot be guaranteed. Nonetheless, the actual writing of the letters, in themselves, with the sense of struggle involved, being beyond precise description, here I know that for me something significant has happened, and the invitation from the soul has been made, and I will not be the same, ever again.

The Psalms and the Letters of St. Paul have addressed God, as well as the human race. As they were written down, through the ages they have conveyed the yearning, hopes, and the fears, but all charged with a deep desire to 'inform' God, to get close to God, and to bypass all those other attributes ascribed to God which hinder personal communication. The Psalms and the New Testament Letters are full of hopes, fears, questions and dilemmas. My own dependence on letters with my own rational imagination, along with and yoked to a pragmatism that demonstrates my own sense of on going urgency, leaves me now quietly waiting for something, though I know not what! But hopefully a deeper perception within, and admittedly perhaps beyond words themselves, there will evolve 'a signal', to say that the messages, the yearning, and the nadir of my soul, have been received.

I identify myself with those who have a ministry of letter writing. This has become an important piece of process and equipment which I wish to use on my journey towards the discovery of God. For me, this is enshrined in the words of Psalm 139 – "Search me, Oh God, and know my heart; try me and know my thoughts". Yes, God, here are my thoughts, and search me as deeply as you wish. My thoughts are open to you and are in these letters. Yes, I'm ready to be searched, as deeply as possible. Further, I hope these letters will enable me to do some searching of you, God. The Very God searching me! And me searching the Very God, the God that is sublime mystery. I'm hoping that God's searching of me, and my own searching will meet!

So I return to my opening image - an image that furnishes a demanding and exciting prospect, and to which these letters are relevant.

'God is the circle whose centre is everywhere
And whose circumference is nowhere'.

However, it is not possible to have a personal relationship with 'a centre', or 'a circumference' no matter how appropriate the metaphor. The goal of my longing and searching remains nothing less than a relationship for me, with God. To love, is to be in relationship. These letters provide a personal focus, and spring from the desire to know and to love.

It is my hope that others will be ready to put into their own letters their desires, dilemmas, doubts, and yes, even their anger and their sadness. Letters also celebrate! I am celebrating the achievement of my struggle by which I have been able, I hope, to offer a path or a process which will provide sensitive and effective communication, for those struggling to have a relationship with God.

There have been, and there are, times when this exploration has felt like a miracle. It's a miracle worth waiting for, no matter how long the time of waiting may be. But the waiting comes first.

Printed in the United Kingdom
by Lightning Source UK Ltd.
119129UK00001B/166-318